Library of
Davidson College

Soviet-Indian Relations

Issues and Influence

STUDIES OF INFLUENCE IN INTERNATIONAL RELATIONS

Alvin Z. Rubinstein, General Editor

Soviet-Indian Relations

Issues and Influence

ROBERT C. HORN

PRAEGER

PRAEGER SPECIAL STUDIES • PRAEGER SCIENTIFIC

Library of Congress Cataloging in Publication Data
Horn, Robert C.
    Soviet-Indian relations.

    (Studies of influence in international relations)
    Bibliography: p.
    Includes index.
    1. Soviet Union—Relations—India. 2. India—
Relations—Soviet Union. 3. World politics—1965-1975.
4. World politics—1975-1985. I. Title. II. Series.
DK68.7.I5H67   327.47054   81-15678
ISBN 0-03-052571-3   AACR2
ISBN 0-03-052576-4 (pbk.)

Published in 1982 by Praeger Publishers
CBS Educational and Professional Publishing
a Division of CBS Inc.
521 Fifth Avenue, New York, New York 10175 U.S.A.

© 1982 by Praeger Publishers

All rights reserved

23456789   145   987654321
Printed in the United States of America

EDITOR'S PREFACE

India has been a target of special Soviet interest ever since it became independent on August 15, 1947. When the decolonization process was just beginning, Moscow recognized India's potential to be a leader of the Asian and African countries whose colonial experience was expected to make them anti-Western and receptive to friendship with the Soviet Union. As early as 1950, it put out feelers for a treaty of friendship and cooperation via the Indian mission in Peking but the Indian ambassador's misjudgment in downgrading the overture, the advent of the Korean War, and Stalin's increasing inflexibility vis-à-vis Third World countries ended the matter. Stalin's successors, however, wasted little time in communicating their desire for better relations. Eager to dissuade India from joining any Western-sponsored military pact and to demonstrate their readiness to assist its economic development, they undertook, in February 1955, to build a steel plant in the public sector at Bhilai. This was the first of many projects that the Soviet Union was to construct in the years ahead, and as Khrushchev later correctly assessed, the projects were a spur to Western aid programs.

Even more significant to India has been the Soviet Union's political and military support on many important issues. On November 16, 1962, Prime Minister Jawaharlal Nehru, addressing the Lok Sabha (the lower house of Parliament) on the Chinese attack, commended Moscow for its sympathetic neutrality: "We do not expect the Soviet Union to do anything which could definitely mean a breach with the Chinese [with whom it was allied militarily]. But we have had their goodwill all along and even very recently and that is a consolation. We certainly hope to have it in the future, too." At Tashkent in September 1965, Moscow successfully mediated an end to the Indo-Pakistani war to India's general satisfaction by gingerly treading the narrow line between advocacy and adjudication on the all-important Kashmir issue. The 1971 Treaty of Peace, Friendship and Cooperation gave India the assurance it needed to handle Pakistan, which was always its primary foreign policy consideration, without having to worry about Chinese or U.S. interference. In the spring of 1980, Moscow and New Delhi concluded a $1.6 billion arms agreement, the largest ever negotiated between them, on very generous concessionary terms that confirmed the USSR position as India's principal arms supplier. There have been many such examples of Moscow's value and liberality.

Moreover, if the United States decides to modernize the Pakistani army (which in the summer of 1981, seems likely) the Soviet arms connection would take on renewed significance for New Delhi.

Since all of this suggests that the Soviet-Indian relationship will grow in the years ahead, Professor Robert Horn's study is particularly timely. It examines the essentially unchanging perceptions and aims that prompt the policies of the Soviet Union and India toward one another and the other principals in the region, that is, Pakistan, China, Bangladesh, and, of course, the United States.

South Asia is an area of considerable significance. It contains more than 20 percent of the world's population, occupies a strategic location, is a potential source of constructive change and dangerous disruption, and is a contentious region where the struggle between Soviet and U.S. conceptions of international order, imperial rivalry, and socioeconomic development is waged against a backdrop of endemic tension and dislocation.

A few geopolitical facts need to be kept in mind. First, the subcontinent is, after all, the Soviet Union's backyard and may yet become its route to warm water ports on the Persian Gulf and Indian Ocean, atavistic aims of generations of Muscovite planners. Second, the Soviet military occupation of Afghanistan has, for the first time in history, brought USSR troops to the Khyber Pass, traditional gateway to the subcontinent, with as yet unforeseen political consequences. Third, India's humbling of Pakistan in 1971 wrought a transformation in the regional distribution of power, but what this will mean in terms of old rivalries is slow to emerge. Finally, how the Himalayan socioeconomic challenges of promoting stability and development in this poor, populous, resource-scarce region are met will determine not only the fate of the legacy of Western ideas and institutions but the alignments and antagonisms of the future. For example, the contradictions of current U.S. policy in South Asia are so offensive to India that it regards Soviet policy as almost benevolent by contrast.

The lack of ideological affinity is not an important consideration. The socialism of Prime Minister Indira Gandhi's Congress Party has little in common with the Marxist-Leninist Soviet variant. Indeed, India is still following a predominately capitalist path of development, and its friendly relations with the Soviet Union have served to weaken and keep isolated the pro-Moscow Communist Party of India. But, as this study demonstrates, none of this constrains Soviet policy preferences since Moscow's aims are primarily diplomatic and strategic in character.

In this meticulously researched account, Professor Horn examines the symmetries and asymmetries in the Soviet-Indian relationship since the late 1960s, highlighting the perceptions and priorities that underlie the policies of Moscow and New Delhi. Why and how each capital influenced policies of the other is analyzed in both domestic and international context, as he follows the evolving influence relationship in a systematic, insightful manner.

What emerges is a sense of the mutual advantages derived from the relationship: without a friendly India, the Soviet Union would lack an effective counter to China in Asia, and without a friendly Soviet Union, India would not have the relatively free hand it now has to deal with Pakistan. Admittedly, relations between nations are expedient and expendable, even interchangeable at times, but for the present, Moscow can do no better in South Asia than to maintain good relations with India, and India can do no better than continue its relationship to the Soviet Union. The author skillfully covers the gamut of knotty issues from Kashmir to Kampuchea, from tension with China to intervention in Afghanistan, and from conventional force buildups to nuclear proliferation; the dilemmas they posed and the behaviors they elicited are examined in detail.

Diplomacy has been called the art of the possible, and in this contribution to the series of *Studies of Influence in International Relations*, Professor Horn offers detailed evidence that over the past generation or so both Moscow and New Delhi have generally been well served by their diplomats.

Alvin Z. Rubinstein
Bryn Mawr, Pa.

PREFACE

What is the reason for another book on relations between the Soviet Union and India? Haven't there been enough, you might well ask. Indeed, the list of books on this subject is impressively lengthy as can be seen from the brief bibliography near the back of the present volume. Many of these, moreover, are excellent studies that can perhaps only be improved upon by bringing them up to date.

The justification for *this* study is more than simply updating previous ones, however. As with the best full-length examinations of Soviet-Indian relations, the present study focuses on a particular conceptual issue, which provides a unique analytical framework for viewing the last 10 to 15 years of relations between the Soviet Union and India. For example, Sen Gupta organized his analysis around Asian perceptions of the USSR, Donaldson focused on ideology, Remnek highlighted the role of Soviet scholars, Barnds' study centered on the behavior of great powers, and Clarkson stressed Soviet economic development theories.[1] This analysis, however, is structured around the question of influence. The ability of one state to exercise influence over another, that is, to affect the other's behavior in a desired direction, is a central dynamic of international politics. A large load of "conventional wisdom" has emerged concerning the ability of superpowers to exercise this influence, or leverage, on the actions of weaker, or Third World, states. This conventional wisdom has dominated many of the perceptions of Soviet-Indian relations, in particular. Ony two briefer studies, a chapter by Barnds[2] and a monograph by Donaldson,[3] have directly confronted this issue of influence in the relationship between Moscow and New Delhi. The purpose of the present study is to examine explicitly and in greater depth the theme of influence in these relations with a focus on the present, and likely future, state of relations in the 1980s. It is my hope that the main body of the book will persuade the reader of the value of this endeavor, and that it will not be "just another study" of Soviet-Indian relations.

There are many people who deserve my thanks for the contributions they have made in one form or another to this book. Among faculty colleagues, there are many, but I would cite, in particular, Roger Rieber, Clifford Edmunds, Uri Ra'anan, William Griffith, Kit Machado, and, of course, Alvin Rubinstein. I would also like to express my gratitude to Indian and Soviet scholars and officials with whom I have discussed this project—here in the United States as well as on trips to India and the Soviet Union, and at various international gatherings, particularly, the Eleventh Congress of the International Political Science Association held in Moscow in August 1979, and the Second World Congress on Soviet and East European Studies in Garmisch, West Germany, in October 1980. I want to thank the librarians and staff at the Oviatt Library at California State University, Northridge for aiding in the search for materials and for providing a small "home away from home" in which I piled stacks of materials and spent countless hours over the past three years. A number of graduate and undergraduate student assistants rendered outstanding service in tracking down various items and helping to gather necessary data; these included Rick Sweeney, Dave Stowe, Bill Belden, and Paula Brumbaugh. Chapter 2 is largely based on an article of mine published in *Orbis* and I would thank the editors of that journal for permission to draw on the analysis presented there.[4] Finally, I offer my most sincere thanks to the secretarial staff of the Department of Political Science—Florence Jameson, Ellen Forman, and Joyce Leu—for their good humor and equally good skills in the face of the veritable mountain of typing I asked them to do.

The book is dedicated to my wife, Judy, and our three children, Jeff, Chris, and Laura, who have all contributed more than they know to the book simply by putting up with it—and with me.

NOTES

1. Bhabani Sen Gupta, *Soviet-Asian Relations in the 1970s and Beyond: An Interperceptional Study* (New York: Praeger, 1976); Robert H. Donaldson, *Soviet Policy Towards India: Ideology and Strategy* (Cambridge, Mass.: Harvard University Press, 1974); Richard B. Remnek, *Soviet Scholars and Soviet Foreign Policy: A Case Study in Soviet Policy Towards India* (Durham, N.C.: Carolina Academic Press, 1975); William J. Barnds, *India, Pakistan, and the Great Powers* (New York: Praeger, 1972); Stephen Clarkson, *The Soviet Theory of Development: India and the Third World in Marxist-Leninist Scholarship* (Toronto: University of Toronto Press, 1978).
2. William J. Barnds, "Soviet Influence in India: A Search for the Spoils that Go with Victory," in Alvin Z. Rubinstein, ed., *Soviet and Chinese Influence in the Third World* (New York: Praeger, 1975).
3. Robert H. Donaldson, *The Soviet-Indian Alignment: Quest for Influence* (Denver: University of Denver Monograph Series in World Affairs, 1979).
4. Robert C. Horn, "Indian-Soviet Relations in 1969: A Watershed Year?," *Orbis*, Winter 1976, pp. 1539–63.

CONTENTS

EDITOR'S PREFACE		v
PREFACE		ix
Notes		x
INTRODUCTION: INFLUENCE AS THE CONCEPTUAL FOCUS		xiii
Note		xviii
1	HISTORICAL FRAMEWORK OF THE CONTEMPORARY RELATIONSHIP	1
	Changing Soviet Perceptions after Stalin	3
	Soviet Capabilities in Seeking Influence	7
	Indian Foreign Policy Issues and the Soviet Union	9
	Soviet and Indian Goals	13
	Notes	15
2	1969. A TURNING POINT IN RELATIONS	16
	The Changing International and Regional Contexts	17
	Indo-Soviet Bilateral Relations in 1968	20
	Shifting Policies in 1969	27
	Who Was Influencing Whom?	40
	Notes	43
3	THE APPROACH OF WAR IN SOUTH ASIA	46
	The Economic Side of Indo-Soviet Relations	48
	The Foreign Policy Side of Indo-Soviet Relations	49
	Closer Ties and Continuing Issues	54
	The Treaty Is Made Public	62
	The Approaching Conflict	66
	War and Influence	71
	Notes	74
4	THE CONFLICT'S AFTERMATH: "THE ARITHMETICS OF SUPER POWER INFLUENCE"	77
	Indian and Soviet Perspectives	78
	Visits and Issues	83
	"India Welcomes a Good and Trusted Friend"	89

   Collective Security, the Indian Ocean, and India's
    Nuclear Detonation 93
   Regional Affairs and Outside Powers 98
   The Postwar Period: Little in the Way of Spoils 112
   Notes 112

5 INDIA'S STATE OF EMERGENCY 116
   Regional and External Concerns 119
   India's Chinese Policy Shift 123
   Mrs. Gandhi in Moscow: "The Best of Friends"? 129
   Indo-Soviet Relations and International Forums 135
   Expanding Economic Cooperation 137
   India's External and Internal Environments:
    Elections and Influence 140
   Notes 143

6 THE JANATA INTERREGNUM 147
   Moscow's Initial Responses 148
   The United States' and Chinese "Challenges" 156
   India and the Great-Power Triangle 163
   Desai's Last Visit to Moscow 171
   Changing Governments 173
   Observations on the Election 176
   Notes 177

7 RETURN TO "NORMALCY"?: INDIRA BACK
  IN OFFICE 180
   India and the Afghan Invasion 181
   Moscow's Multifaceted Strategy 185
   Resurgence of the Chinese Factor 190
   The Continuing Afghan Issue and the Exchange
    of Visits 194
   1981: The State of Relations 200
   Influence and Continuing Issues 208
   Notes 209

8 THE PARAMETERS OF AN INFLUENCE
  RELATIONSHIP 213
   Notes 222

BIBLIOGRAPHY 223
INDEX 229
ABOUT THE AUTHOR 233

INTRODUCTION
INFLUENCE AS THE CONCEPTUAL FOCUS

The significance for world politics of relations between the Soviet Union, a superpower with growing global interests and capabilities, and India, a major Third World state, does not seem open to doubt. Indeed, primarily out of a recognition of India's potential as a leader in Third World and nonaligned affairs, the Soviet Union chose India in the mid-1950s as one of the major focuses of its policies in the developing world. Over the course of the more than two and a half decades since USSR efforts began in earnest in India, that country has continued to rank among the top two or three Third World states in terms of Soviet attention and emphasis. India was the recipient, for example, of the greatest amount of Soviet economic credits and grants to developing countries between 1954 and 1976. Soviet attention has also been apparent in such policies as military assistance, trade, and diplomatic, political, and propaganda support, all of which India has received in large quantities. India rapidly became a major factor in a broad range of Soviet foreign policies; this is exemplified not only in the Soviet Union's global competition with the United States, which the inclusion of Pakistan—India's chief adversary in South Asia—in the Western alliance system facilitated, but also in the Soviets' growing rift with the People's Republic of China (PRC) due to Moscow's implicit support of New Delhi in the Sino-Indian border clashes of 1959 and 1962.

It is evident, then, that the Soviet Union has placed high hopes on India and has made a considerable investment of material and political resources in that country. It is far less clear what kind of return the Soviets have received on this investment. There may have been developments that redounded to Soviet advantage, but which Soviet policy had little to do with. On the other hand, there may have been Soviet efforts, which may have failed or succeeded, to obtain a direct return. What is certain, however, is that any such successes cannot simply be assumed based on the scale of the investment; that is, the input of Soviet resources does not necessarily give us an indication of the Soviet return.

What we are faced with, in short, is the question of influence: the ability of one state to affect the behavior of another to the former's advantage in policy. We can assume that the Soviet Union, like all states, expends its resources with some return in mind. Fundamentally, what we are asking is what kind of return—that is, influence over Indian behavior—did it obtain? In examining this issue, we need to investigate a number of questions. These include: What goals is the Soviet Union seeking? How did, and does, the Soviet Union seek to influence India? That is, what instruments or capabilities does it use? What factors have been conducive to the establishment of such influence? What factors have been obstacles? How has the Soviet Union succeeded or failed and why? Throughout these questions and particularly in the last one, we must also reverse the perspective and analyze Indian influence attempts: What goals has India pursued? How has India tried to influence the Soviet Union? What capabilities does it use? What factors have worked to New Delhi's advantage and which ones have served as constraints? To what degree has India been successful and why? In sum, we are concerned with who influenced whom, when, how, and why.

What we are looking for in this study are examples of either the Soviet Union or India affecting the other's behavior to its advantage. This might mean *modification* or *reinforcement* of behavior. In either case, our definition of influence requires that we have indications that the state being influenced would not have acted that way without the influencer's input. Moreover, we must be sensitive not only to instances of manifest influence—where the Soviet Union, for example, directly gets India to behave a certain way—but also to implicit influence, where India anticipates the Soviet Union's application of influence or leverage and adopts the desired mode of conduct prior to the application. We must also look for examples of positive influence, i.e., getting New Delhi to take some action, as well as negative influence (deterrence), i.e., getting it to refrain from or stop some behavior. Finally, we need continuously to be aware that influence is a process, not only an outcome, and that it can be reciprocal. Thus, the Soviet Union could simultaneously be influencing India while being influenced by it.

What does the success of an influence-building attempt depend on? There are several indicators of success. For the Soviet Union, these include capabilities, goals, the will to allocate capabilities in this regard, and the effectiveness and skill in mobilizing and applying these resources. For India, these include capabilities and goals, predisposition toward the Soviet Union, perception of the issue and of Soviet policies, and the degree of need or dependence (which in turn depends on the importance of the product, whether it is economic assistance or diplomatic support, and the availability of alternative sources of supply). The role of external conditions, including the capabilities, goals, and policies of third states then combines with these other factors to determine the outcome.

How do we assess influence? Where do we look for evidence of the existence or exercise of influence? Basically, we are searching for information on the policies of the Soviet Union and India on bilateral and international issues and, particularly, for indication of any changes in those ship of the creation of Bangladesh. Chapter 4 examines the years 1972 to June 1975, which encompasses the period from the end of the war until the declaration of the state of emergency by Prime Minister Indira Gandhi. Foreign policy changes in New Delhi and Moscow are analyzed as is the Soviet rejuvenation of the collective security idea and the November 1973 visit to India of Communist Party of the Soviet Union (CPSU) leader Leonid Brezhnev. The increasing pressures of Indian internal developments are also considered.

Chapter 5 focuses on the period from June 1975 to March 1977; it explores the impact of the emergency rule situation in India on the influence relationship. The Soviet attitude is analyzed as is Indian foreign policy, particularly the June 1976 visit of Mrs. Gandhi to the Soviet Union. The following chapter analyzes the impact on Indo-Soviet relations of other changes in India's domestic political situation: Mrs. Gandhi's stunning electoral defeat in March 1977 and the emergence to power of the Janata. Of particular concern here is the Soviet attitude prior to and after the election, the new Indian policies under the new Janata government, and the Soviet response. Chapter 7 covers the most recent period, beginning with Mrs. Gandhi's return to power early in 1980, and bringing the nature of the Soviet-Indian influence relationship up to date as of the time of writing (May 1981). Especially important insights into the status of Moscow's and New Delhi's attempts to influence one another can be drawn from India's reaction to the Soviet invasion of Afghanistan and the behavior of both states toward the nonaligned foreign ministers' meeting in Delhi in February 1981.

Chapter 8 concludes the book by seeking to pull these threads together for an overall assessment of the nature of the influence relationship between the Soviet Union and India. Who influenced whom and on what issues? How is the presence or lack of influence explained? What role did the goals and capabilities of the two states play? What factors were conducive or obstacles to the exercise of influence by either state? Finally, what does our evaluation tell us about the future of the Soviet-Indian influence relationship?

Two further intoductory notes are in order. First, in the interests of consistency, I have utilized throughout the book the United States' spellings of words—such as "favor" rather than "favour"—rather than switch back and forth between this and the Indian/British spellings. Also, I have maintained the pre-1978 spelling of Chinese names—Peking and Teng Hsiao-ping, for instance—throughout the book, rather than switch in midstream to Beijing and Deng Xiaoping.

Second, I should comment on sources. Only the most directly helpful secondary sources are listed in the bibliography. However, the overwhelming percentage of the data analyzed in the study came from primary sources, such as official communiqués, government statements, and speeches by political leaders. The texts of these, and to some extent analyses of them, came mostly from Indian and Soviet press sources. For India the daily newspaper *Statesman* was consulted for the entire period while others, especially *Hindu* and *Hindustan Times*, were used extensively. The weekly *Overseas Hindustan Times* was relied on for the recent periods as well. The Indian government publication, *Indian and Foreign Review*, published twice a month, often carried texts of documents and speeches. The Pakistani daily newspapers *Dawn* and *Morning News* were also used heavily. Western analyses were drawn particularly from *The Times* (London), *New York Times*, *Los Angeles Times*, and *Christian Science Monitor*. Of course, the Soviet press was subjected to intensive and extensive reading, particularly the daily *Pravda*. In addition, Moscow's foreign affairs journals, the weekly *New Times* and the monthly *International Affairs*, both published in several languages, were extremely useful. Also useful was *Soviet Review*, published by the Soviet Embassy in India in various Indian languages. On Asian affairs generally, the weekly *Far Eastern Economic Review* has been indispensable as has the annual *Military Balance* from the International Institute for Strategic Studies in London for examining the military relationship. The Indian journal *International Studies* began a few years back to publish reviews by Indian scholars reporting on India's foreign relations during specific six-month periods; these were of great value in helping to fill in the broader context in which Soviet-Indian relations operated. *Asian Survey's* annual studies of the past year's developments for each Asian state were also helpful in detailing that context.

NOTE

1. See his discussion of the nature, assessment, and measurement of influence in his "Introduction" to Alvin Z. Rubinstein, ed., *Soviet and Chinese Influence in the Third World* (New York: Praeger, 1975), pp. 1–22.

Soviet-Indian Relations
Issues and Influence

1
HISTORICAL FRAMEWORK OF THE CONTEMPORARY RELATIONSHIP

It is obvious that India did not just suddenly emerge on the horizon of Soviet foreign policy in 1969. Indeed, although the period of the most intense USSR involvement did not begin until after Stalin's death in 1953, Soviet interest in the Indian subcontinent can be traced as far back as the seventeenth century when trade links with the Mogul Empire were established and Peter the Great (1682–1725) began the intermittent tsarist dream of expansion in that direction. Growing competition and rivalry between the Russian and British Empires kept such dreams alive. The Russians attempted various unsuccessful schemes in the nineteenth century, all designed to weaken Britain by triggering an anti-British uprising in India. While the area did not acquire primary importance for the new Bolshevik leaders after 1917, Marxism and its application by Lenin and later Stalin as heads of the new USSR regime added crucial new elements to the Soviet view of and approach toward India.

Marx's writings reflected a concern both with how British policies furthered India's social and economic revolution and with how India, like other colonies, served British capitalism as a source of raw materials and a market for manufactured goods. It was Lenin who took this fundamental Marxist analysis one step further by applying it to conditions during and after World War I. In his writing on *Imperialism, The Highest Stage of Capitalism* (1916), Lenin argued that colonies were weak links in the imperialist system. For Lenin this added a "scientific" justification to the historically based Russian interest in India. Other Marxists, in particular the Indian M.N. Roy, argued that this analysis demanded that the primary focus in the global struggle against imperialism be on colonial areas. Fomenting anticolonial rebellion there would bring the inevitable collapse of European imperialism. Lenin, as the leader of the fledgling Soviet government, drew different conclusions from his own emphasis on the importance of the colonial world. While the new forces of nationalism there held promise and efforts should be made to develop and strengthen these forces, the primary focus of Soviet foreign policy had to be on Europe. The threat to the new regime's existence originated in Europe and it was there that the proper proletarian revolutionary conditions—which were not present in the colonies—existed.

Under Stalin there was no change in this order of Soviet priorities. With the stalemate in Europe in the mid-1920s, there was an upsurge of Soviet interest in the "East," but most of this was directed toward the nationalist Kuomintang in China and its relations with the Soviet Union and the Chinese Communist Party (CCP). After the failure of Soviet policy in China, Stalin's new suspicions of bourgeoisie-led nationalist movements in colonial areas spread to India. Despite the 1927 visit to the Soviet Union of Indian nationalist leader Jawaharlal Nehru and his favorable comments on developments in the Soviet Union, Stalin expressed deep suspicions of the Indian National Congress (INC), which was the leading element of India's struggle against the British. Continuing the practice of subordinating Soviet policy in India to Soviet interests elsewhere, Stalin in the mid-1930s had no sympathy for anti-British forces when he sought British support against the rise of Nazi Germany and Fascist Italy; nationalists had to fight against the primary danger, fascism, and leave the struggle for emancipation until later.

Only with the end of the war and the disintegration of the allied relationship with Britain did the Soviet focus begin to change. Moscow established diplomatic relations with India in April 1947, about four months prior to its complete independence. Soviet sympathies clearly were with the new states of the developing world and with those colonies struggling to become independent. In an important speech in September 1947, one of Stalin's leading associates, Andrei Zhdanov, included India among those exceptional states that, while not socialist, were not part of the imperialist camp either. India (along with Egypt and Syria) was seen to be "sympathizing" with the anti-imperialist (i.e., Soviet) camp. However, the "new era" in Soviet-Indian relations that this seemed to point to was short-lived. By early 1948 East-West Cold War positions had been rigidified and India was to fall victim to these new tensions. The Soviets enunciated their new suspicion of continuing British imperialism in areas like India, and the Indian bourgeoisie were once again, as in 1928-35, viewed as reactionary and in "the camp of imperialism." India was a semicolony that was not truly independent. Nonalignment was perceived as an "imperialist device." Not only was India's independence seen as a sham, but Pakistan was viewed as an artificial and unviable entity created by British imperialism on the principle of "divide and rule" in the subcontinent. A communist insurrection in the Telengana area of India in 1948 was encouraged. Once again, the Soviet approach toward India appears to have been determined by Moscow's relations elsewhere—with the West in this case—and to have little or nothing to do with changes within India.

In the early 1950s, prior to Stalin's death, there were signs of change in the Soviet perception of India. Gradually lessening their militant stance, the Soviets softened their appraisal of Nehru. Cultural exchanges were begun, and the Soviets sent greatly needed shipments of wheat to India. In 1952, Stalin gave his first interview to a foreign diplomat in two years to the departing Indian ambassador, Dr. S. Radhakrishnan. In 1953, in a further "gesture of good will" Stalin granted an interview to the new Indian ambassador, K.P.S. Menon.[1] The Soviet leadership began to perceive that its anti-Indian hostility had not reaped benefits. The Soviets had isolated themselves and the Communist Party of India (CPI) from Indian nationalism. The 1951-52 election illustrated this harsh reality for the CPI, and Nehru's 1949 visit to the United States warned of this potential for isolation for the Soviet Union as well. The Soviets also saw encouraging signs in Indian foreign policy, particularly in: (1) New Delhi's support for the seating of Communist China in the United Nations; (2) its refusal to condemn China in the Korean War and its offer to mediate that conflict; and (3) its refusal to sign a Japanese peace treaty in San Francisco in 1950. These policies indicated that nonalignment might not be an obstacle to Soviet interests and that India was further from being an "imperialist lackey" than previously assumed.

CHANGING SOVIET PERCEPTIONS AFTER STALIN

The clearest sign of further change in Soviet perceptions of India after Stalin's death was seen in the address of G.M. Malenkov, chairman of the Council of Ministers, to the USSR Supreme Soviet in August 1953:

> The position of so large a state as India is of great importance for strengthening peace in the East. India has made a considerable contribution to the efforts of peace-loving countries aimed at ending the war in Korea, and relations with India are growing stronger; cultural and economic ties are developing. We hope that relations between India and the Soviet Union will continue to develop and grow, with friendly cooperation as the keynote.[2]

As Ambassador K.P.S. Menon noted, this was the "first occasion on which so friendly a reference to India, or indeed to any noncommunist state, has been made by so important a personage in the Soviet Union . . . "[3] This was followed by the appointment of a new Soviet ambassador, a foreign trade specialist with an excellent command of English. The first trade agreement was signed in December 1953. In the May Day 1954 slogans of the CPSU, India made its initial appearance and was listed first among noncommunist countries in Soviet greetings. Meanwhile, visits between the two became more significant. After the unofficial visit of Nehru's daughter, Indira Gandhi, in 1953, Nehru himself came in June 1955, and Soviet leaders, Khrushchev and Bulganin, returned the honor in November.

Importantly, these signs of adjustment in the perception of India were part of a larger process of change in Soviet foreign policy. Basic to this change was Moscow's altered perception of the nature of its competition with the West. The emergence of large quantities of nuclear weapons had encouraged, in the post-Stalin Soviet leadership, an appreciation of the very real danger of East-West confrontations having catastrophic results. The area of greatest potential explosiveness naturally was Europe where tensions were already high and the situation was stalemated. However, while the status quo should and could be maintained there, Soviet leaders sought other arenas where the struggle or competition—albeit peaceful—with the West could be waged. It was in the Third World, Khrushchev and others enthusiastically and optimistically believed, where the West seemed particularly vulnerable. In varying degrees, countries in these regions were involved in the decolonization process and, in numerous cases, had stored up vast reservoirs of anti-Western sentiments. The nationalist movements that were growing there would be amenable to the Soviet goal of breaking their countries' dependence on the West, particularly economically. They would be emotionally receptive to Soviet appeals to peace and the struggle for independence and against Western imperialism and neocolonialism. In other words, in Khrushchev's view, the Third World offered a pragmatic and flexible Soviet policy enormous opportunities with little cost and, most importantly, little risk. Moreover, the Kremlin leaders must have seen a necessity in acting quickly, since the West had already joined the struggle in the Third World in the form of military pacts in the Middle East, and South and Southeast Asia.[4] Finally, there was the emerging factor of Communist China. While Moscow and Peking were not yet engaged in an outright struggle in the early 1950s, their competitive relationship in the Third World was already evolving.

The crux of the changing Soviet analysis of the role and potential of the developing countries was presented in Nikita Khrushchev's report of the Central Committee to the Twentieth Congress of the Communist Party of the Soviet Union in 1956.[5] This Congress, a watershed in Soviet foreign and domestic policy, gave confirmation, formal sanction, and additional impetus to policies and ideas that had been developing and accelerating since the last years of Stalin's life. In his report, Khrushchev emphasized the importance in international relations of the accelerating disintegration of the world colonial system and the concomitant "political and economic upsurge of the peoples of Southeast Asia and the Arab East." The outcome of the anticolonial wars in Korea, Indochina, and Indonesia "has demonstrated that the imperialists are unable ... to cope with the peoples who are resolutely fighting for a life of freedom and independence." According to Khrushchev, the power of these new nations was rapidly growing more significant. In short, the period predicted by Lenin "when the peoples of the East play an active part in deciding the destinies of the whole world and have become a new and mighty factor in international relations, has arrived."

Then what was to be the basis of Soviet policy toward this "new and mighty factor" of the East? Khrushchev said that Soviet policies were to be encompassed within the "general line" (that is, a fundamental principle, not merely a tactical maneuver) of Soviet foreign policy: "peaceful coexistence." He asserted that countries with different social and political systems, that is, the Soviet Union and the newly emerging countries of the East, could coexist peacefully in friendship and cooperation. Furthermore, by means of cooperation between the Soviet Union and these developing countries, war was no longer inevitable. The First Secretary said that there had been established a vast "zone of peace," which consisted of both socialist and nonsocialist peace-loving states in Europe and the East. The Soviet Union stood in support of the people and countries of the East who sought peace. Khrushchev promised that the Soviet Union would "tirelessly" seek to strengthen friendship and cooperation with those countries "which stand for peace, ... refuse to be involved in military pacts, and seek to preserve peace."[6]

Khrushchev argued that countries that had gained their independence since World War II still faced serious problems: "the aftermath of the colonialists' misrule." The basic difficulty was the lack of economic independence of these countries, for key economic positions continued to be controlled by "foreign monopoly capital." Western "aid" and "technical assistance" were seen and depicted by the Russians as efforts to keep these struggling new nations as suppliers of raw materials and markets for Western products. However, he asserted, it was precisely here that the Soviet Union could play a crucial role by offering these new nations an *alternative* to their Western ties. Modern equipment and techniques (including capital equipment that the West was reluctant to give) and mutually beneficial trade "free from any political or military obligations" would be forthcoming from the Soviet Union, which was a state powerful enough politically and militarily to be able to do so without attempting to interfere with these countries' independence. In the words of Khrushchev's Central Committee report:

> These countries, although they do not belong to the socialist world system can draw on its achievements in building an independent national economy and in raising their peoples' living standards. Today they need not go begging to their former oppressors for modern equipment. They can get it from the socialist countries.... The very fact that the Soviet Union and the other counties of the socialist camp exist, that they are ready to help the underdeveloped countries with their industrial development on terms of equality and mutual benefit, is a major stumbling block to colonial policy. The imperialists can no longer regard the underdeveloped countries as merely potential sources for the extraction of maximum profits. They are compelled to make concessions in their relations with them.[7]

In short, said a later but typical *Pravda* editorial, the West's "colonialist aspirations" and its efforts to apply economic pressures to developing countries were neutralized: "It is increasingly difficult for the imperialists to use the lever of economic pressures against the liberated countries."[8]

A critical aspect of this new Soviet appraisal of the Third World has been the emphasis placed on the international orientation of these potential "allies" of Moscow rather than on internal situations in the countries. As an authoritative analysis in *Kommunist,* the theoretical and political journal of the Central Committee of the CPSU, stated in December 1956, the fight of the countries of the East for their "political and economic independence, for their sovereign rights, is objectively an anti-imperialist fight and shakes the big imperialist powers' domination in international relations...."[9] Both Khrushchev's report to the Twentieth Congress and the *Kommunist* article gave scant attention to the role of internal developments in the countries of the Third World. Undoubtedly this was partly a reflection of the poor state of Soviet scholarship concerning the East as of 1956; significant steps were soon taken to correct the situation.[10] Nevertheless, it gradually became clear that the foreign policies of national/bourgeoisie regimes took precedence over both internal developments as well as the needs and programs of communist parties.

Within the context of this changing Soviet perception of the Third World, India stood out as an important and attractive "target." It was large in size and population and it occupied a strategic location vis-à-vis Soviet borders and the Indian Ocean. It was more economically developed than other states in Asia and politically it appeared impressively stable. Moreover, India's policies of nonalignment and anticolonialism and its emphasis on morality in foreign affairs had given it an important position in world politics. That is, India was one of the most significant, and most potentially powerful Third World nations and was most likely to be responsive to Soviet overtures among those states that fit the Soviet "framework."

SOVIET CAPABILITIES IN SEEKING INFLUENCE

One of the most crucial differences in the Soviet approach to India and the Third World in the mid-1950s compared to any previous period was that the Soviet state now had the capabilities to project itself dramatically into these regions. Soviet tools in seeking influence in India ran the gamut from economic aid, foreign trade, and military assistance to an enormous variety of cultural, educational, and informational exchanges and agreements.

Since its beginning in 1955, the Soviet economic aid program (as compared to that of the United States) has had an impact far out of proportion to its size. This impact has been due to several factors. For one, Soviet aid has reduced Indian dependence on the West. In the case of the first Soviet project, the Bhilai steel mill, Moscow moved quickly where German and British interests had dragged negotiations on fruitlessly for two years. The Soviet offer of crude oil at a low price in 1960 forced the Western cartels to lower their price. For Indian nonalignment, the political value of having the Soviet Union as one of its donors had a further practical value: more generous Soviet terms forced more favorable Western terms, amounts, and end-uses in numerous cases. The Soviets had agreed to 2.5 percent over 12 years, after completion of the project, to be repaid in rupees or Indian exports, while the Western offer was 4.5–6.3 percent over a shorter length of time to be repaid in convertible currency. The Soviet Union also was willing to help with projects, particularly in the public sector, where the West was reluctant to give assistance. Moscow offered to aid in the construction of the steel plant at Bokaro after years of negotiation with the United States had led nowhere.[11] In addition, the Soviets allowed repayment in Indian commodities. This provision had several advantages for New Delhi: it represented export expansion, meant that products were sold that India might otherwise have trouble selling in the world market, and conserved precious foreign exchange. The Soviets aided India in its economic planning and trained Indians to run Soviet-developed projects. Finally, the timing of Soviet aid offers—for example, immediately after the Sino-Indian border clash in the fall of 1959—was indicative of Soviet efforts to create a favorable impression in New Delhi. Overall, the Soviet Union offered approximately $1.5 billion in credits to New Delhi between 1955 and the late 1960s and had financed an impressive array of heavy industrial and oil-related public sector projects. The overall Soviet technical record was good although, as with any donor, there were problem areas.[12] The political value of Soviet aid seemed even more impressive.

Trade between the Soviet Union and India has undergone tremendous growth. In 1953 total trade turnover between the two countries was only $1.6 million, a total surpassed in the closing days of tsarist Russia. By 1958 this trade had grown to $94.6 million; Indian imports from the Soviet Union were 2.5 percent of its total imports and its exports to the Soviet Union were 4.2 percent of its total exports. By 1965 these figures had grown to 6 percent and 11.5 percent respectively, and India had emerged as the largest noncommunist trade partner for the Soviet Union.[13] Over the years, the change in the composition of the trade has been as important as the growth in trade. While the Soviet Union initially took India's traditional exports, by the early 1960s Moscow was taking an increasing share of India's new manufactured and semimanufactured goods. Moreover, many of these items were unmarketable in the West. Finally, settlement of imbalances in the bilateral trade could be made in rupees; this arrangement has taken the burden off India's limited foreign exchange reserves. As with the aid program, there have been problem areas, such as the Soviets reselling Indian goods for hard currency, difficult bargaining over prices, and often arduous negotiations regarding purchase of certain products the Soviets desired to sell. But these issues should not obscure the fact that the growth and composition of trade have generally been perceived in both Moscow and New Delhi as very positive factors in the developing Soviet-Indian friendship.

Soviet use of the tool of military aid lagged behind the use of economic aid and foreign trade programs. It was not until the fall of 1960 that the two states agreed to military credits. In 1961 the first Soviet shipments of transports and helicopters arrived (along with the training of crews for fighting in mountain areas and the provision of road-building equipment). As with this first agreement, subsequent ones seemed designed to aid India in its border conflicts with China and, to a lesser extent, with Pakistan. A new agreement in 1962 brought MiG aircraft a year later along with plans to establish a plant to manufacture MiG-21 engines and frames in India. Impressive quantities of such material as sophisticated aircraft, surface-to-air missile sites, submarines, and tanks followed during the 1960s. Although reports vary, it would appear that by the end of the 1960s India had received more than $700 million worth of military equipment from the Soviet Union (again to be repaid in goods or rupees).[14]

Finally, the Soviets have engaged in what might be called "personal diplomacy" in an effort to cultivate India. In 1955 Prime Minister Nehru undertook a precedent-setting 16-day trip to the Soviet Union. Never before had the Soviets so warmly welcomed a noncommunist leader, nor had they ever before allowed noncommunists to speak their views publicly before Soviet audiences. The Soviets were sensitive not to engage in any criticism of the United States or Great Britain, which would have made Nehru's nonalignment awkward, and they even allowed the Indian delegation to draft the joint communiqué independently at the close of the visit.[15] The Khrushchev-Bulganin visit to India, which followed in 1955, seemed equally successful. The Indian reception was warm and enthusiastic, and the two Soviet leaders took every opportunity to hail Soviet-Indian friendship and cooperation. They offered further economic aid, enunciated a pro-Indian position on Kashmir, and offered no help to the CPI. These two visits set the framework and tone for the dozens of high-level visits that were to follow in the next decade and a half. Furthermore, they set the stage for closer Soviet-Indian ties, particularly on foreign policy issues of critical importance to the two states.

INDIAN FOREIGN POLICY ISSUES AND THE SOVIET UNION

India entered world politics with a set of principles that were to serve as a guide for its foreign policy. These principles were closely tied to India's domestic situation and needs and also reflected the ideals of the leader who thoroughly dominated Indian foreign policy decision making—Prime Minister Nehru. By virtue of being India's nationalist leader and also its first prime minister (and by holding the external-affairs portfolio during his entire term, 1947–64), Nehru formulated and articulated India's interests and put into practice Indian policies.

Among the principles underlying Indian foreign policy, the best known has been that of nonalignment. To Nehru, this meant that India would avoid military alliances or being tied too closely to either "camp" in the Cold War struggle. At the same time, it did not mean noninvolvement in world affairs. In Nehru's view, the Cold War itself threatened world peace as well as the independence and economic well-being of new states in Asia and elsewhere. Therefore, Nehru envisioned an active role for India in world politics: a moralistic, crusading, internationalist approach where India would play an important role as a spokesman for Asia and indeed for all nonaligned new states. India would champion an end to imperialism and colonialism, and the need for peace, stability, and nonviolent change. Without these, development and nation building in the Third World would be impossible.

These fundamental principles in Nehru's perception of India and its role in world affairs led to differing outlooks on the two power centers of the time—the United States and the Soviet Union. Indian perception of the United States and the West in general was mixed. On the one hand, the West was responsible for colonialism, imperialism, and the capitalist economic system (which Indian socialist economic aspirations conflicted with). On the other hand, New Delhi was dependent on the West economically and militarily and was sympathetic to the liberalism and political democracy present there. The Soviet Union had the distinct advantage over the West of having no historical "devil image" and no bitter legacy to overcome. India had been insulated from Russian expansion by Great Britain and was, moreover, impressed by the anti-imperialist overtones of the Bolshevik revolution. Certainly during his visit in 1927, Nehru had been sympathetic to Soviet aspirations, and later he developed an admiration for Soviet economic development. Moscow was not seen as a threat; it espoused many views that Indians agreed with and could serve as an important counterweight to the West (and later to China).[16]

The three areas of Indian foreign policy where the Soviet role became the most significant in New Delhi's and Moscow's mutual efforts at influence were relations with the West, with China, and with Pakistan. On the first, the previously discussed similarity in Indian and Soviet views seemed likely to bring them together in opposition to certain Western policies. The Soviet policy change toward India was combined with U.S. policy initiatives in the region and the Indian reaction to them. U.S. policies included the creation, in 1954 and 1955 respectively, of the anticommunist Southeast Asia Treaty Organization and the Baghdad Pact. The U.S.-armed Pakistan (proceeding more on an anti-Indian basis than an anticommunist one) was a member of both. The Indian reaction was hostile on several grounds: the Cold War was being brought into South Asia, military blocs were being formed, and its rival, Pakistan, was to be armed. Washington's goal of anticommunism had little to do with Indian goals. Soviet support for New Delhi, including a Security Council veto at the United Nations, when India invaded the Portuguese enclaves of Goa, Daman, and Diu in December 1961, contrasted markedly with Western hostility. Only under the Kennedy administration did the United States seek to be more responsive to Indian needs and security concerns. After the border clash with China in the fall of 1962, India found Washington very forthcoming with aid and support. However, with the administration of Lyndon Johnson, the growing U.S. involvement elsewhere in Asia, and the apparent futility of seeking peace and positive relations with *both* India and Pakistan—as signified by the 1965 war over Kashmir—U.S. attention to India again declined.

The coincidence of Soviet and Indian views regarding the People's Republic of China has been equally significant. Prior to the 1959 Sino-Indian border clash, relations between Peking and New Delhi had been unstable. Despite the fact that India was the second noncommunist country to recognize the PRC, China adopted a hostile and virulent attitude toward newly independent India. The PRC "liberation" of Tibet by force in 1950 further added to Indian suspicions of China. The 1954 agreement in which India recognized Tibet as part of China seemed to resolve this issue. The agreement then on Panch Shee1, which contained the five principles of peaceful coexistence, at the Bandung Conference in 1955 seemed to augur well for close relations between the two Asian giants. However, growing changes in Chinese foreign policy soon began to strain relations. The forceful Chinese crushing of the Tibetan revolt in March 1959 and the border clashes with India at the end of that summer and into the early fall signified a basically hostile Sino-Indian relationship. It is at this point that the Soviet Union entered this area of Indian foreign policy. Not wanting to jeopardize relations with such an important focus of their Third World policies as India, and experiencing an accelerating escalation of Sino-Soviet antagonisms by the summer of 1959, the Soviet leaders enunciated a position of neutrality on the clash and called for talks bewween New Delhi and Peking. The Indians were pleased but the Chinese were furious. Over the next few years, Moscow became increasingly critical of Peking's attitude toward India; it intensified its economic and cultural relations with New Delhi, and initiated a military assistance program.

The timing of the 1962 Sino-Indian border war caused Moscow temporary difficulties in its support for India against China. China's massive attack in October came at the height of the Cuban missile confrontation between the Soviet Union and the United States. Apparently unwilling to risk a major feud with China at this sensitive time, *Pravda* gave approval to the PRC position and ceasefire proposals. It was not until the end of the missile crisis that the Soviets returned to their neutralist (pro-Indian in the eyes both of New Delhi and Peking) line of 1959. This temporary Soviet equivocation at so critical a time for Indian security did serve to stir up anti-Soviet feelings and to decrease Soviet prestige in India. Although Nehru avoided criticizing the Soviet Union, a certain degree of coolness crept into the relationship. In addition, substantial U.S. and British military assistance meant that New Delhi was not totally dependent on Moscow in standing up to Peking. This other assistance against Peking was soon to decline, however, while the Soviet Union's was to continue and indeed, with the exacerbation of the Sino-Soviet split, became more significant. As we shall see, this "triangular" Sino-Soviet-Indian relationship as well as the Soviet-United States-Indian one will again come to play a crucial role in 1969 and through the 1970s.

Fundamental to India's internal and external behavior has been its relationship with Pakistan. There were many problems associated with the

1947 partition of the Indian subcontinent into the separate and religiously based states of Pakistan and India. In addition, the disputed status of Kashmir has been a source of major conflicts in 1947 and 1965 and of constant friction over the entire period. With Pakistan's membership in the U.S.-sponsored Baghdad Pact, the Soviet Union gave its support, announced by Khrushchev during his 1955 visit, to the Indian postion on the dispute. In 1957 and 1962 the Soviet Union vetoed resolutions opposed by India in the Security Council of the United Nations. In addition to the Kashmir question, the Soviet Union, into the early 1960s, was clearly on India's side against Pakistan in general foreign policy questions, such as relations with the West, and all Indian-Pakistani issues.

During the mid-1960s, however, there was a change in this one-sided orientation of Soviet policy. The beginnings of this shift can be seen after India's 1962 border clash with China. New Delhi's demonstrated weakness in that conflict certainly must have reduced Soviet enthusiasm and encouraged Moscow to develop other options. As the Cold War waned in the aftermath of the Cuban missile crisis, Moscow recognized that new opportunities existed for reducing U.S. influence in treaty states such as Pakistan. A less pro-Indian policy might help move Pakistan away from its close relationship with the United States. Pakistan's chief objective of developing alliances and allies in opposition to New Delhi (or at least denying them to India) led Pakistan to accelerate its search for greater options among the major powers. Formerly tied exclusively to the United States, Pakistan began to pursue relations with both China and the Soviet Union, while trying to maintain ties with Washington. The U.S. policy of refusing to aid Pakistan actively in response to the Indian "threat" was crowned by Washington's suspension of arms sales to the region during (and after) the 1965 Indo-Pakistani war over Kashmir. This and the subsequent U.S. "disengagement" from affairs of the subcontinent were substantial blows to Pakistan. Meanwhile, already improving relations with China, in which military aid played an important role, warmed considerably when China supported Pakistan in the conflict with India. This growing relationship provided an additional, and increasingly significant, incentive for Moscow to seek to woo Pakistan.

Changes in Soviet policy were subtle but crucial. Alterations were to be seen first in the Kashmir question. Moscow's support for the Indian position was so diluted that the issue was not even mentioned in joint communiqués published after visits of Indian leaders to the Soviet Union in 1964 and 1965. Another sign was that Pakistani leaders began to visit the Soviet Union and these meeting were hailed enthusiastically by the Soviet media. The most significant signal was Moscow's adoption of a position of evenhandedness in the 1965 clash between the two states. Premier Kosygin's role of mediating the dispute at Tashkent in early 1966, was indicative of Moscow's new assessment of the South Asia scene: (1) India was too weak a link on which to base Soviet regional interests exclusively—as seen from the 1962 clash with China and the mounting internal problems with the death of Nehru in 1964; (2) Pakistan might be weaned away from its ties to Washington and Peking; and (3) the Khrushchevian policy of "overcommitment" to one state in a conflict-prone region would be avoided by his successors. Although the Tashkent agreement led to no real settlement, and the decline in Indo-Pakistani hostility was to be only short-lived, it is clear that Moscow now sought a stable South Asia where Soviet policy might influence all states. Further steps to develop influence in Pakistan—such as changes in the May Day slogans in 1966, increasing visits back and forth, and finally the offer of arms to Pakistan in July 1968—began to threaten Soviet-Indian relations. This "triangle" too—between India, the Soviet Union, and Pakistan—will provide a major part of the framework for developments in the influence relationship from 1969 through the 1970s.

SOVIET AND INDIAN GOALS

There is no way an analyst can hope to determine the existence of influence of one state over another unless there is some idea of the goals of the two states. That is, how could we know that the Soviet Union influenced India in a particular circumstance unless we knew what the Soviets were seeking in that situation? One of the major tasks of this study is to reassess continually each state's goals as the analysis proceeds. We need to infer Soviet and Indian goals from their policies and behavior. On that inference, we can attempt to assess degrees of success, i.e., influence.

Based on Soviet policy toward India up until 1969, what preliminary inference can be made regarding Soviet goals in India and South Asia?[17] First, Moscow's approach has been dominated here by the same motivation that spurred the initial Soviet "offensive" throughout the Third World: the reduction and, hopefully, elimination of Western influence in particular states and regions. This goal can be seen in the beginning of Soviet-Indian ties and in the attitude toward Pakistan and its ties to the West. A second primary goal of the Soviet Union has been to reduce, or at least contain, China's involvement in the area. This has been a major USSR goal since 1959, as the Soviets sought to develop India into a counterweight to China. Since the early 1960s, with the emergence into public view of the full-blown Sino-Soviet rift and the almost simultaneous decline of U.S. interest and involvement in South Asia, this goal has likely replaced the first one as the most critical in the Soviet perspective. Third, the Soviet Union has sought to advance its close relationship with India as a justification for its claims to be a global as well as an Asian power. Moscow seeks to be recognized as a "natural" and powerful voice in the region's affairs. A fourth goal of the Soviets has been to utilize India as an intermediary in the Third World and world politics as a whole. Again, a model relationship with New Delhi might well serve as Moscow's entree to other Third World capitals. Although they have never been heavily emphasized, security or strategic goals ought to be ruled out. That is, while the Soviet Union does not share a direct border with either India or Pakistan, South Asia does form the Soviet Union's southern frontier. Moreover, the region presents the possibility of Soviet access to the Indian Ocean, the Arabian Sea, and the Bay of Bengal, and raises the question of the establishment of Soviet naval and shipping facilities and, perhaps, bases. Finally, there is a variety of goals that includes Indian stability, commercial ties between the two countries, and socialist economic development. Of particular concern here would be India's success in following some sort of "noncapitalist path" and, at minimum, in illustrating the value of Soviet economic assistance. In the period when Moscow sought a balanced relationship with India and Pakistan, these goals could all be applied to Soviet policy toward Pakistan as well. Especially motivating Moscow in that issue was the goal of reducing China's role in South Asia.

Indian goals have been similarly diverse and complex. First, India has sought security from external threats. In the history of independent India this has been very much a real concern. It has meant defenses primarily against Pakistan and, secondarily, against China. There has been ongoing tension with both countries, highlighted by the outbreak of actual conflict in 1947 and 1965 with Pakistan and in 1959 and 1962 with China. Second, India has sought independence and nonalignment. India has striven to avoid being dominated by any other power. A third goal of New Delhi has been to insulate South Asia and the Indian Ocean from great-power activity except where that activity might be necessary or beneficial to the pursuit of the first or second goal. The third objective might be permissible also when it is conducive to a fourth goal: establishing Indian leadership in the region. Last, and highly significant to India and its other goals, India has sought assistance in economic development. While avoiding excessive commitments or dependence, successive administrations in New Delhi have sought substantial aid for ambitious development plans.

As has been seen in this discussion on the background of contemporary Soviet-Indian relations, there have been situations both of agreement or coincidence of these goals of the two states as well as divergence. It is now necessary to evaluate: (1) the extent to which any of these goals changed from 1969 to the present; (2) to what degree the goals of the two states coincided or diverged; (3) what influence-seeking efforts were made by each; and (4) what were the end results—influence or leverage—developed by either India or the Soviet Union.

NOTES

1. For a first-hand description of his meeting with Stalin, see K. P. S. Menon, *The Flying Troika* (London: Oxford University Press, 1963), pp. 26–32.
2. *Pravda*, August 9, 1953.
3. Menon, *The Flying Troika*, p. 58.
4. See Uri Ra'anan, "Tactics in the Third World," *Survey*, no. 57, October 1965, pp. 26–27; and also his *The USSR Arms the Third World: Case Studies in Soviet Foreign Policy* (Cambridge, Mass.: M. I. T. Press, 1969), esp. pp. 13–26.
5. N. S. Khrushchev, "Report of the Central Committee of the Communist Party of the Soviet Union to the 20th Party Congress," *Pravda*, February 15, 1956.
6. Ibid.
7. Ibid.
8. *Pravda*, August 7, 1963.
9. V. Semenov, "The Collapse of the Colonial System of Imperialism and Problems of International Relations," *Kommunist*, no. 18, December 1956.
10. See William Zimmerman, *Soviet Perspectives on International Relations, 1956-1967* (Princeton: Princeton University Press, 1969), esp. pp. 32–38; O. Edmund Clubb, "Soviet Oriental Studies and the Asian Revolution," *Pacific Affairs*, December 1958, pp. 380–89; and W. Z. Laqueur, "The Shifting Line in Soviet Orientalogy," *Problems of Communism*, March-April 1956, pp. 20–26.
11. See John Kenneth Galbraith, *Ambassador's Journal* (New York: New American Library, 1969), passim.
12. For example, see Asha L. Datar, *India's Economic Relations with the USSR and Eastern Europe, 1953 to 1969* (Cambridge: Cambridge University Press, 1972), passim.
13. See Arthur Stein, *India and the Soviet Union: The Nehru Era* (Chicago: University of Chicago Press, 1969), p. 297.
14. For one source, see Jyotirmoy Banerjee, *India in Soviet Global Strategy* (Calcutta: South Asia Books, 1977), p. 157.
15. See the discussion in Richard B. Remnek, *Soviet Scholars and Soviet Foreign Policy: A Case Study in Soviet Policy Towards India.* (Durham, N.C.: Carolina Academic Press, 1975), pp. 16–18.
16. For example, see the discussion in Bhabani Sen Gupta, *Soviet-Asian Relations in the 1970s and Beyond* (New York: Praeger, 1976), pp. 136 ff.; and Geoffrey Jukes, *The Soviet Union in Asia* (Berkeley: University of California Press, 1973), pp. 116–20.
17. For an excellent discussion of each state's goals, see Robert H. Donaldson, *The Soviet-Indian Alignment: Quest for Influence* (Denver: University of Denver Monograph Series in World Affairs, 1979), esp. pp. 5–9.

2
1969: A TURNING POINT IN RELATIONS

The new policy of striving to achieve a balance in relations with India and Pakistan, which Moscow undertook in the mid-1960s, had to be at least temporarily abandoned in 1971 when events on the subcontinent forced the Soviet Union to choose sides in the growing conflict between New Delhi and Islamabad. The result was the 20-year Treaty of Peace, Friendship and Cooperation signed in August 1971 by the Soviet Union and India. This treaty represented a Soviet commitment—in political, economic, and military terms—to India against Pakistan. Suddenly Indo-Soviet relations had reached a level of closeness previously thought highly unlikely in New Delhi, probably in Moscow, and certainly in the rest of the world.

The hypothesis of this chapter is that the changes witnessed in 1971 in Soviet-Indian relations and in Soviet policy in South Asia as a whole actually began primarily in 1969. In fact, it could even be argued that the treaty was drawn up in this year.[1] Even if it cannot be *proved* that the treaty was drawn up during 1969, and it probably cannot, strong evidence that points to significant alteration in the Soviet-Indian relationship in 1969 can be assembled and analyzed. The first objective of this chapter, then, is to assess the extent to which Indo-Soviet relations and Soviet policy in South Asia changed two years ahead of when "conventional wisdom" tells us it did. Secondly, we need to examine what conditions had changed—in international politics, in other areas of Soviet foreign policy, and in the relationship between India and Pakistan—to inspire such a shift in 1969. If Soviet policy during that year reverted to emphasizing a greater reliance on India rather than a balanced posture between the two South Asian rivals, what could have motivated such a shift? Was it a change in Soviet perceptions of factors external to South Asia? Or did Soviet motivation arise from a changing situation within the subcontinent? The argument here is that both external and regional factors played important roles. After viewing the former, primarily through major shifts in Soviet perceptions of the threat from China and changes in U.S. policies, we will move to an examination of the latter, the impact of the changing regional conditions on USSR goals in 1968 and 1969. With the stage thus set, we will analyze the record of Soviet-Indian relations during 1969 for indications of change and influence. The key question, as it is throughout this study, is "who was influencing whom?"

THE CHANGING INTERNATIONAL AND REGIONAL CONTEXTS

There seems to be hardly any doubt that the threat from a "militaristic and aggressive" China dominated the entire Soviet foreign policy outlook in 1969 from the first border clash on March 2. From that time on, the Soviet press and Soviet leaders' statements allowed no opportunity to pass without denouncing China for its latest "provocations" and its "hegemonistic aims." Warnings of the dire consequences of continuing such activity included application of the Brezhnev Doctrine and the possibility of nuclear war against China, and other states were warned to beware of China's designs. CPSU leader Brezhnev sought support against China from foreign communist parties in his speech to the international conference in Moscow in June, and Foreign Minister Gromyko used his address on foreign policy to the Supreme Soviet in July to lash out at PRC policies. China had clearly emerged as the Soviet Union's main enemy, and Moscow was searching anxiously in a number of directions for ways to respond to this heightened challenge.

Complicating the USSR efforts to counter the perceived threat from China were rapidly increasing indications of a possible rapprochement between China and the United States. Moscow's sensitivity to U.S. politics made it unlikely that Soviet analysts would have missed Richard Nixon's foreshadowings of a change in the U.S. policy toward China even before his election; Nixon's hints also appeared in his inaugural address and continued thereafter. Moreover, initiatives were coming from the Chinese side as well. On November 25, 1968, China proposed a renewal of the ambassadorial talks in Warsaw and reportedly suggested a Sino-United States agreement on the basis of the five principles of peaceful coexistence. Asian visitors to China in the early weeks of the Ninth Congress of the CCP in April 1969 left with the impression that United States-Chinese relations might soon improve. President Nixon took a small but significant step in July when he relaxed trade and travel restrictions to China. Soviet discomfort was actually expressed as early as December

1968 when an issue of *Literaturnaya Gazeta* analyzed Peking's suggestion for talks in Warsaw as an attempt to begin a serious dialogue with Washington for the purpose of "combining forces against the Soviet Union." The author concluded that "Sino-American coexistence is merely a hypocritical screen for planned cooperation on an anti-Soviet basis."[2] Moscow's suspicions were only partially allayed by Peking's cancellation of the U.S. talks on February 19—one day before they were to be held. Soviet radio broadcasts and diplomatic briefings continued to stress the dangerous ramifications of Sino-United States "collusion." On July 25 *Pravda* articulated Soviet fears: "It goes without saying that any designs to use the contact between Peking and Washington for some pressure on the Soviet Union . . . are nothing but the results of loss of touch with reality."

President Nixon's increasingly clear intention of withdrawing from Vietnam and reducing the U.S. presence in Asia confronted Moscow with an additional consideration. These changes had been indicated before the president's inauguration and were brought into sharper focus with his Asian trip of July-August 1969 and the enunciation of the "Guam Doctrine." While the Soviets expressed substantial skepticism regarding any U.S. "withdrawal" and warned of the need for constant vigilance against the likelihood of U.S. perfidy,[3] Moscow realized it was faced with the possibility of a reduced U.S. role in Asia coupled with renewed, post-Cultural Revolution Chinese activity in the area. Given the intensity of the conflict with China in 1969, this uncertain situation produced both dangers and opportunities for the Soviet Union.

It is within this context of rapid and significant shifts in the interrelationships among the major powers that the developments within South Asia were perceived by the Soviet leadership. The Sino-Soviet-United States triangle thus provides the framework for the alterations in the Soviet Union's South Asian triangular relationships: with India and the West, India and China, and India and Pakistan. On this regional level, too, there were unchanging constraints and new developments that combined to create an increasingly discouraging context for the successful operation of the USSR approach. What one analyst had implicitly predicted seemed indeed to be happening:

> The present [Soviet] policy, which seems to be based on the theory of maintaining a military balance in the subcontinent, may eventually create an explosive situation and thus defeat Russia's basic objective of stabilizing her southern flank through a determining role in the politics of the subcontinent.[4]

One of the keys to this looming possibility of failure for Soviet policy was the major constant of Indo-Pakistani friction. Relations between the two states had steadily worsened since the Tashkent agreement in 1966. Continuing Soviet efforts at mediation and appeals to the "Tashkent spirit" met with no success and seemingly had no impact on either New Delhi or Islamabad. The Kashmir dispute had continued and new differences had arisen. An example of the latter was the "Farakka Barrage" dispute that occurred between India and East Pakistan regarding the distribution and diversion of water from the Ganges River. Communal riots between Hindus and Muslims in India aggravated tensions, as did the increasingly unstable political situation in Pakistan in the last quarter of 1968. Moscow's goal of playing a primary role in regional affairs by means of having an important voice in *both* India and Pakistan was obviously threatened by this escalation of tension.

Moscow's lack of success in weaning Pakistan away from China, which was a fundamental aim of the new Soviet policy adopted in the mid-1960s, was at least as significant to the Soviets as the failure to resolve differences between India and Pakistan. While the Soviet goal of reducing Pakistani dependence on the United States was being achieved (due to Washington's policies as much as Islamabad's), ties with China had not weakened. Indeed, the relationship with Pakistan was one of the few foreign ties that Peking was determined to maintain during its diplomatic isolationism of the Cultural Revolution period. Continued assertions by leaders from both Pakistan and China of their "powerful community of interests" and reference by both countries to Pakistan's need of China "as a counterpoise to India" made Moscow's inability to swing Islamabad away from Peking obvious.

While India had difficulties with China—over Peking's relations with Pakistan, its support for separatists and insurrectionists in India ("Naxalites" and "Nagas"), and continuing differences over their mutual border—Indira Gandhi's government looked at the development of better relations with China, or playing the "China card," as a way of increasing India's options vis-à-vis its central and immediate adversary, Pakistan. New Delhi sought to avoid isolation in its opposition to its neighbor amid concern over Chinese economic and military assistance to Pakistan, fears of a resumpton of U.S. arms aid to that country, and apprehensions about the arms deal Islamabad concluded with the Soviet Union in July 1968. Consequently, despite its quarrels with China, India issued peace feelers in China's direction in the summer of 1968 and again in the beginning of 1969. From Moscow's point of view, of course, any improvement in Sino-Indian relations would be at its expense.

Thus, the Soviet Union seemed faced with disconcerting developments in its triangular relationships with India and Pakistan as well as India and China. The only triangle where developments seemed basically positive was the Soviet-United States-Indian one. There had been no improvement in United States-Indian relations, and the Indian government was becoming increasingly convinced of the Nixon administration's lack of interest in and commitment to Asia. Although Moscow could find some solace in this, the danger signs elsewhere must have seemed far more significant.

INDO-SOVIET BILATERAL RELATIONS IN 1968

These developments were at least as disconcerting in Moscow's perception as the ominous, yet mixed, indications of a deterioration in the direct Soviet-Indian relationship. These indications were observable on (1) foreign policy issues, including Kashmir and the Soviet invasion of Czechoslovakia in August; (2) Soviet criticisms—and the Indian reaction to them—of internal developments within India; (3) Indian concern over Soviet maps of the Sino-Indian border; (4) problems in the economic relationship; and (5) most significantly, the Indian reactions to the Soviet-Pakistani arms deal of July.

Soviet Premier Kosygin's visit in January 1968 illustrated some of these difficulties. On Indo-Pakistani relations, in one Indian newspaper's words, Kosygin continued "the significant shift . . . from outright support of India's position to benevolent neutrality as between India and Pakistan, even overlooking the latter's aggression in 1965 . . . "[5] The joint communiqué signed at the conclusion of the visit was instructive in this regard: while the Indian prime minister "recounted the efforts which India has been making to improve relations between India and Pakistan . . . " the Soviets did not acknowledge New Delhi's efforts. Rather, they only expressed hope that the "Governments of India and Pakistan will exert all their efforts in order to bring about a further normalization of . . . relations and the creation of an atmosphere conducive to the solution of the existing outstanding problems. . . . "[6] The communiqué, while it illustrated various areas of Soviet-Indian agreement such as Vietnam, disarmament, and European security, also demonstrated by omission India's refusal to join in sharing Soviet denunciations of the United States, Israel, and West Germany.[7]

The signing on July 1 of the Nuclear Non-Proliferation Treaty (NPT) created another area of some friction in Soviet-Indian relations. Despite the Soviet Union's sponsorship of the accord and its repeated urgings to other states, including India, to endorse it, New Delhi opposed the agreement on various grounds. In the words of one Indian journalist:

> India's objection was that the treaty sought only to prevent the nonnuclear countries from acquiring or manufacturing nuclear weapons or

nuclear explosive devices while permitting the existing nuclear countries to develop and stockpile more weapons. Again, the treaty required only the non-nuclear countries to undertake certain obligations—not to manufacture, acquire or receive nuclear weapons or explosive devices, and to expose their nuclear reactors and other facilities to international inspection and safeguards. The nuclear Powers were not required to assume corresponding obligations. They were free to proliferate weapons, and their nuclear reactors and facilities were immune from international inspection and safeguards.

Furthermore, the treaty prohibited non-nuclear countries from developing explosive devices for peaceful purposes. The sponsors of the treaty contended that a nuclear explosive device was indistinguishable from a nuclear weapon. India felt, however, that distinction could and should be made between explosive devices that were used only for peaceful purposes and others that were used for testing weapons.[8]

Soviet efforts to get India to sign continued for several years but without success. Since adherence by all states to the NPT was an important goal of Soviet foreign policy in 1968 and thereafter, Moscow's inability to get New Delhi's signature clearly represents a lack of influence over India, at least on that issue.

It is possible that one reason the Soviets were unable to get India's support on the NPT was that the Soviets were unwilling to put substantial pressure on India in the aftermath of the invasion of Czechoslovakia, which took place in August. There was an angry reaction in India to the Soviet-led Warsaw Pact action that ended the short-lived "Prague Spring." A senior member of the ruling Congress Party, with the support of the noncommunist opposition, had proposed a resolution condemning the Soviet Union for its aggression and committing Parliament to the position that the Soviet Union and the allies had violated the U.N. Charter. Morarji Desai, deputy prime minister, and Ram Subhag Singh, communications minister, had also favored an outright condemnation of the Soviet Union. Indira Gandhi, however, sought to play down the invasion and avoid censure of Moscow. She substituted a resolution, which was accepted by the Lok Sabha, the lower and far more important house in India's Parliament, that said only: "This House will no doubt wish to convey to the Soviet Union and its allies our view that they should carefully consider all aspects of the situation which has arisen as a result of the action by their armed forces, and its possible consequences."[9] India also abstained on the seven-nation resolution in the U.N. Security Council. (Pakistan also abstained and the Soviet Union vetoed it.)

Nevertheless, Indian disapproval was clearly registered. Mrs. Gandhi's statement in Parliament was stronger than the initial Indian positions had been on the Hungarian crisis in 1956.[10] Among other things, she said:

> Our relations with the Soviet Union, Poland, Hungary, and Bulgaria are close and many sided. We value these friendships and wish to preserve and extend them. However, we cannot but give expression to our anguish at the events in Czechoslovakia.... I am sure I reflect the opinion of the House when I express the hope that the forces which have entered Czechoslovakia will be withdrawn at the earliest possible moment and the Czech people will be able to determine their future according to their own wishes and interests, and whatever mutual problems there may be between Czechoslovakia and its allies, will be settled peacefully. The right of nations to live peacefully and without outside interference should not be denied in the name of religion or ideology.... We have always stood for the right of every country to its own traditions, aptitudes and genius. India has always raised her voice whenever these principles have been violated.[11]

In the Security Council, India had been willing to support all operative clauses of the resolution except those that condemned the Soviet Union. As Mrs. Gandhi told Parliament, India's concern was for "the withdrawal of foreign troops, restoration of the legitimate government to power and the restoration of the sovereignty of the people," and provocative language gained nothing.

That Moscow was sensitive to this Indian reaction was clearly seen during the September visit of a Soviet delegation led by Deputy Foreign Minister Firyubin. Firyubin delivered a lengthy presentation on the Soviet action, ignored the fact that India had abstained on the Security Council resolution, and, in general, implied Soviet displeasure with the degree of disapproval New Delhi voiced. Nevertheless, much has been made about the existence of Soviet influence over India on the Czech question given various Indian statements about "political realities"—as Mrs. Gandhi said, "after ... we have given expression to our feelings, ... political realities remain and the government will have to deal with them"[12]—and the frequent references at that time by Indian political leaders and journalists to India's military dependence on the Soviet Union. Yet New Delhi's reaction to the Soviet-led invasion was somewhat more outspoken in 1968 than it had been in 1956 when the Soviet-Indian relationship was just beginning. Certainly, Moscow took note of this as seen in Firyubin's visit. Ultimately, moreover, the issue was not of major concern to India. Much more important for Indian foreign policy were Soviet actions that had a direct impact on India's interests, such as ties with Pakistan. Thus, there does not seem to be sufficient evidence to demonstrate the existence of Soviet influence in this case. Although New Delhi did not condemn the Soviet Union as many in the West would have liked, Indian behavior was similar to its posture in 1956, in fact a little stronger, and was sharp enough to cause the Soviets some concern.

Another growing area of friction included Soviet criticism of internal developments in India. This had never been Moscow's primary focus in its relations with New Delhi; foreign policy was a far higher priority. The Soviets had seemed to pay attention to the pro-Soviet Communist Party of India (CPI) only to ensure that it would support the ruling Indian National Congress (INC) on whose leader (Nehru followed by Shastri and then Indira Gandhi) the Soviets based their own policy. In any case, there began in the mid-1960s a gradual decline in the previously positive nature of Soviet perceptions of the Indian domestic scene, reflected both in academic and policy-oriented writings. The years 1965–69 were marked by food shortages, regional autonomy movements, communalist tensions, and generally growing instability and social discontent. Splits within the Congress deepened and right-wing forces, "monopoly capital" in Soviet parlance, increasingly asserted themselves. Moscow lamented the poor performance of the INC in the 1967 elections and its failure to implement meaningful economic reforms. By 1969 the increasingly severe polarization between right and left factions within the Congress threatened to split the party and lead to further instability. The Soviet radio station, *Radio Peace and Progress*, beamed critical broadsides on these issues into India, a practice denounced by many in Delhi.

Many Indians also raised objections to Soviet maps that appeared to take China's side on the Sino-Indian border question. These maps showed the disputed areas of the Aksai Chin and the Northeast Frontier Agency (NEFA) as belonging to China. Such "generous cartographic concessions to China"[13] were seen as unfair by India, particularly since New Delhi had accepted Moscow's version of the Sino-Soviet border, and were also an embarrassment to the government since the issue was frequently raised in Parliament. When this issue was brought up with Firyubin in September, the Soviet deputy foreign minister simply replied that surveyors, not political leaders, were responsible for the maps; Moscow's attention had already been drawn to these complaints, he added, and the current complaint "would be noted."[14]

Although Soviet-Indian aid and trade relationships had continued to develop, by 1968 there was evidence of problems in this area too. Kosygin reportedly indicated his concern with the poor performance of some Soviet-sponsored projects and called for greater efficiency during his January visit to India.[15] In December 1968, a high-powered Soviet delegation led by Chairman of the State Committee for Foreign Economic Relations Skachkov was dispatched to India. A major concern in this visit was the operation of the Heavy Engineering Corporation at Ranchi, which was built with Soviet assistance. (The problems in this plant were seen as crucial, since the Soviet-built Bokaro steel plant depended on deliveries from Ranchi.) Heavy losses by other Soviet plants, such as the pharmaceutical ones, were also a concern. Although Skackhov's visit did not signify an actual crisis in the Soviet aid program, there were reports that he was brusque in this meeting with Indian officials, that he recommended further nationalization, particularly in the steel industry, and that he demanded greater Indian efficiency in following through on the projects.[16] His pressure on the Indians was substantial enough to lead to false reports that further Soviet aid had been discontinued until these projects were functioning smoothly and at capacity; these reports continued to circulate despite being repeatedly denied by the government.

The final step in this new, post-1964 policy of developing friendship with Pakistan in order to establish influence in *both* India and Pakistan produced the most severe Indian reaction and held the greatest potential for the disruption of Soviet-Indian relations. This step was the Soviet decision in 1968 to supply arms to Pakistan. Islamabad had sought Soviet military assistance ever since the U.S. cutoff in 1965. The Pakistani argument was simple: if Moscow hoped to balance its relations with the two leaders of the subcontinent, it could not provide military aid to just one; it had either to stop its assistance to India or undertake a similar program with Pakistan. This argument plus assurances that Islamabad would not use the arms to disturb the peace in South Asia were reiterated by President Ayub Khan when he made his third and last trip to the Soviet Union in September 1967. When the USSR leaders asked for more time to consider the request, Ayub replied that Pakistan had already waited for two years. According to an "inside" Pakistani source, Brezhnev responded that "now that period may be reduced by one-fourth, *i.e.*, wait for another six months." In fact, Moscow seems to have recognized that arming Pakistan within that time frame was unavoidable; tentative agreement was reached on Kosygin's visit to Pakistan, the first by a Soviet premier, in April, 1968. In late June, a Pakistani military delegation under Army Commander Yahya Khan journeyed to Moscow and negotiated the final details. While earlier agreements had provided for Soviet army jeeps and trucks and later a few helicopters, this one was to include MiG jets, Il-28 bombers, tanks, and guns.[17]

What is important here is not the scope of Soviet-Pakistani arms relationship—it would still have a long way to go to equal the Soviet-Indian one—but rather its impact on relations between Moscow and New Delhi. The Indian reaction was immediate. The cabinet subcommittee on foreign affairs met on July 7 after the Soviet chargé d'affaires informed Prime Minister Gandhi of the Soviet decision. Although the displeasure of the prime minister was evident, there was a reluctance to condemn the USSR move or to take such actions as cancelling President Zakir Hussain's forthcoming trip to the Soviet Union. Mrs. Gandhi sent Kosygin a letter on July 10 in which she warned of the strain an arms deal would place on Soviet-Indian relations. Kosygin promptly assured the prime minister that nothing would undermine the friendship between the Soviet Union and New Delhi and that such questions as arms for Pakistan "are decided from the point of view of friendship between India and the Soviet Union."[18] President Hussain reiterated India's concern—the talks were described as frank, which is a certain indication of disagreement—as did the Indian team that met with Firyubin's delegation in September.[19] Soviet leaders continued to deliver the same assurances: friendship with India would be maintained; Moscow would not let Pakistan use the arms against India; the establishment of Soviet influence in Pakistan would pay dividends for India since this influence would be used to restrain Pakistan; and the arms were modest in scope (and, specifically, did not include missiles).

Although the Indian government continued to handle the issue in this direct, less-emotional way of expressing concern through letters and official delegations, within the Indian political system there was less restraint. At the meeting of the Congress Parliamentary Party on July 21, Desai asserted that "it is not the quantum of supplies Pakistan gets from Russia which is significant but the change in the attitude of the Soviet Union." Even Mrs. Gandhi said that "the government had been noticing a shift in the Soviet thinking ever since the Tashkent agreement."[20] On July 22 the Lok Sabha considered an opposition measure to condemn the Congress government for "its failure to foresee the shift in Soviet policy in favor of Pakistan over the years and shape the country's foreign policy to meet the changed conditions." Various members of the major right-wing opposition parties, the Swatantra and Jan Sangh, rejected Soviet assurances and denounced Moscow's creation of a Cold War atmosphere in South Asia. "When the U.S. could not stop Pakistan from using American arms against India," remarked Jan Sangh leader A.B. Vajpayee, "what was the guarantee that Russia would be able to . . . ?" In partial agreement, Mrs. Gandhi delivered a sharply worded statement that, among other things, stated:

> In these circumstances, we cannot but view with concern this further accretion of armed strength to Pakistan. The unavoidable consequence would be to accentuate tension in the sub-continent and to add to our responsibilities in regard to the defense and security of our country. It will make Pakistan even more intransigent than it has been. Indeed, some recent pronouncements made by leaders of the Pakistan Government confirm this.
>
> The Soviet Union, like any other country, is entitled to form its own

judgment as to where its interests lie and how to promote them. But we are bound to express our misgivings and apprehensions to the Soviet leaders in all frankness. We do not question either the motives or the good faith of the Soviet Union, but we are convinced that this development cannot promote the cause of peace and stability in the subcontinent.[21]

After thus joining in the attack on the Soviet policy, Mrs. Gandhi balanced her assessment by citing the significance of the totality of Soviet-Indian relations and USSR assurances regarding friendship with India. In sum, she said that the government opposed the resolution deploring the Soviet action for two reasons: first, Parliament had not passed a resolution in 1954 when the United States decided to supply arms to Pakistan; and, second, "the Government's reaction to the Soviet move had been conveyed already." The resolution was then defeated by a vote of 200 to 61.

This rather restrained reaction of the Indian government has been interpreted by many as evidence of USSR influence over Indian behavior. India's economic and military dependence on the Soviet Union led to repeated emphasis, in the Lok Sabha as well as the Indian and Western press, on New Delhi's lack of options. What is also significant, however, is that the negative Indian reaction exceeded Soviet expectations.[22] Official protests continued into 1969 and led to greater friction. Moreover, Soviet arms deliveries to Pakistan ended early in 1970, a development that seems to suggest Indian influence over the Soviet Union. Thus, while Moscow may have influenced New Delhi in mid-1968 on arms to Pakistan, this influence was slight, limited—in return for continuing Soviet economic and military aid to India—and short-lived.

What is clear is that, by the end of 1968, a number of serious strains were showing up in the Soviet-Indian relationship. The September visit to India of the Firyubin delegation demonstrated the new situation. In the words of one Indian journalist, based on a "leaked" report of the meeting:

> In sum, the leaders and members of the Soviet delegation conducted themselves in the manner of *representatives of an imperial power in their dealings with a dependency*. They did not observe even elementary diplomatic courtesies.... Whether the issue was the supply of Soviet arms to Pakistan, or Moscow's stand on Kashmir, or the malicious propaganda against leading Indians by... Radio Peace and Progress, or the generous cartographic concessions to China regarding its borders with India, the Soviet delegation, according to these reports, was generally evasive, non-committal and even rude.[23]

In many ways, Moscow had succeeded in placing itself halfway between India and Pakistan just as Washington had and was now suffering the same consequences as Washington.

Moreover, there was an increasing trend in India toward a reevaluation of the question of influence or leverage in Indo-Soviet relations. One example of this growing, if often implicit, reevaluation stated that "the extent of Soviet dependence on Indian friendship has not been properly appreciated in this country with the result that the unfortunate impression has gained ground that Indo-Soviet friendship is a one-way street."[24] The one issue to which Firyubin, for example, had seemed sensitive was the one of Sino-Indian relations. He made it clear that the Chinese issue had become paramount in the Soviet perspective and "innocent references to the desirability of resuming [India's] dialogue with China in the Indian press provoked his ire." The significance of this, as Indian leaders perhaps were beginning to realize, was that "the Soviet Union is not invulnerable" and "that India is not without leverage in its relations with Moscow...." Thus, at a time when strains were showing in the Soviet-Indian relationship and when India's dissatisfaction with its lack of options vis-à-vis Moscow began to develop, the Chinese issue was soon to aid in an adjustment of that relationship. The phenomenon of influence could be limited, short-lived, and as was soon to be seen, very much a "two-way street."

SHIFTING POLICIES IN 1969

During 1969, the Soviet Union increasingly perceived the need for firm allies responsive to the Chinese "threat." Whatever influence the Soviets had in India was too limited to enable them to include India as such an ally. Steadily this need was to move Moscow toward closer relations with New Delhi, yet the Soviets were unwilling either to admit failure publicly or to give up on "weaning" Pakistan away from China. Evidence that the Soviets did not give up quickly or entirely on their recent approach could be seen in several aspects of Soviet behavior in South Asia in the first half of 1969. Urging Pakistan and India to settle their differences peacefully continued to be a major theme of USSR policy. To do this soon "in accordance with the Tashkent Declaration" would be "in the interest of peace in the subcontinent," Kosygin said during a visit to Pakistan in May.[25] Moreover, the Soviets continued their efforts to identify themselves with Pakistani viewpoints and policies. Foreign Minister Gromyko sounded positive and hopeful when he referred to relations with Pakistan in his July address to the Supreme Soviet:

> There are excellent grounds for expressing satisfaction with the continued broadening of the Soviet Union's relations with Pakistan, and there is a desire and a readiness on the part of both sides to exert further efforts to consolidating mutual friendly ties, and developing cooperation

in the economic, cultural, and other spheres in the future too. This is also furthered by the coinciding points of view of the Soviet Union and Pakistan on a number of important international problems and by growing mutual confidence, in which a large role belongs to the establishment of contacts at the summit.[26]

The Soviets intensified their emphasis on the Chinese "threat" to South Asia during 1969. This was done partly in the effort to split Pakistan from China. A *Pravda* editorial of June 3 hammered at the theme of Chinese responsibility for Pakistan's difficulties asserting that Pakistan (as well as India and Afghanistan) wanted peace but the Chinese created tensions in the area of the interests of "their hegemonic aims." Peking sought to "mislead people," authors V. Nayevsky and A. Filiipov warned, in order to "draw them against their will in adventures and pointless actions."

Due to Sino-Indian friction, moreover, Moscow was able to go further in its effort to convince India of the severity of the threat from China and of the need to do something about it. Among the high-level visits where this issue was a featured item of discussion was the visit to India (which was "balanced" by talks in Pakistan later in the month) of the Soviet Defense Minister Marshal Grechko in early March. Arriving in New Delhi just after the first major Sino-Soviet clash on the Ussuri River, Grechko focused his talks on the "Asian scene with special reference to India-Pakistan relations and China" and "international problems having defense implications."[27] Grechko may also actually have discussed coordinating policy toward China and it was significant that he included in his delegation General N. G. Lyashchenko, head of the Turkestan Military District, which is the district that adjoins China's Sinkiang province. Moscow was anxious to obtain some indication of Indian sympathy or support, particularly in view of Mrs. Gandhi's January offer to China of border talks with no preconditions. *Implicit* Indian support was only forthcoming in April. In early May, Premier Kosygin made a surprise visit to New Delhi on the occasion of the funeral of Indian President Zakir Hussain. This visit of a much higher rank delegation than had been expected may have been prompted by Mrs. Gandhi's April letter to the Soviet premier. In this letter she had emphasized to Moscow that the attempt to maintain a balance between India and Pakistan was wrong, because India had wider commitments to meet and Pakistan would only become more intransigent. While this visit was certainly in part an attempt by Kosygin to reassure Mrs. Gandhi regarding Soviet arms to Pakistan, the USSR leader also prominently featured China in his conversations with her.[28] The Soviet Union, Kosygin said, wanted "no one to encroach on India's interests" and he called for closer Indian support in the anti-Chinese crusade: "in view of the complex international situation, no really peaceloving state could withhold its active participation in the fight against imperialism and expansionism."[29] Peking certainly saw the Kosygin visit as an effort to further the "anti-China alliance" and "intrigues." *NCNA* reported on May 8:

> On May 6 and 7, Kosygin held lengthy secret talks with Indian Prime Minister Gandhi [and] their discussions centered around "the two countries' mutual border problems with China." In the talks, Kosygin took pains to spell out the "case" of Soviet social imperialism in launching aimed provocations against China. The Soviet revisionists wanted the Indian reactionaries to "form a common approach" towards the strenthening of the anti-China military alliance.

In sum, it seems clear that both Grechko and Kosygin utilized their visits to stress the danger that China represented. Their message was that no "neighboring country—least of all India with an unsettled border dispute—could afford to take any chances by ignoring or even minimizing the dangers of a sudden conflict" with China.[30]

In early June, the Soviets added a new element to their anti-Chinese campaign when Leonid Brezhnev advocated the creation of a collective security system in Asia at the Moscow International Meeting of Communist and Workers' Parties. Rather cryptically, the general secretary stated, "We are of the opinion that the course of events is also putting on the agenda the task of creating a system of collective security in Asia."[31] The proposal was to remain vague and was only slightly elaborated during 1969. Nevertheless, judging from the fact that the Kremlin called home 15 USSR ambassadors to Asian countries for briefings and discussion of the proposal, it would appear that the Soviet leadership placed significant hopes on it.

The proposal clearly had at least two important goals. The first was to establish the Soviet Union as a major voice in Asian affairs by virtue of membership in this system. The second was to create some kind of grouping against China. While the Soviets denied that the proposal was directed against any state—and instead emphasized that such a system would stabilize Asia, insure peace and peaceful coexistence, guarantee the equality, sovereignty, and territorial integrity of Asian states, and thus be in the interest of *all* states—the context of their statements pointed in an anti-Chinese direction. *Izvestia's* initial broaching of the subject on May 29, for instance, was basically an outline of the dangers inherent for Asia in PRC foreign policy; China was depicted as the greatest threat to peace in Asia. In one of many Radio Moscow broadcasts to South Asia calling for some kind of collective security, the commentator on July 8, Vladimir Volokholansky, asserted that "mankind cannot but feel anxiety at the world tensions created by some states which seek to capture foreign territory so as to dominate other countries." The "expansionist courses" of

China and the United States were the dangers. Crucial to peace in Asia, he concluded, was the utilization of Soviet international weight and influence to decide Asian problems by peaceful means, such as had happened at Tashkent in 1966.

Significantly, during his May travels to India, Afghanistan, and Pakistan, Kosygin had been busy proposing a related idea—regional economic cooperation. As reactions to the colletive security idea continued to be cool if not skeptical, the Soviets turned increasingly toward the regional cooperation approach. Indira Gandhi's response, for example, to the Brezhnev proposal was one of opposition to its "military overtones" and disagreement with its assumptions of a "power vacuum" facing Asia with the planned British withdrawal in 1971.[32] Since India was a major target of the anti-Chinese thrust of Asian collective security, Moscow obviously had to reorient its approach. As Mrs. Gandhi told the Congress Parliamentary Executive, "India has responded favorably" to the USSR suggestion for a conference of the countries of the region, even including the Soviet Union, "to discuss economic collaboration." This proposal was "in keeping with India's policy that economic cooperation was the best way to strengthen the economics of the Asian countries" and was, then, fully "in accord with India's own consistent stand in the matter."[33]

Despite all of these Soviet efforts, by the end of June, Moscow's relations with both India and Pakistan still seemed to be tense. Assertions of PRC support in Pakistan's "struggle to oppose foreign aggression and interference and safeguard national independence"[34] indicated the continuing close ties between Islamabad and Peking. Significantly, the Pakistanis chose the time of Kosygin's visit to India to make public a letter from Chou En-lai to the new president (since March), Yahya Khan, reiterating China's firm support of Pakistan and Pakistan's position on Kashmir. Islamabad expressed no enthusiasm, furthermore, about either the economic cooperation or the collective security schemes. The Soviet Union's difficulties with Pakistan may best be summed up by the reference to an "exchange of opinions"—a term in Soviet diplomatic parlance indicative of disagreement—in the joint communiqué signed at the end of Kosygin's visit with Yahya at the end of May.[35]

Meanwhile, friction in the relationship with India seemed to be increasing. Indian leaders were agitated by Kosygin's stop in Pakistan despite claims in the communiqué that Soviet-Pakistan relations were not directed against any third state. (This was a message that the Soviets hoped would reassure India while the Pakistanis hoped for the same with respect to China.) One Indian newspaper even claimed that Pakistan's anti-Indian propaganda "has tended to assume more strident tones since Soviet Prime Minister Kosygin visited Pakistan . . . ."[36] Moreover, while the

Indians had welcomed the regional economic cooperation idea, they had remained cool toward the collective security one.

New Delhi's major concern, however, continued to be Soviet arms aid to Pakistan. Moscow may well have underestimated the degree of Indian concern on this issue as it increasingly irritated Indo-Soviet relations in the first half of 1969. The March visit to Pakistan of Soviet Defense Minister Grechko served only to fuel the fire when he was reported as saying that Pakistan should be strengthened against its "enemies." In response to Indian questioning, "the Soviet Embassy in Pakistan confirmed that Grechko had said those words" and later USSR assertions that the remarks had been taken out of context did little to reassure New Delhi.[37] During the same visit, the deputy chief of staff of the Soviet navy, Vice-Admiral N. I. Smirnov, stated at an official dinner that a strong Pakistani navy "would be a powerful precondition for peace in this part of the Indian Ocean."[38] During June rumors circulated in India that the Soviets had promised to develop the port of Gwador in West Pakistan and convert it into a base for use of Soviet submarines, both those of the Soviet fleet and those to be given to Pakistan.[39] This report was denied by Moscow, but Indian skepticism remained high and Mrs. Gandhi repeatedly warned that an "unavoidable consequence" of Soviet arms aid to Pakistan "would be to accentuate tension in the subcontinent and to add to our responsibility in regard to defense and security of our country."[40] Defense Minister Swaran Singh admitted to the Lok Sabha in April that he had been unable to convince the Soviet Union of the dangers of its policy during Grechko's visit in early March. In April Prime Minister Gandhi sought reassurances in her secret letter to Kosygin. Neither his reply nor his subsequent visit for President Hussain's funeral comforted Indian fears. During the visit Mrs. Gandhi is reported to have argued that USSR arms would not move Pakistan away from China.[41] Still the Soviets would not budge. While in Washington, External Affairs Minister Dinesh Singh conveyed India's concern over both U.S. and Soviet military supplies to Pakistan and, regarding the latter, "indicated that the Soviet actions had affected harmonious relations that had existed long between India and the USSR."[42] Thus, Moscow may well have had sufficient influence in India to complete the arms deal with Pakistan, yet it clearly did not have enough leverage to keep the issue from causing considerable friction in Indo-Soviet relations.

By mid-1969 then, Moscow was faced in South Asia with a radically altered set of circumstances from those that had fostered the change in Soviet policy in 1964–65. The Chinese "threat" was greatly increased and the heretofore unimaginable possibility of Sino-United States cooperation against Soviet interests was now very real. Pakistan had moved closer to

China and had proved unresponsive to Soviet entreaties. In addition, Indo-Pakistani relations had worsend since 1966 and Soviet efforts to be evenhanded had led to increasingly strained relations with India. From the Kremlin's perspective, there was now the growing possibility of losing in both states of the subcontinent by having its previously significant role in India reduced *and* not gaining a more influential position in Pakistan. The events of July and August were to make this clearer, to limit Soviet policy options, and to force Moscow into a new, even if secret, direction.

Mid-Year Clarifications

Two of the relationships that seemed to crystallize in the middle of 1969 were the Soviet-Pakistani and the Sino-Pakistani ones. Moscow had held out hopes that Islamabad, although opposed to Brezhnev's collective security idea, might be responsive to Kosygin's proposals regarding regional economic cooperation. These hopes were dashed, however, when a Pakistani Foreign Office spokesman on July 10 rejected talks on the topic as "unrealistic" given the strained bilateral relations with India.[43] Indicating that Islamabad was aware of the anti-Chinese nature of this proposal, he added that the idea was also rejected on the grounds that it "may be interpreted as a step towards the creation of a system of collective security to be directed against China; and Pakistan has no intention of getting involved in any arrangement which may cast doubts on Sino-Pakistan relations."

In case Pakistan's position in Sino-Soviet relations was not clear, the visit of Air Marshal Nur Khan as head of a goodwill mission to China in mid-July confirmed emphatically the failure of the USSR policy. Nur sat through a vitriolic attack by Chinese Premier Chou En-lai on the "modern revisionist renegade clique" in Moscow and received China's unqualified support for Pakistan's stand on Kashmir.[44] Nur Khan responded by asserting at the end of his visit that China's strength "has been and will remain a stabilizing factor in the maintenance of peace in the region. It is our belief that China does not pose a threat to any nation."[45] In light of the ongoing Sino-Soviet border clashes, Pakistan's distance from the Soviets on the question of relations with China could not have been greater. Nur finished off Soviet hopes by rejecting, on the basis of both Sino-Pakistani friendship and Indo-Pakistani enmity, the Soviet proposals for collective security and regional economic cooperation.[46] Moreover, two factors certainly must have aggravated the discouragement and growing fears felt by Moscow and New Delhi: (1) the Pakistani representative's enthusiasm about the nearly completed highway, a new version of the old "Silk Route," linking the two countries through the Aksai Chin area—a region claimed by India, but held by China, and a source of substantial tension in Sino-

Indian relations—and (2) the constant presence during the visit of Huang Yung-sheng, chief of the General Staff of China's People's Liberation Army.

The status of India's foreign relations seemed also to be crystallizing during the middle of 1969. Not only were New Delhi's relations with Moscow undergoing certain strains, but there were also major issues with Peking, Washington, and, of course, Islamabad. With China, Indian suspicions were significantly heightened by the progress in Sino-Pakistani road building. The political significance of the roads, in addition to the presence of large numbers of Chinese working on them, plus PRC military aid to Pakistan convinced many anew in New Delhi of collusion between these two hostile neighbors of India. Those in India who had argued in favor of overtures toward China had little to stand on when "Lin Piao's speech to the [CCP] Ninth Party Congress took as tough a line on the border disputes with India as before" and when Chinese statements and broadcasts contrived "to revile India as a tool of the imperialists and revisionists" (the latter being the Soviet Union).[47] Finally, and most ominously for New Delhi, there was a new clash on the Sino-Indian border in mid-July. Reports indicated that Chinese troop concentrations and activities all along the Indian border had increased in recent weeks and that, in this particular incident, the Chinese had fired on Indian soldiers well inside Indian territory. Officials undoubtedly did not fail to notice that the PRC involvement in this incident came during Nur Khan's visit to China. The implications for the Sino-Pakistani-Indian triangle were unmistakable.

The continued U.S. disengagement from Asia, and particularly South Asia, made it impossible for India to turn to the United States for help. An Indian proposal, discussed by Mrs. Gandhi in Tokyo and Jakarta in June, that the United States and the Soviet Union underwrite peace in Asia for an interim period following a Vietnam settlement, was rejected by Washington. President Nixon, while on an Asian trip in mid-1969, announced his "Guam Doctrine," which implied a fundamental U.S. disengagement from Asia. In India, he repeated that Asian countries themselves would have to be responsible for their own security.[48] Subsequently, in Pakistan, the U.S. leader seemed sympathetic, despite Indian warnings, to his hosts' appeals for renewed arms aid. Also while in Pakistan, Nixon endorsed the Sino-Pakistani relationship and secretly "asked Yahya Khan to explore the possibility of providing links between Washington and Peking."[49] Given India's and Pakistan's intelligence about one another, it is unlikely that New Delhi was unaware for long of the nature, even if not the full extent, of the change in this triangular relationship. Moscow eagerly sought to highlight these developments and threats to India, especially those that might result from Sino-American "collusion" for "division of their spheres of influence in Asia."[50] That this perception was not alien to the Indian outlook seems obvious from the report by *The Indian Express* of February 18, 1972:

> In an interview given to C.L. Sulzberger, Prime Minister Indira Gandhi was asked where Indo-U.S. relations went wrong "after the talk all these years of an American desire to rely on India as a counterpoise in Asia to China." She said she supposed that U.S. policy towards India changed when "U.S. policy towards China changed."[51]

The final relationship, which became clarified during mid-1969, was between Pakistan and India. In June Prime Minister Gandhi had sent a secret letter to Yahya Khan proposing the signing of a "no-war pact" and the setting up of joint machinery to examine all aspects of normalizing relations between India and Pakistan. Yahya's government procrastinated for several weeks. After finally assenting to the talks, Pakistan and India began to meet at the end of July. By early August the fruitless talks had already ground to a dismal halt.

In order to complete this picture of change and clarification during 1969, it is necessary to examine briefly the highly significant political developments that took place in this year in both Pakistan and India. These developments were to have an impact on regional and international alignments not only during 1969, but also through the 1970s. Thus, although the political trends within these countries have never been Moscow's primary focus, it was inevitable that Soviet policies would be affected by them. Indeed, the "turning to the right" and growing instability in post-Nehru India had contrasted unfavorably with Pakistan's stability and had been a contributing factor leading to the USSR policy of seeking a balance in its relationship with New Delhi and Islamabad.

In the case of Pakistan, stability proved during 1969 to have been only temporary. The year opened on a note of severe tension between the eastern and western wings of the country. The growing conflict forced Ayub to step down as president in late March. He was replaced by a man the Soviets believed they could probably get along with, Yahya Khan. (Yahya, as commander of the armed forces, had negotiated the 1968 arms deal with the Soviet Union.) The Soviets announced that they were in support of Yahya, sympathized with the problems he faced, and hoped he would be able to return stability to Pakistan. Each side sought to assure the other of continuing friendship during Kosygin's visit in May. Despite Yahya's apparently well-intentioned efforts, however, little progress was made in mitigating the discontent of East Pakistan. Both the Soviet Union and India, then, were faced with an increasingly unstable situation. For Moscow this growing instability was very discouraging given its goals in the region. For New Delhi this development was even worse; an unstable and unpredictable Pakistan posed new threats to Indian security.

In the meantime, the trends in India were running in quite the opposite direction in Moscow's perception. In the summer of 1969, Mrs. Gandhi took initiatives that stunned her opponents, enhanced her own security and "left-wing" credentials, and greatly enhanced India's position in the Soviet view. First of all, in mid-July she announced that the government would proceed with the nationalization of 14 major Indian banks. This was a step the left wing of the Congress had sought for years. Second, and relatedly, she forced Morarji Desai's resignation as deputy prime minister by taking the finance portfolio from him. Desai was the leader of the Congress' right wing and was considered by the Soviets and many others inside and outside India to be the most significant spokesman and representative of Indian monopoly houses. The polarization within the Congress that the Gandhi-Desai struggle precipitated led to still another Gandhi initiative in August: the prime minister proposed her own candidate, 75-year-old V.V. Giri, to be president of India in opposition to her party's nominee, Sanjeeva Reddy, who had been supported by the right-wing party bosses, generally known as the "Syndicate." Mrs. Gandhi's victory in this confrontation, too, meant she was in a more secure position than at any time during her tenure and that she had carried India further to the left than most had thought likely or possible.[52]

The Soviet reaction was one of guarded optimism. Moscow clearly approved of the bank nationalizations and Mrs. Gandhi's victories over Desai and over the Syndicate in the presidential contest. Her greater power and move to the left were considered to be highly progressive. As the London *Observer's* correspondent in Moscow noted:

> ... there is genuine pleasure here at the routing of the old guard by her [Mrs. Gandhi]. For the Soviet Union has a good deal at stake in India, and the galloping march of the right-wing forces has worried Moscow greatly in recent years. Mrs. Gandhi's victory is the first positive sign that the trend is not reversible and this comforts Moscow.[53]

These trends were to become increasingly significant from Moscow's viewpoint, and from Indira Gandhi's, with the formal split in the Congress in November 1969 and then with Mrs. Gandhi's landslide electoral victory in March 1971. Later Soviet commentary was to look back on the events of 1969 as the "showdown between Mrs. Gandhi, who was backed by the many adherents to the Nehru line, and the conservatives who were dragging the INC and the country to the Right...." The "right-wing splinter group" in the Congress and "other domestic reactionary forces" had tried "to seize power," but Mrs. Gandhi and her followers, "in keeping with the mood of the people, announced a number of progressive socioeconomic measures" such as nationalizations, agrarian reforms, and policies to consolidate the state sector.[54]

The point here is that Moscow was sensitive to these new developments even in their initial stages in July-August 1969. Moreover, the Soviets were also sensitive to the impact these events might have on Indian foreign policy. India might be able to move more decisively and act less passively in world affairs, but whether or not this development would be in Moscow's interest was impossible to predict. Therefore, the Soviets undertook significant efforts to support Mrs. Gandhi and to strengthen Soviet-Indian ties. In 1973 two Soviet analysts of the South Asian scene were able to assert that included among Mrs. Gandhi's praiseworthy "progressive measures" of 1969 was the policy to develop "friendship and cooperation with the Soviet Union and other socialist countries."[55]

The September Meetings

The events of September indicate that Moscow was willing to respond to any change in the subcontinent. And changes were plentiful within India and Pakistan and also in Indo-Soviet relations. The need for new Soviet responses was only underlined by the areas where there was little change—Chinese relations with Pakistan and India, Soviet-Pakistani ties, and Indian-Pakistani enmity. Moscow was looking for an answer to its problems in policy in South Asia, and India also sought to cope with an external situation running generally counter to its interests. Given the Kremlin's renewed enthusiasm about the Indian domestic scene, it seems hardly surprising that the two states sought each other out.

The death of North Vietnam's Ho Chi Minh created an opportunity for further Soviet-Indian discussion. When the Soviets announced that Premier Kosygin would stop for refueling in Calcutta, Mrs. Gandhi requested that this be changed to New Delhi so that the two could confer. The Soviets rearranged Kosygin's flight and the two held talks at the Delhi airport. These talks began at 6:45 A.M. and lasted for one hour (twice as long as had been anticipated) and involved no aides to either prime minister. Kosygin again tried to reassure Mrs. Gandhi of the benefits of USSR efforts to befriend Pakistan. The Soviet premier referred to the meeting as "useful, important and necessary."[56] The circumstances do indeed point to this as an important meeting, perhaps not a completely cordial one, but one that was to be an important foundation for what was to come.

After attending the ceremonies in Hanoi, Kosygin stopped in Calcutta on September 10 on his way back to Moscow. (This refuted rumors in the

Indian press that Kosygin would keep India and Pakistan in balance by refueling in Lahore since he had stopped in New Delhi en route to Hanoi.) Amid reports in the press that Yahya Khan would be going to the Soviet Union in the second half of September to press for more military aid, Kosygin called for an Asian security agreement, something Pakistan had already rejected due to its anti-Chinese thrust, to preserve peace and deter "would-be aggressors." He also denounced the issue surrounding the Soviet-Pakistani arms deal as "being artificially created by those who did not relish the friendly ties that existed between India and his country." But, he underlined, "we would never exchange our friendship with India [for] anything else." Perhaps foreshadowing the developments to come, he added, "We will keep this friendship, as we value it above everything else."[57]

These brief stopovers, in addition to possible contact in Hanoi, may have laid important groundwork for Dinesh Singh's journey to Moscow. This trip, which had been delayed due to Ho's funeral, was crammed in immediately thereafter. Perhaps indicating some degree of urgency, Dinesh returned from Hanoi the evening of September 10 and left for the Soviet Union and Yugoslavia early the very next morning. In any case, both the Indians and the Soviets[58] treated the visit as highly significant. New Delhi reported that Foreign Minister Singh was to conduct "high level talks" with Kremlin leaders "on the question of stabilizing peace in Asia, India-Pakistan relations and a Soviet supply of arms to Pakistan."[59] In Moscow, he met with Foreign Minister Gromyko within two hours of his arrival on September 11 and again on the following two days. He also met with Defense Minister Grechko as well as with Kosygin and Brezhnev. He was briefed on Kosygin's talks with Chou En-lai, which had occurred at the Peking airport after Kosygin had left Calcutta on his way back to Moscow following Ho's funeral. (This strange itinerary was brought about by the delay in China's response to Kosygin's request for a meeting.) Brezhnev and Kosygin explained that Soviet plans for Asian collective security were not for a defense pact "but a system of Asian cooperation and renunciation of the use of force." Dinesh replied that "these ideas are in line with our own and we support this." It was revealed that relations with China had ranked high in the talks.[60]

Perhaps of greatest significance was the composition of the delegations that met in Moscow. The Indian foreign minister was accompanied by the Indian ambassador to the Soviet Union, D.P. Dhar; the secretary to the External Affairs Minister, Kewal Singh; the head of that ministry's Foreign Policy Planning Department, K. Narayanan; a special assistant to the minister, and two advisors to the Indian Embassy. However, neither the head of the Foreign Policy Planning Department nor the advisors were reported present after the first session of talks. This seems very strange, particularly for Narayanan, an important official who had traveled all the way from New Delhi for the visit.

The Soviet side in the initial talks was also unusually constituted. In addition to Gromyko, it consisted of the deputy minister of Foreign Affairs, N.P. Firyubin; the Soviet ambassador to India, N.M. Pegov; head of the Foreign Ministry's South Asia Department, A.A. Fomin; head of the Ministry of Foreign Affairs' Treaty and Legal Department, O.N. Khlestov; and the deputy head of the Ministry's Press Department, I.I. Marchuk. All except Khlestov could normally be expected to be included in such talks. Firyubin and Fomin, indeed, had been members of delegations to India earlier in the year. It is highly unusual, however, for a man such as Khlestov, head of the Treaty and Legal Department within the Foreign Affairs Ministry, to be present at conventional ministerial talks. Of further interest, he was not present at any subsequent reported meetings during the Indian delegation's stay.

It seems entirely feasible that Dinesh Singh's visit was meant to inaugurate a substantive change in Soviet-Indian relations. If so, there would have been reason to assign Khlestov, the Soviet official in charge of treaties and legal documents, and Narayanan, the Indian head of foreign policy planning, to finalize at least the rough aspects of some kind of Soviet-Indian treaty or agreement. Official Soviet reports of the foreign minister's visit were full of references to the "warm and friendly atmosphere" of the talks and the "particular attention" devoted "to questions of the bilateral relations of the USSR and India."[61] Discussions of mutual concerns, which most likely referred to China and Pakistan, were held by Dinesh with Brezhnev and Kosygin. General Secretary Brezhnev and Foreign Minister Dinesh dealt with "questions of strengthening and further developing relations between the Soviet Union and the Republic of India, as well as [with] certain urgent questions on the international situation, including the situation in Asia . . . ."[62] With Premier Kosygin "questions of the further development and strengthening of Soviet-Indian relations in the interests of the peoples of both countries and world peace were considered . . . ."[63]

The joint statement issued at the end of the visit cited the "atmosphere of cordiality and mutual understanding" and went on to say in part:

> The two sides examined all the aspects of the friendly cooperation that exists between the Soviet Union and India and noted with satisfaction that in the political, economic, cultural, scientific and other fields this cooperation has received substantial development and has great possibilities for further expansion. They are convinced that this cooperation corresponds to the fundamental interests of the people of both

countries and serves the cause of the strengthening of peace in Asia and throughout the world....

During the talks, the two sides exchanged opinions on urgent international problems and noted with satisfaction the coincidence or closeness of the positions held by the Soviet Union and India on these problems.[64]

Most significantly, in perhaps the clearest indication of where negotiations were actually leading at that precise moment, Dinesh Singh was reported to have said at a banquet on September 12 that:

... the friendship between the two countries [India and the USSR] was indeed many-sided. He said further that we were all living today in a world torn by conflict and that many of those present had probably witnessed both world wars in their lifetime. *He felt that if we were to avoid a conflict in the future it was necessary to enter into a closer and more intimate relationship.*[65]

Was this statement by the foreign minister a conscious or unconscious clue to the outside world? In any event, Soviet Foreign Minister Gromyko capped his banquet speech by replying that "talks on international politics with representatives of India are not difficult."

Concrete indications of a major and definitive change in USSR policy coinciding with Dinesh Singh's visit took the form of efforts to resolve rapidly the problem areas in Soviet-Indian relations. In particular, Indian concerns over Pakistan's relations with the Soviet Union were apparently allayed. The Indian foreign minister had expressed concern over Yahya Khan's impending visit to Moscow and was told that no date had yet been fixed. Indeed, the lack of eagerness on Moscow's part for Yahya's visit continued into 1970 and it was only in June of that year that the trip was undertaken. In reference to India's more immediate concern regarding Soviet arms supplies to Pakistan, the *Times of India* reported on September 20 that "contrary to reports in some quarters," no Soviet arms had been delivered since May. Apparently the first two deliveries under the 1968 agreement were made in March and May (tanks on both occasions) and the third was to be in August, "but there are no signs of it being sent yet." Moscow had apparently reconsidered its arms policy and was now making an important concession to India. (Significantly, Yahya Khan sought further arms during his 1970 visit to the Soviet Union but was turned down.)

Concerning the threat from China, a firmer commitment on India's behalf seemed to be indicated, according to another September report: "Soviet sources here [Moscow] are appreciative of Indian fears that to rehabilitate the morale of the Chinese Army [which] suffered in recent clashes with the Soviet Union, the Chinese leadership might well attempt another spectacular thrust towards India."[66] Moreover, on his return to India, Dinesh declared that India welcomed (quite temporarily, as it turned out) the Soviet proposal on the creation of a system of collective security in Asia.

A final bit of circumstantial evidence pointing toward the new nature of Indo-Soviet relations was the October visit of Defense Minister Swaran Singh to Moscow. (Interestingly, he was external affairs minister in 1971 and signed the treaty with the Soviet Union on India's behalf.) There was remarkably little about his visit in the Indian press and he was reported to have been "tight-lipped on the outcome of his talks." There had been speculation that China would be a major topic in his talks, and he did report that he was "highly satisfied" with the visit, the strength of Indo-Soviet friendship, and the *"remarkable coincidence of views and complete understanding* between the two countries."[67] Significantly, for the first time since mid-1968, there was no report that the issue of Soviet arms to Pakistan had been discussed. This may well have been an indication that India was satisfied at this time with USSR assurances.

WHO WAS INFLUENCING WHOM?

The evidence presented points to a significant change in Soviet-Indian relations—the establishment of a relationship at least as close as in the pre-1965 period, and probably closer—in the fall of 1969. September of that year seems to be the key month in which developments and pressures of the previous 6 months (more than 12 months if one begins with the Soviet-Pakistani arms deal of 1968) culminated in a new mutual commitment between the Soviet Union and India. The fundamental factor leading to this "alliance" was the linkage of the threats Moscow perceived from China, and New Delhi perceived from Pakistan. For the Soviets the Chinese threat had grown so acute, in the form of tense bilateral relations and the potentiality of a Sino-United States rapprochement, to necessitate the mending of relations with India. Pakistan had proved unreceptive to Soviet overtures, had rejected Moscow's proposal of regional economic collaboration, and had strengthened its ties with China. Thus, Moscow's attempt to befriend Pakistan had failed but its courting of Islamabad had strained relations with New Delhi. The Kremlin had to shore up its position in the region and needed at least one firm and reliable ally; the Soviets could not afford to risk having little or no support in *both* Pakistan and India.

On India's part, the constant threat from the main adversary had to be dealt with even at the cost of a "distortion" of nonalignment. India needed the Soviet Union so as to have a reliable friend vis-à-vis Pakistan. China's close relationship with and substantial assistance to Pakistan, in addition to the threat China itself represented to India, provided the crucial linkage that brought New Delhi and Moscow together. The United States hardly appeared as a viable ally for India in a period of increasing tension. A closer relationship with the Soviet Union offered the only possible alternative.

There is one question that stands out from the trend of this analysis: why was such secrecy maintained regarding any new Soviet-Indian relationship? Certainly, public acknowledgment of a new agreement would have served better as a deterrent to China and Pakistan than secrecy. However, just as the desire for an agreement or treaty seems to have been mutual, with perhaps the stronger motivation coming from the Soviet Union, so may the desire to keep it secret have been mutual. It may generally have been felt that the agreement ought not to be made public unless Sino-Soviet and Pakistani-Indian confrontations over a common issue proved unavoidable (which became the case in 1971.)

New Delhi would seem to have had the strongest reasons for secrecy. One factor would be the desire to maintain as great a degree of nonalignment as possible. Another is that domestic political conditions probably would not have permitted the kind of Indian commitment that was implied in a treaty. More positively, Indira Gandhi's government undoubtedly wished to keep its options open in case of the possibility of improved relations with Pakistan and China. For the Soviets, it seems clear that they wished to continue trying to wean Pakistan away from China. Although they were willing to make important concessions to India, in the form of delaying Yahya's visit and especially by halting arms aid, they were unwilling to give up completely on their efforts of several years to build a more influential position in Pakistan. This seems to be supported by the fact that the Soviets used the treaty in the fall of 1971 (it had been officially signed in August) as a means of encouraging restraint and caution in India's policy toward Pakistan.

For both Moscow and New Delhi, therefore, the new relationship represented security and the avoidance of isolation in the event of a threat. To a significant extent, however, the threat perceived was not the same for both partners. China clearly was the central danger for the Soviets, while for the Indians it was Pakistan. This difference may account for both the delay in the Soviet Union and India coming to terms in the first half of 1969 and for the motivations to keep the agreement secret. The large number of references to an "exchange of opinions" during Dinesh Singh's otherwise extremely successful Moscow visit in September may also point to the principals' differing views. This could also mean that when either bilateral relationship—Sino-Soviet or Indo-Pakistani—changed in the future, Soviet and/or Indian policy toward one another might also change significantly.

This significant turn in Indo-Soviet relations, which took place in 1969, may well represent a case of joint influence or coincidence of interests. That is to say, both New Delhi and Moscow considered moving toward closer relations with one another to be beneficial. Soviet influence might be said to have existed since the new relationship represented something of a break with India's traditional posture of nonalignment. However, Indian influence on Soviet policy was also operative: Moscow was now clearly lining up with India rather than seeking to balance its ties with India and Pakistan. The fact that this mutual influence was limited and qualified, however, is attested to by the maintenance of secrecy regarding the new relationship.

Certain clauses of the treaty, made public in August 1971, also support the conclusions reached here as to the motivations for and limitations of the new relationship.[68] Article 9 guaranteed that neither India nor the Soviet Union will give any assistance "to any Third Party taking part in an armed conflict with the other Party" and that, if either was attacked or threatened with attack, the two would begin mutual consultations "with a view to eliminating this threat..." Thus, India is assured of Soviet support—or, at minimum, nonsupport for Pakistan—in case of an Indo-Pakistani conflict, and the Soviet Union is assured of India's support—or, at least, nonsupport for China—in case of a Sino-Soviet clash. Article 10 reinforces the same interrelationships when it declares that neither side will "undertake any commitment, secret or open, with regard to one or more states incompatible with the present Treaty." Article 4 seems to illustrate well the limits of each side's influence: the Soviet Union "respects India's policy of nonalignment..." and India "respects" USSR policy "aimed at strengthening friendship and cooperation with all peoples." Thus, each side was giving recognition to the other's position that the treaty would not completely change basic foreign policy tenets—for India, nonalignment, and for the Soviet Union, the attempt to woo Pakistan.

Finally, it needs to be emphasized that the interplay of the factors discussed here was to influence the evolution of Indo-Soviet relations after 1969 up to the present. The interrelationships between and within the various triangles—particularly the Sino-Soviet-Indian one—have continued to be crucial. Chinese policies, Pakistan's internal and external developments, the U.S. posture, and, of course, India's domestic and foreign policy developments have continued to impinge in various ways on relations between the Soviet Union and India. How these relationships changed in the 1970s and how these changes affected the influence of

Moscow and New Delhi over one another must now be analyzed, beginning with the period leading to the India-Pakistan war over Bangladesh.

NOTES

1. I have made this argument in my article "Indian-Soviet Relations in 1969: A Watershed Year?," *Orbis*, Winter 1976, pp. 1539–63. Much of the discussion in this chapter is based directly on this article.
2. O. B. Bulatov, "Peking and Washington: A New Round," *Literaturnaya Gazeta*, December 11, 1968.
3. For a good example, see Yury Zhukov, "The United States and Asia," *Pravda*, August 12, 1969.
4. S. P. Seth, "Russia's Role in Indo-Pak Politics," *Asian Survey*, August 1969, p. 624.
5. *Hindu* (Madras), January 29, 1968.
6. From the text of the communiqué; see *Hindu*, February 1, 1968.
7. Significantly, these denunciations had been present in the Soviet draft of the communique but do not appear in the final version; *Hindu*, February 4, 1968.
8. Kuldip Nayar, *Between the Lines* (Bombay: Allied Publishers, 1969), p. 127.
9. Cited in ibid., p. 101.
10. On this point, see Arthur Stein, *India and the Soviet Union: The Nehru Era* (Chicago: University of Chicago Press, 1969), pp. 267–69. As Stein points out, pp. 85–97, in 1956 Nehru hesitated to express disapproval initially due to the uncertainties of the Hungarian uprising for East-West relations. In the U.N. General Assembly, India generally abstained on resolutions dealing with Hungary, being particularly opposed to any condemnatory tone in the resolutions. Later India did call for the entry of U.N. observers into the country and self-determination for the Hungarians.
11. *Indian and Foreign Review*, September 1, 1968, p. 5; cited in ibid, p. 267.
12. *New York Times*, August 27, 1968; cited in Stein, *India and the Soviet Union*, p. 268.
13. *The Times of India*, September 26, 1968.
14. Nayar, *Between the Lines*, p. 109.
15. Elizabeth Kridl Valkenier, "New Trends in Soviet Economic Relations with the Third World," *World Politics*, April 1970, p. 427.
16. See *Hindu*, December 22, 1968; and Nayar, *Between the Lines*, p. 126.
17. Information on these visits and negotiations comes from G. W. Choudhury, *India, Pakistan, Bangladesh, and the Major Powers: Politics of a Divided Subcontinent* (New York: Free Press, 1975), pp. 56–57. Choudhury was, at this time, head of the Research Division of the Ministry of Foreign Affairs of Pakistan and he accompanied Ayub to Moscow. He later was communications minister in President Yahya Khan's Cabinet and accompanied Yahya on a visit to China.
18. See *Hindu*, July 11, 1968.
19. See *Hindu*, July 19, 1968, for the text of the communiqué.
20. *Hindu*, July 22, 1968.
21. *Hindu*, July 23, 1968.
22. See Nayar, *Between the Lines*, pp. 99–106.
23. *Times of India*, September 26, 1968. Emphasis added. The Skachkov visit in December was hardly any better. One correspondent wrote that the Soviet leader "must be the rudest Russian to visit the subcontinent since the two countries started diplomatic relations," *Financial Times* (London), January 22, 1969. Another reported that he

"expressed himself abrasively and behaved like a viceroy on an inspection tour," *The Guardian* (London), December 18, 1969.
24. *Times of India*, September 26, 1968.
25. *Hindustan Times*, June 1, 1969. Pakistan seemed to be rejecting Tashkent as a model for Indo-Pakistani relations, as the declaration was not mentioned in the joint communiqué signed by Yahya Khan and Kosygin.
26. *Pravda*, July 11, 1969.
27. *Hindustan Times*, March 4, 1969.
28. See *Hindustan Times*, May 6–8, 1969; and Nayar, *Between the Lines*, p. 119.
29. Ernst Kux, "Is Russia a Pacific Power?" *Pacific Community*, April 1970, p. 506.
30. *Hindu*, October 24, 1969. See also *Hindu*, April 6, 1969. The Soviets clearly sought to link Sino-Soviet with Sino-Indian territorial problems; see, Radio Moscow, in *Bengali to India*, August 27, 1969.
31. *Pravda*, June 8, 1969.
32. See her remarks while in Tokyo and Jakarta, *Hindustan Times*, June 19 and July 1, 1969, respectively.
33. *Hindustan Times*, June 17, 1969.
34. *Peking Review*, no. 13, March 28, 1969, p. 27; cited in Vijay Sen Budhraj, *Soviet Russia and the Hindustan Subcontinent* (Bombay: Somaiya Publications, 1973), p. 173.
35. See *Hindustan Times*, June 1, 1969.
36. *Hindustan Times*, June 8, 1969.
37. See Nayar, *Between the Lines*, p. 118. For reports on the visit see *Dawn* (Karachi), March 11–16, 1969.
38. Nayar, *Between the Lines*, p. 118.
39. See *Hindu*, June 30, 1969. See also Avigdor Haselkorn, *The Evolution of Soviet Security Strategy* (New York: Crane, Russak, 1978), pp. 107–8; and K. R. Singh, *The Indian Ocean: Big Power Presence and Local Response* (New Delhi: South Asia Books, 1978), pp. 61–62.
40. See Bhabani Sen Gupta, *The Fulcrum of Asia: Relations Among China, India, Pakistan, and the USSR* (New York: Pegasus, 1970), p. 273. See also *Hindustan Times*, June 12, 1969.
41. *Hindustan Times*, April 10, and May 8, 1969. See also Nayar, *Between the Lines*, p. 119.
42. *Hindustan Times*, July 13, 1969.
43. *Dawn*, July 11, 1969.
44. *NCNA*, July 13, 1969.
45. *NCNA*, July 16, 1969.
46. Ibid.
47. See Dilip Mukerjee, "Sleepless Nights," *Far Eastern Economic Review* (hereafter cited as *FEER*), July 10, 1969, pp. 114–15.
48. For example, see *Hindustan Times*, August 1 and 2, 1969.
49. Choudhury, *India, Pakistan, Bangladesh*, pp. 141–42.
50. Radio Moscow, in English to South Asia, August 23, 1969.
51. Cited in William H. Overholt, "President Nixon's Trip to China and its Consequences," *Asian Survey*, July 1973, p. 709.
52. See Dilip Mukerjee, "Indira Rules Supreme," *FEER*, September 11, 1969.
53. Dev Murarka, "Moscow Applauds Mrs. Gandhi's New Strength," *The Observer Foreign News Service*, August 28, 1969.
54. See *New Times*, no. 7, February 1973, p. 13; and P. Kutsobin and V. Shurygin, "South Asia: Tendencies Toward Stability," *International Affairs*, April 1973, pp. 43–48.
55. See Kutsobin and Shurygin, "South Asia," p. 44.
56. *Hindustan Times*, September 7, 1969.
57. *Hindustan Times*, September 11, 1969.

58. See *Pravda*, September 12, 14, 16, and 18, 1969; *Izvestia*, September 14 and 20; and *TASS*, International Service in Russian, September 11-13 and 15, 1969.
59. *Hindustan Times*, September 12, 1969.
60. *Hindustan Times*, September 16, 1969, see also *Pravda*, September 21, 1969.
61. For example, see *Pravda*, September 14, 1969.
62. *Pravda*, September 15, 1969.
63. *Pravda*, September 16, 1969.
64. *Pravda*, September 18, 1969.
65. *Information Service of India*, September 13, 1969. Emphasis added.
66. *Times of India*, September 11, 1969.
67. *Hindustan Times*, October 27, 1969. Emphasis added. See also *The Hindu*, October 24, 1969.
68. For the text of the treaty, see *New Times*, no. 33, August 1971, pp. 4–5.

―――――――――――――――――― 3

THE APPROACH OF WAR
IN SOUTH ASIA

Indo-Soviet relations entered the decade of the 1970s on a more positive note than had been the case for the past several years. Indeed, there seemed to be a potential for a return to the close relationship that existed between New Delhi and Moscow in the late 1950s and early 1960s. Sino-Soviet tensions had escalated, Indo-Pakistani friction was on the rise, relations between Pakistan and China were growing closer, and the United States continued to play only a marginal role in the region's affairs. All of these external conditions had brought India and the Soviet Union closer together by September 1969 and, excluding abrupt changes, appeared likely to continue to act as forces for cohesion.

Moreover, the internal developments within India were also serving to strengthen ties between the two states. Just as negative trends in Indian politics had been a factor in leading Moscow to seek a balance between India and Pakistan in the mid-1960s, more positive signs contributed to another USSR reassessment of its India policy. The Soviet Union's prominent India specialist, R. A. Ulianovsky, reviewing the past decade in Indian politics, argued that it was only when the right-wing elements tried to push too far, in the late 1960s, that Mrs. Gandhi, with left and center support, moved ahead with reforms that led to the split in the Indian National Congress (INC).[1] It is clear that, as Richard Remnek has remarked, "the Soviets saw the split as a decisive shift in domestic politics in a direction they found desirable, and one which they were actively encouraging . . . ."[2] The foreign affairs weekly, *New Times*, and other Soviet media published frequent articles expressing sympathy for Mrs. Gandhi and INC and other progressive and democratic forces in their struggle against the "right-wing" Syndicate, which had split off from the INC, and the "ultra reactionary" Jan Sangh and Swatantra parties. A continuing theme, as before, was the perceived link between progressive internal reforms and progressive foreign policy as opposed to the one between rightist domestic policies and an end to nonalignment in foreign policy.

Not all was sanguine in Moscow's view, of course. The Soviets repeatedly warned that the struggle in India was by no means over. All Soviet analyses emphasized the decisive importance of the unity of the left—including Indian communists—and center forces in the face of the threat from the right, while recognizing certain divisions *within* the INC. Moscow's concern was greatest when India's relationship with the Soviet Union became a domestic political issue in New Delhi, which happened periodically in the conflict between the Old and New (Mrs. Gandhi's) Congress. For example:

> President of the Old Congress, S. Nijalingappa . . . accused Mrs. Gandhi of "subordinating" India's policy to the Soviet Union's to gain the support of communists at home, while Morarji Desai, former deputy prime minister, maintains the government has been deviating increasingly from the policy of non-alignment to accommodate Moscow.
> S. K. Patil, the most outspoken rightist in the Old Congress, goes even further: He says that Soviet Prime Minister Alexei Kosygin has jumped at every opportunity to visit India "to advise Mrs. Gandhi on the leadership structure here" . . . [3]

A real concern for the Soviets was that such a conflict might lead New Delhi to back away from its relationship with Moscow. One Indian reporter revealed that:

> The Soviet Embassy in Delhi is making no secret of its feeling that possibly as a reaction to the new anti-Soviet stance of the right-wing parties in India, Mrs Gandhi's Government has been shying away from too close contacts with the Soviet Union for fear of giving some degree of credibility to the oft-repeated accusation that it had become excessively dependent on Communist support.[4]

While there is little evidence to support the charge that Moscow had been exercising influence in Indian domestic politics, it is clear that the Soviets felt they had a stake in the New Congress government of Indira Gandhi. The Kremlin's extremely restrained response to the uproar caused by the Indian discovery, due to an on-site accident that killed nine workers, that the Soviets had been building an unauthorized cultural center in Trivandrum, the capital of Kerala, seemed to be an example of an attempt to minimize as much as possible the embarrassment to Mrs. Gandhi's government. Soviet efforts to have this lead to a crackdown on U.S. cultural centers were successful but seemed to be due more to Indian predilections than to Soviet influence. In essence, the Soviets could rather comfortably support Mrs. Gandhi's government and its policies. Yet the opposition was strong enough that care had to be taken not to undermine the regime by allowing Indo-Soviet differences or "Soviet influence" to become too visible. The agenda for Moscow in this environment was to find those areas where relations could be improved and strengthened, and to meet Indian interests and needs while not violating the Soviet Union's own objectives.

THE ECONOMIC SIDE OF INDO-SOVIET RELATIONS

Further clarification of Moscow's perception of India was forthcoming in the February visit of a significant economic delegation from the Soviet Union. The delegation, led by S. A. Skachkov, chairman of the State Committee for Foreign Economic Relations, took part in the fifteenth-anniversary celebration of the signing of the first Indo-Soviet agreement on economic cooperation. He was joined later by another prominent Soviet official, V. E. Dymshits, first vice-chairman of the USSR Council of Ministers and the head of the Bhilai steel mill when it was set up. It was announced early that both sides were "attaching considerable importance" to the talks. Dymshits' arrival was said to set the stage for an "extensive review of the working of some of the major Soviet-aided projects..."[5] The Soviet officials held talks with Kewal Singh, external affairs secretary (and former ambassador to the Soviet Union), and with Mrs. Gandhi, in addition to engaging in lengthy discussions with Indian ministers and other officials. At the conclusion of the visit, two protocols were signed that pointed to a further extension of Soviet economic assistance. In one the Soviets agreed to an expansion of Bokaro's capacity. In the other, the Soviets pledged further orders for products from two major Soviet-aided projects and agreed to help in setting up new petrochemical and fertilizer plants in India.

However, there were clearly problems as well. A long-term effort by New Delhi had been to wrap up a large-scale Soviet purchase of Indian-built railway wagons. These negotiations had dragged on for months but Dymshits reiterated that the Soviet Union was interested only if it were commerically feasible; that is, India's price was still not internationally competitive and would have to come down in order for a deal to be made. A second Indian goal had been for Moscow to place orders with Soviet-aided plants in India for Soviet projects elsewhere in the Third World. Dymshits said only that this would be studied at a later stage. India was also pressuring the Soviets to escalate their orders from Soviet-aided plants. Although Dymshits demurred here, too, indicating that Moscow already had placed a great many orders, one of the protocols did take a step toward meeting India's interests on this question.[6]

As with many such meetings, it is often true that what is not said is more important than what is said. As will be remembered, Skachkov's last visit to India, in December 1968, was hardly a congenial one. Then he was critical of Indian officials and their handling of Soviet-aided projects and made various demands on New Delhi. There was no hint whatsoever of such a tone on this visit. While there was a recognition of problem areas, Skachkov and Dymshits, on more than one occasion, expressed their satisfaction with the progress of the projects and explained that many of the difficulties were natural growth problems that were not peculiar to India. Thus, there was a significant change in the nature of the economic relationship in slightly over one year. Change in the operation of the projects themselves seems to have been too limited to account for this alteration in the relationship. In that 13-month period, however, Indian domestic politics and foreign policy had taken substantial turns for the better from Moscow's viewpoint. The Soviets now had reason to de-emphasize the negative aspects of their ties with India, while not ignoring them or making any costly concessions, and to accent the positive aspects of the relationship.

THE FOREIGN POLICY SIDE OF INDO-SOVIET RELATIONS

The broad political aspects of Indo-Soviet relations were revealed in a little noted visit to Moscow at the end of May by a team from the External Affairs Ministry. Led by Foreign Secretary T. N. Kaul, the group consisted also of Secretary Kewal Singh and the Indian ambassador to Moscow, D. P. Dhar. Billed as the annual meeting, or periodic consultation between foreign offices, it was supposed to be routine. However, not only did Kaul deliver a personal message from Mrs. Gandhi to Premier Kosygin, but the Indian delegation also had a 90-minute session with Kosygin and another later with Foreign Minister Gromyko. The Indian delegation also had talks with Firyubin, the Foreign Ministry official most concerned with India (and who had conducted an unpleasant visit to India in September 1968). The joint statement issued after the conclusion of the visit testified to the success of the meeting. It had been held in a "warm and friendly atmosphere"—language indicating closer relations than in Kosygin's 1968 visit, for example—and the two sides "noted with satisfaction that there has been a marked strengthening of cooperation in all fields and particularly in trade, industry, education, science, and technology."[7] Indian and Soviet experts were to meet soon to explore prospects for further bilateral cooperation in many fields. This was clearly a follow-up to the positive tone of the Skachkov-Dymshits visit in February.

Moreover, discussion on international issues, apparently the major focus of the talks, was also encouraging. The joint statement asserted that on "most" of the issues discussed there had been "identity of views or proximity of approach."[8] Although the statement mentioned no specifics on these issues, one issue that undoubtedly was a major topic was Indochina. Both sides were grappling with the fluid situation in Cambodia—the new Lon Nol regime and Prince Sihanouk's appeal for recognition as a government in exile. Both New Delhi and Moscow sympathized more with the ousted Sihanouk yet found "it difficult to back Sihanouk unequivocally" because he seemed to be "making himself increasingly dependent on China."[9] India had still taken a far milder position than the Soviet Union vis-à-vis the U.S. "incursion" into Cambodia. In addition, India also remained less supportive of North Vietnam, which was probably due to Hanoi's perceived ties with Peking, than the Soviets desired. Indian concern with the developments in Vietnam, particularly the resumption of U.S. bombing of the North, was expressed in mild terms. Although it is not clear whether the Soviets were able to influence India's behavior on the issue at this meeting, it is true that Indian policy began to shift. New Delhi was soon to host Madame Binh, foreign minister of the People's Revolutionary Government, and the invitation must have been extended at approximately this time.

A related but much more fundamental issue for both parties was the China question. The *Hindustan Times* of New Delhi reported after the meeting that the two sides have a "*near* identity of views on the character of the threat posed by Communist China."[10] Both viewed China's behavior, the daily went on, as "aimed at promoting hegemonistic domination of Asia . . . " While there were no further details available concerning the nature of their views and the substance of the differences that made their views near rather than identical, there are some clues provided by the annual report of the External Affairs Ministry published just two months earlier.[11] While the report saw signs of a return to "revolutionary normalcy" following the Cultural Revolution, it emphasized that it would be "unrealistic to anticipate any fundamental change in Chinese foreign policy particularly towards India." Undoubtedly strengthening this skepticism and wariness toward China were the visits of an important Chinese delegation to Pakistan, the opening of a Chinese-assisted ordnance factory in East Pakistan, and Peking's launching of a satellite, which all occurred during April. Thus, it is likely that India's perception of threat from China was not lessening, and may have increased, despite some change toward moderation in Chinese foreign policy. Yet New Delhi sought to keep the option open of improving relations with Peking—"We cannot say when this [reversal] will happen but we can say that when it does happen we shall not be wanting in responding to it," stated the report—and this remained a point of some significance with Moscow. Having only a "near identity of views" would enable India to retain the possibility of usable leverage in its relationship with Moscow.

Moscow's role in Asia was another point of discussion. Once again the positions of the two were close and once again the External Affairs Ministry report provides some clues. The report contained unusually strong support for the Brezhnev collective security proposal. Referring to it as a "new development of some significance," the report went on to hail it as "a declaration of the fact that the Soviet Union is as much an Asian as a European power." What Dinesh Singh and the foreign ministry seemed to be saying was that the Brezhnev proposal would serve as a bulwark protecting states like India from China and even from the United States. Nevertheless, the report did not give unqualified endorsement to the proposal, thus keeping the door to better relations with China open.

Undoubtedly, the major item under discussion was the Soviet relationship with Pakistan. The evidence indicates that the major purpose of the Indian delegation was to dissuade Moscow from further arms deliveries to Islamabad. Prior to the meeting there were numerous reports in the Indian press, "according to information available from official sources in New Delhi," that the Soviets were planning to supply Pakistan with SU-7 bombers and missile boats. The government, reported the *Statesman* on May 29, had so far been unsuccessful in its entreaties to Moscow and was afraid the Soviets would come to a final agreement on the deal when Yahya visited the Soviet Union in June. The Indian delegation, continued the *Statesman*:

> ... is expected to try to make the Soviet government realize that the arms supplied to Pakistan has added to the tension in the Subcontinent and increased Pakistan's intransigence in not implementing the Tashkent accord.

It seems hardly coincidental that the Kaul-Singh mission preceded Yahya's visit by barely more than three weeks (or that the Pakistani ambassador had an audience with Kosygin the day Kaul and Singh arrived). Despite some editorials in the Indian press that argued that India had been "shamefully ineffective" in getting Moscow to stop arms shipments to Pakistan, other observers stated that the Indians had noticed "some signs of receptivity" to India's arguments against the arms deliveries.[12] Later in June it was revealed that indeed the Soviets had assured the Indian delegation that it would not give fresh military aid to Pakistan.[13]

It would appear that the Kaul-Singh mission was a highly successful one. Much as the Skachkov-Dymshits visit had indicated the more positive nature of the economic side of the relationship, this one revealed that political ties were also growing significantly closer. While this appears to have represented a growing coincidence of interests between the two countries, it is conceivable that influence was being exercised. If so, it would appear to be a case of mutual influence, or a tradeoff, where one state was shifting certain policies in return for alterations on other issues by the other. Mutual, or two-way, influence and growing coincidence of interests became extremely difficult to differentiate at this point.

Insight into the evolving nature of the Soviet-Indian-Pakistani triangle was provided by the visit of the Pakistani president to Moscow in June. Indian leaders scrutinized this summit for confirmation of the indications that the Kremlin had given Kaul and Singh of Moscow's position in the affairs of the subcontinent. Despite a number of superficial indications of a successful meeting, especially the Soviet agreement to finance a $200 million steel mill, the visit appears to have been a failure from the Pakistani point of view. An indication of Moscow's failing hopes for its Pakistan policy appeared on the eve of the visit. In the foreword to a new book, entitled *Pakistan and the Soviet Union*, Mikhail Kapitsa, a Soviet Asian expert in the Foreign Ministry and ambassador to Pakistan when Moscow had begun to seek a closer relationship in the mid-1960s, warned obliquely that Soviet friendship could not be taken for granted by Pakistan. In particular, Kapitsa warned Islamabad to resist too close a relationship with both the imperialists, the United States, and the "leftist adventurist forces," meaning, of course, China.[14] However, it was precisely these external ties that Islamabad was seeking to further, particularly as the middleman in United States-China relations. According to G. W. Choudhury, a high-ranking foreign ministry official who helped prepare Yahya for the visit, the Soviets linked the question of arms to those of collective security and attitude toward China.

> But when Yahya raised the question of continued arms shipments to Pakistan, the Kremlin leaders demurred. Kosygin told Yahya, "you cannot expect Soviet arms while you are unwilling to endorse our Asian Security System."[15]

Kosygin then got even more explicit by asserting that the collective security system would be the best guarantee of Pakistan's territorial integrity, *especially vis-à-vis China*. When Yahya replied that "China is sincerely interested in Pakistan's territorial integrity and sovereignty," thus politely but firmly rejecting the Soviet proposal, he ended the prospects for an era "of better understanding and warmer relations."[16]

The other area of Soviet-Pakistani relations that constituted a major focus of the talks revolved around disputes in the subcontinent and the bilateral Indo-Pakistani relationship. The Pakistani press had made it clear prior to the meeting that Yahya would seek some kind of USSR mediation, if not USSR support, in the Farakka Barrage and Kashmir disputes. However, Yahya failed to persuade the Soviets that it was India that had to change its attitude. The joint communiqué was particularly revealing of Soviet-Pakistani differences in this area.[17] On the question of Indo-Pakistani ties, Yahya "informed"—that is, the two sides were not in agreement—"the Soviet leaders of the present state of relations between Pakistan and India, with particular reference to the continued existence of the unresolved disputes to which Pakistan attaches special significance." Moscow ignored the Pakistani claim and instead urged the two to settle their differences in the "Tashkent Spirit," recalling an agreement that had never been popular in Pakistan and that Yahya refrained from referring to in any of his speeches.

All of these differences explain Podgorny's banquet reference to "frankness" in the talks—which implies actual disagreements—and the communiqué's mention of "exchange of views"—implying a difference of opinions. Not only had the Soviets refused further military arms but they also had refused to seek to influence New Delhi toward a resolution of its differences with Islamabad. The *Statesman* appreciated these results and editorialized cautiously on July 14 that the "law of diminishing returns has begun to apply to their [Soviet] efforts to befriend both sides in the Indo-Pak subcontinent."

Barely two weeks after Yahya's visit to Moscow, a Soviet envoy made a surprise appearance in New Delhi. Nikolai Firyubin, the same Soviet deputy foreign minister who had behaved in an "imperial" manner during a September 1968 visit to India, arrived on July 11 from Hanoi with less than three days notice. Although the meeting was billed as merely "a good will stopover," the length of his stay (four days), the size and composition of his delegation, which included experts on India and Pakistan, his lengthy meetings with the new foreign minister, Swaran Singh, and with Mrs. Gandhi, and the secrecy surrounding the visit all indicated that it was much more.[18] Certainly, an important concern of the talk was Indochina. Moscow, increasingly agitated over Chinese gains as the war dragged on, was seeking support for pressure on the United States to make new initiatives for peace. Although Firyubin obtained India's backing, it was with a notable lack of enthusiasm regarding an early settlement of the conflict.

There were other, probably more significant, aspects to Firyubin's supposed "mere stopover." Since the visit apparently took place at Soviet request, we need to look at what might have changed in Indian behavior. The one event that had marked the period since the Kaul-Singh visit to Moscow was Mrs. Gandhi's Cabinet reshuffle in late June, which included the removal of Dinesh Singh as external affairs minister and his replacement by Swaran Singh. Dinesh, considered a "Moscow favorite," had seemingly been playing a significant role in relations with the Soviet Union. He had led the 1969 negotiations in Moscow, which at least laid the basis for the 1971 Indo-Soviet treaty, had been virtually the only noncommunist Indian leader to endorse (and more than once) Brezhnev's Asian collective security idea, and had worked to deflect criticism of the Soviet Union on the Trivandrum cultural center issue. In light of the rumors that his replacement was "seeking to reverse some pro-Moscow policies,"[19] Moscow's concern likely revolved around its direct relationship with New Delhi and also that government's attitudes toward Indochina and China. All indications are that Firyubin received the assurances he was seeking and that he provided some to India in return. As if to demonstrate that Indian policy was not about to backslide, the government announced the forthcoming visit of Madame Binh on July 14, which was the day Firyubin headed home. She had been invited as a personal guest of Dinesh, but she was now to be the official guest of new External Affairs Minister Swaran. In return for these assuarances and other promising continuity in India's China policy,[20] Firyubin confirmed Indian perceptions of the nature of Yahya's talks in Moscow. Moreover, he was "understood to have assured India that the Soviet Union would not begin a new arms supply program for Pakistan."[21]

It is tempting to try to read more into Dinesh Singh's removal than is there. Although the actual motivations for Mrs. Gandhi's move are not clear, most Indian analysts stressed that there were no obvious policy differences between her and Dinesh. Rather, Mrs. Gandhi was seen as wanting someone less independent and "controversial" in the position because she was interested "in more directly shaping the country's foreign policy herself."[22] It is also likely that Mrs. Gandhi sought to punish Dinesh for his political behavior domestically, particularly in the state of Uttar Pradesh where his "political freelancing" upset the prime minister. These motivations and Indian assurances, however, should not mask the fact of Soviet concern with the change. Firyubin's unheralded visit indicates clearly the importance of Indian policy to Moscow as well as the Kremlin's uneasiness regarding the possibility of change in this policy. The rather steady nature of Indo-Soviet ties through the rest of the year also seems to point to the fact that relations did not depend on Dinesh.

CLOSER TIES AND CONTINUING ISSUES

Indian President V. V. Giri's 11-day visit to the Soviet Union in late September 1970 was one more of atmospherics than substance and revealed little of the evolving nature of the Indo-Soviet relationship.[23] Mrs. Gandhi's three-hour stop in Moscow in October and subsequent developments, however, were more enlightening. On her way to New York for the General Assembly session, the prime minister was met at the airport in Moscow by Kosygin. That this was more than a courtesy call is attested to by several aspects of the brief visit. For one, the welcoming ceremonies at the airport were cut short to save time for talks, and Mrs. Gandhi was whisked away to a villa in the Lenin Hills, overlooking Moscow. Indian officials present at the talks, which ran over and delayed Mrs. Gandhi's departure by 40 minutes, were Swaran, Kaul, and Ambassador Dhar. On the Soviet side, Kosygin was assisted by Acting Foreign Minister Kuznetsov (Gromyko had already left for the United States), Firyubin, who was Moscow's chief political negotiator with India, Skachkov, who was the chief economic negotiator, and Ambassador Pegov. After the meeting, Mrs. Gandhi said the two delegations had "exchanged views" on "various problems confronting the world." Kosygin expressed satisfaction at the steady development of bilateral relations and added that "he regretted that the time was short but nevertheless, they succeeded in exchanging opinions on developments in both countries."[24]

How is one to assess this cryptic visit and the mutual reference to an exchange of views, a phrase that indicates each side presenting its version and not reaching agreement? On foreign policy issues, such as Indochina and the Middle East, their positions continued to be close. Indeed a later Soviet commentary seemed to confirm this by asserting that "while discussing a host of important *international* problems, the identity of views of both countries was noted."[25] The Soviets, for example, were undoubtedly pleased with the "leftist" anti-imperialist swing of the nonaligned movement and India's role in that shift as seen in the recently concluded summit in Lusaka, Zambia. More significant was the fact that after her appearance at the United Nations, Mrs. Gandhi would be talking with U.S. leaders. As she later revealed on the U.S. television program "Meet the Press," the main subject of her talks with Secretary of State William Rogers was that of U.S. arms to Pakistan in the wake of President Nixon's announcement earlier in the month that Washington was offering "limited defense equipment" to Pakistan as a "one-time," partial lifting of the embargo. She expressed herself then as "not satisfied" with the U.S. explanation of seeking to wean Pakistan from China, which was the same one "we *used to* receive from the Soviets."[26] The message here seems to have been that Mrs. Gandhi discussed U.S. and Soviet policy toward Pakistan while in Moscow and received partial reassurances; Kosygin was unwilling to scrap entirely Soviet efforts to establish influence in Pakistan but continued to disavow any intention to send arms to Islamabad.

An additional issue that seems to have been the source of the exchange rather than identity of views has to do with Soviet maps of the Sino-Indian border. New Delhi's protests in 1956, 1958, 1966, and 1968 had brought no alteration in the maps that favored the Chinese position in the territorial dispute. During 1970 opposition groups in the Lok Sabha had challenged the government on the issue and in early September the External Affairs Ministry finally agreed to draft a strong protest to the Soviets on their "cartographic aggression." Giri was to have broached the issue during his visit and Mrs. Gandhi reported that she raised the issue with Kosygin, receiving the same assurances Giri had been given.[27] That the issue was not resolved during her visit is revealed by the report that T. N. Kaul made a visit to Moscow at the end of October on his way home from the United Nations and explicitly discussed the issue again with Firyubin. This time the Indians got some changes, which produced the most favorable version so far: Kashmir was made entirely Indian, part of the Northeast Frontier Agency went to India, while the rest of it and the disputed Aksai Chin area were still shown as Chinese. Despite this improvement, the issue was hardly resolved and was soon to reappear.

On the Soviet side, the persistent Indian feelers to the Chinese may also have been an irritant in the relationship. Moscow was certainly aware of the constraints the 1962 war put on India's Chinese policy. Moscow also encouraged coordinated Indian *and* Soviet gestures toward China, which were intended to put pressure on Pakistan; for example, mutual calls for normalization within a day of each other in August. Nevertheless, calls for improvement of ties with China at other times by leading Indian officials including the prime minister and her defense minister, Jagjivan Ram, as well as the October Sino-Indian ambassadorial talks in Cairo were somewhat unsettling to the Soviets. Moscow undoubtedly wanted these carried out under its guidance, and India just as surely wanted autonomy in its playing of any "China card."

While Mrs. Gandhi's Moscow stop may have indicated certain points of friction in relations, the overall relationship stood in marked contrast to New Delhi's relations with either Washington or Peking and to Moscow's ties with Pakistan. Relations were drawing closer and perhaps the stage was being set for even stronger ties. For instance, knowledgeable sources were quoted after the prime minister's stop in Moscow as reporting that "on bilateral relations both sides expressed the view that time had come to investigate greater possibilities and new areas of collaboration and cooperation."[28]

A major impetus to a closer relationship was provided by Pakistani President Yahya Khan's visits to the United States and China. Yahya's talks with U.S. officials, following his appearance at the U.N. General Assembly in October, were far more successful than Mrs. Gandhi's. President Nixon reaffirmed U.S. support for Pakistan and reiterated his offer of "limited defense equipment" to Islamabad, which was precisely the offer that Mrs. Gandhi had sought to have withdrawn.[29] On the heels of this trip, Yahya journeyed to Peking where his lavish reception, "one of the biggest welcomes in Peking ever accorded a foreign chief of state on a visit to Communist China,"[30] far outdid those he received both in Washington and particularly, in Moscow.

The visit to China stood in marked contrast to Yahya's USSR trip substantively as well. At minimum, China pledged to continue its military assistance, which was the very pledge the Soviets had refused to make. On the economic side, the new Chinese offer of $200 million equalled Moscow's, but the terms were easier—interest free, and no repayment for 20 years. Peking also expressed support for Pakistan's position on Kashmir, implying that India was responsible for the lack of a settlement. On the Farakka dispute, Peking was much more circumspect in its support: having been apprised of the issue by Yahya, China only "appreciated Pakistan's stand for a peaceful solution of this question and hoped for an early settlement of this dispute."[31] Yet even this degree of support for Pakistan was far more than Moscow had been willing to grant.

Pakistan's major worry had been rapprochment in Sino-Indian relations. What it had seen as India's "persistent efforts to improve its relations with China and, simultaneously, spoil, if possible, Sino-Pakistan relations"[32] coupled with reports that China was warming toward India had made the Pakistanis wonder whether Peking would continue to take their side against India as strongly as before. Consequently, the Pakistani press was quick to highlight all aspects of the talks that tended to disprove any such change in Sino-Pakistani ties. China also expressed *its* appreciation that Pakistan had resisted outside pressure, undoubtedly referring to the Soviet Union, in order to "firmly adhere to the policy of friendship towards China..."[33] At the banquet on November 11, Yahya asserted that Sino-Pakistani relations were not based on expediency nor directed against others but that their growing friendship served the interests of the two states as well as of peace and stability in the region. The Chinese vice-chairman, Tung Li-wu, responded that China would always stand by Pakistan and denounced efforts to sow seeds of dissension between the two. Clearly referring to both India and the Soviet Union, Tung proclaimed that "although some people are displeased with the continuous development of Sino-Pakistani friendly relations, we firmly believe that the joint effort of our two governments and people would frustrate all their attempts."[34]

Yahya's pilgrimage to Peking thus seems to have clarified the evolving interrelationships in the subcontinent. New Delhi's and Moscow's efforts to divide China and Pakistan for their own separate objectives had clearly failed. With their major adversaries thus closely aligned, and with that alignment being supported by Washington, India and the Soviet Union had nowhere else to turn but to each other and, in the wake of these events, New Delhi and Moscow did indeed take a significant further step in their bilateral relationship. At the conclusion of a visit to India by Soviet Foreign Trade Minister Patolichev in December, the two states signed a new five-year trade agreement. While this pact was a continuation of a long-term trade relationship, it was also a qualitatively new stage, a "landmark" in "the development of Indo-Soviet relations."[35] One reason was that new items were to be included in each country's exports. The Soviet Union, for the first time, agreed to trade such needed items as ships and tankers, as well as more steel, various metals, and new industrial goods. Perhaps even more significantly, India was now to export a larger percentage of manufactured goods, including those from Soviet-aided projects, which was a development that reflected changes in the structure of the Indian economy and would provide important markets for India's new products. The share of manufactured goods in India's total exports to the Soviet Union was set to increase from 44 percent in 1970 to 60 percent by 1975. Another significant provision of the new agreement was for production collaboration and joint marketing in third countries. This was a breakthrough for New Delhi after long years of negotiations, and something the Indians had failed to achieve in the February agreement. Finally, the new pact called for an annual increase of 15 percent in total trade turnover. Since the Soviet Union was emerging at precisely this time as India's number-two trading partner, the realization of this ambitious target would challenge Washington's role as number one.

In this period, what dominated the agenda in Indo-Soviet relations from Yahya's PRC trip through the end of 1971, however, were internal developments in India and Pakistan and the growing friction between the two neighbors. In India, 1970 was a year of political turmoil for Indira Gandhi's government. Due to the defection of the "Syndicate" from the Indian National Congress, and its formation of the rival Congress Organization, the prime minister's majority of 284 seats in the Lok Sabha (of a total of 523, 520 of which are elected) had been reduced to a plurality of 222. Mrs. Gandhi had been forced to rely on minor parties, particularly the pro-Soviet Communist Party of India, in order to remain in power. In an attempt to alter that situation, she dissolved the Lok Sabha in December and called new elections for March, which was a year ahead of schedule. In these first midterm elections in Indian history, Mrs. Gandhi confounded most experts and won a massive victory. She emerged with a two-thirds majority, a whopping 362 seats in the new Lok Sabha.

Moscow, which had sympathetically followed Mrs. Gandhi and the "left forces'" struggle against "the pressure of reaction," was also outspokenly supportive during the campaign of 1971. Mrs. Gandhi's victory was enthusiastically greeted as a "defeat for Indian reaction" and a victory not only for Mrs. Gandhi and the "New Congress," but also for progressive policies.[36] General Secretary Brezhnev even devoted a paragraph to these "inspiring" developments in his Central Committee report to the Twenty-fourth Congress of the CPSU in late March. Brezhnev also had positive things to say about Soviet-Indian bilateral relations:

> Our friendly relations with India have received considerable development. The Indian government's pursuit of a peace-loving, independent course in international affairs, the feelings of friendship that traditionally link the peoples of our two countries—all this helps to deepen Soviet-Indian cooperation.[37]

Moscow was clearly cheered by Mrs. Gandhi's victory and the large-scale rout of rightist forces that were demonstratively anti-Soviet. Yet it would seem that the Kremlin was also concerned that Mrs. Gandhi no longer needed communist support and thus perhaps Soviet support as well; hence, there were frequent references in Soviet analysis to the need for democratic reforms to be enacted and assertions that Mrs. Gandhi won not only due to her own popularity, but also due to the masses' demands for change. The Soviets greeted evidence of Mrs. Gandhi's socialist intention, such as the nationalization of the insurance business in May, with enthusiasm but cited the need for further progress, particularly in the area of agrarian reform.[38]

In stark contrast to the new stability the March vote brought to India, the situation in Pakistan had deteriorated rapidly following the December election for the constituent assembly there. The election results confirmed the growing fissure between the country's two wings: in East Pakistan, Sheik Mujibur Rahman's Awami League, whose Six Point Program featured a demand for autonomy, won 167 of the 169 seats; in the West, Ali Bhutto's Pakistan People's Party, which stood for a strong central government, won the majority of seats. Given Yahya's own precarious position within the military leadership, as well as Mujib's dependence on a broad and diverse coalition and the pressures on Bhutto to emerge as a *West* Pakistani neutralist, Pakistan seemed destined for a time of conflict if not disintegration, a fate many had long predicted. By the end of February, Yahya had been forced by events to postpone indefinitely the national assembly meeting that was to begin drafting the constitution. Further talks broke down and before the end of March the West Pakistan army was unleashed on the Bengalis of East Pakistan. Civil war had begun.

Relations between New Delhi and Islamabad had been deteriorating along with the conditions within Pakistan. Friction over Kashmir had escalated early in 1971. Despite Pakistani efforts to get Moscow to pressure New Delhi, the Indians would not budge.[39] As Pakistan moved toward civil war, tension between the two countries grew. The "massive attack" against "the entire people of East Bengal" was quickly condemned in a resolution of March 31 in the Lok Sabha which warned Pakistan that India "cannot remain indifferent to the macabre tragedy being enacted so close to our border," expressed "its profound sympathy for and solidarity with the people of East Bengal," demanded the "immediate cessation of the use of force, and the massacre of defenseless people," and assured the people of East Bengal that "their struggle and sacrifices will receive the whole-hearted sympathy and support of the people of India."[40] The conflict that was tearing Pakistan apart thus seemed likely to spill over to more of South Asia.

The major trauma in the subcontinent coincided with various trends at the great-power level. The most removed of these, yet one fraught with dangers for both India and the Soviet Union, was the beginning of change in Sino-United States relations. In March Washington further relaxed travel restrictions to China, and in April it did the same with trade. In that month, Peking initiated its "ping-pong diplomacy" by inviting a U.S. table-tennis team to China. Further U.S. steps toward China followed and there were increasing hints, mixed with continued Chinese attacks on U.S. imperialism, of Chinese reciprocity. While the tentative steps toward a normalization would obviously be viewed with genuine trepidation in Moscow,[41] China's seemingly unwavering support for Pakistan made this development a source of real apprehension in New Delhi as well. On April 13, Islamabad published a letter to Yahya from Chou En-lai, which accused New Delhi of "gross interference in the internal affairs of Pakistan" and promised that "should the Indian expansionists dare to launch aggression against Pakistan, the Chinese Government and people will, as always, firmly support the Pakistan Government and people in their just struggle to safeguard State sovereignty and national independence."[42] Early in May, the Pakistanis reported that China had offered to increase its aid in the face of Islamabad's battle against rebels in the East.

Meanwhile, Indian-United States relations continued their downward slide. Trade and aid were undergoing a steady decline. Indian hostility to the U.S. role in Vietnam was escalating. The United States-China thaw raised real questions about whether Washington would assist New Delhi, as it had in 1962, if another war with China broke out. The United States' lack of support for Bengali nationalism in East Pakistan and its lack of sufficient concern for the refugees who began pouring out of Pakistan's eastern wing shortly after the beginning of the war on March 25 deepened India's skepticism regarding the U.S. role. The one step Washington took that should have pleased India—the embargo placed on U.S. arms sales to

Pakistan in March—had little impact due to the continuing evidence that U.S. arms were reaching Pakistan.

India was thus being put progessively into a more difficult position during 1971. On the local level, the events in Pakistan quickly became the overriding issue in Indian internal politics. Most observers were soon to agree with one analyst's view that "no government could have survived in New Delhi if it had taken a neutral, hands-off attitude to the political upheaval in East Pakistan."[43] Moreover, this crisis was becoming intermingled with Sino-United States developments that threatened to leave India isolated. The Kremlin leaders were undoubtedly aware of India's perception and certainly shared its concerns regarding Chinese and U.S. backing of Pakistan. Yet to completely support India would thoroughly alienate Pakistan, as well as offend Moscow's Arab friends. Moreover, complete backing for India would certainly invite war in the subcontinent. The avoidance of that was something Moscow had strenuously worked for at least since Tashkent in 1966. A new conflict in South Asia would upset the balance there, weakening both India and Pakistan, and strengthening reactionary forces in both. It might also invite foreign intervention, either from China or the United States or both.

Faced with these kinds of problems and options, it is hardly surprising that Moscow sought to find a policy that would lessen, if not remove, the crisis before the situation deteriorated further. One prong of this approach was to encourage Islamabad to resolve the issues with the eastern wing peacefully. On April 2, Soviet President Podgorny sent a letter to Yahya that was "an insistent appeal for the adoption of the most urgent measures to stop the bloodshed and repression against the population in East Pakistan and for turning to methods of a peaceful political settlement." While the Soviets were opposed to any use of force, including that by India, the clear appeal was to Islamabad to resolve these problems before they did "great harm to the vital interest of the entire people of Pakistan."[44] When Yahya maintained a hard-line position in response, the Soviets chose not to escalate the tension but to work behind the scenes. The Soviet media gave wide publicity to the meetings Premier Kosygin had with Indian and Pakistani ambassadors in April, and Kosygin sent a more restrained letter to Yahya at the end of that month. At no time did the Soviets indicate an interest in the breakup of Pakistan—indeed in Podgorny's letter, his references to the "entire people of Pakistan" seemed intended to convey the opposite—nor a lack of concern in the heightening India-Pakistan friction.

At the same time, Moscow pursued a policy of urging restraint on India. Although, within India, pressures intensified rapidly to adopt policies regarding the flood of refugees into the country, it was not until early May that *Pravda* even mentioned the problem and still later before the Soviets promised help to India on the refugee issue. Early in June the "unofficial" visit of External Affairs Minister Swaran Singh to Moscow revealed the gap between the Indian and Soviet positions on the overall situation. Although the two sides reiterated their agreement that Pakistan should be urged to take measures to restore peace and security, there were continuing areas of disagreement as testified to by the reference to an "exchange of views" in Soviet commentary on the meeting.[45] In the joint statement, Swaran is reported to have "explained"—that is, he was unable to obtain complete Soviet support and differences remained—to the Soviets the "social, economic and political problems created by the course of events in East Pakistan."[46] The Indian press was quick to perceive Swaran's mission as a failure. The visit, commented the *Indian Express* on June 11, "surely had the purpose of persuading the Soviet Union that the crisis has deepened and continues to deepen with the passage of time," but it had been unable to bring about even a marginal change in Moscow's policy. The Soviets would not insist on the need for a "specifically political settlement" in Pakistan, but kept to more general formulations, which were sure to be less offensive to Islamabad. Indeed, the *Indian Express* editorial even saw the final statement as a Soviet effort to reassure Pakistan publicly that Swaran's visit had not caused any abrupt shift in Soviet attitudes. Moscow was willing to side with India in calling for an end to the influx of refugees from East Pakistan and the creation of conditions that would lead to their return, but was not willing to go so far as India in calling for specific kinds of settlements in East Pakistan or in making political demands on Islamabad.

THE TREATY IS MADE PUBLIC

As the crisis in East Pakistan and between India and Pakistan deepened in the summer of 1971, further clarification of the role of external powers took place. Early in July, Henry Kissinger stopped in New Delhi on his way to Islamabad. He was conciliatory toward India, warning that "China would intervene on behalf of Yahya Khan if India intervened on behalf of Mujib," but added reassuringly that Washington "would support India in the event of a Chinese attack."[47] He also soothingly explained that the continuing arms flow from the United States into Pakistan was merely a "bureaucratic muddle."[48] Far more significant for Indian security, however, were Kissinger's subsequent actions and words. He reportedly was ill while in Pakistan, but President Nixon revealed in mid-July that his national security advisor had in fact flown secretly to Peking, met with Chinese leaders there, and laid the groundwork for a presidential visit to China in 1972. This large step toward normalization of relations between an "unfriendly neighbor" and an increasingly untrustworthy supporter, both of which were also Pakistan's main supporters, sent a shock wave through India. Kissinger soon gave concrete substance to New Delhi's heightened concerns: meeting with the Indian ambassador upon his return to Washington, Kissinger reiterated his belief that China would intervene in the subcontinent if India did *and* reversed his earlier pledge by asserting that the United States would stay neutral in the event of such a conflict.[49]

New Delhi's intitial response to its growing predicament came quickly even if it was largely futile: a flurry of rumors leaked out of official quarters regarding the possibility of a normalization of relations between India and China. The Defense Ministry's annual report near the end of July "pointedly skipped specific mention of China in outlining India's new military budget—giving new credence to signs of a shift in New Delhi's attitude to Peking."[50] Rather than indicating any diminishing of concern about the China "threat," this seemed to have two purposes: first, to offer China some incentive to modify its support of Pakistan and perhaps pledge its noninvolvement if an Indo-Pakistani conflict should develop; and second, even if that failed as it was likely to, to heighten Moscow's concern about the reliability of India's anti-Chinese stance. Mrs. Gandhi's letter in July to Chou En-lai, explaining India's position and offering to hold talks with China on the East Pakistan issue, was another effort along these lines. Finally, former Indian ambassador to the Soviet Union, D.P. Dhar, was dispatched to Moscow at the end of July to attempt one further effort in China's direction. At New Delhi's request, Dhar held at least two secret talks with the Chinese ambassador in Moscow.

Either during Dhar's meetings with Chinese Ambassador Lin Hsin-chuan—which led to no change in Sino-Indian relations—or subsequent to them, there was a flurry of Indian-Soviet meetings. Soviet Ambassador Pegov called on the External Affairs Ministry on two consecutive days, the Indian ambassador in Moscow went to the Soviet Foreign Ministry, and Dhar himself held unpublicized meetings with Soviet officials. It is unclear whether these meetings dealt primarily with the Chinese talks or with a possible change in New Delhi's attitude toward West Pakistan. The immediate effect, however, became clear when, on August 6, *TASS* announced that Foreign Minister Gromyko would be traveling to India two days later.

Gromyko's hastily arranged trip, evidently at Indian request, testifies to the sense of urgency in the Indo-Soviet relationship at this time. Upon his arrival on August 8, the foreign minister announced his purpose as promoting "the cause of further developing and deepening the friendly cooperation" between India and the Soviet Union, which would aid in "the consolidation of peace in Asia and throughout the world."[51] Within 24 hours, Gromyko and Swaran Singh produced a significant bilateral agreement, the Treaty of Peace, Friendship and Cooperation. Why was the treaty drawn at this time? Just as a confluence of events and a coincidence of perceptions had brought New Delhi and Moscow closer together in September 1969, when the treaty was probably drafted, so another confluence brought the two to the point of making their agreement public. From India's point of view, dangers were increasing all around. The United States-China rapprochement boded ill and China had proven unreceptive to Indian overtures. Second, the possibility of war with Pakistan was growing in light of Yahya's recent statements warning of total war with India. Moreover, Islamabad, with Washington's help, seemed to be making progress in obtaining United Nations involvement in East Pakistan, which was an interference India did not want. New Delhi, under intensifying domestic pressure to recognize a new state of Bangladesh in Pakistan and to resolve the issue with Pakistan once and for all, thought that a treaty would grant "public" security. The Soviet Union was still anxious to avoid a conflict in the region and was also interested in underlining its relationship with India as a bar to Chinese influence. The treaty would certainly do the latter but it would also hopefully accomplish the former. By convincing India of Soviet support, perhaps the pressures on Mrs. Gandhi's government would be eased—in particular, the recognition of Bangladesh, a sure trigger of war, would be delayed—China would be deterred, and Yahya would be pressured to find a solution acceptable to India and the other parties involved.

The treaty itself consists of a preamble—which focuses on Indo-Soviet friendship and cooperation and the need for world peace—and 12 articles.[52] The first declares lasting friendship, respect for sovereignty and territorial integrity, and noninterference in internal affairs in relations between the two states. The next two articles are concerned with disarmament and state their position against colonialism and racism. Article Four pays public homage to India's policy of nonalignment, indicating that the Soviet Union "respects" it, and also confirms India's respect for Moscow's "peaceful policy," which is seen as aimed at "strengthening friendship and cooperation with all peoples" (Pakistan included). Articles Five through Seven deal with the maintenance of regular contacts and economic, scientific, technical, cultural, and other kinds of cooperation between the two parties. Article Eleven sets the term of the treaty at 20 years and provides the means for its renewal, termination, and ratification. Article Twelve provides for the means of resolving any differences in interpretation.

Of particular significance for the Soviet-Indian relationship are Articles Eight through Ten.[53] Article Eight pledges the two "High Contracting Parties" not to "enter into or participate in any military alliances directed against the other Party." The first part of Article Nine goes a step further—and seems directly related to Indian concerns about Soviet behavior in the growing conflict with Pakistan—by stating that each side would "refrain from giving any assistance to any third Party taking part in an armed conflict with the other Party." Article Ten underlines this, and perhaps is intended to give comfort particularly to the Soviet Union in its concerns about a possible Indian rapprochement with China (and also to India regarding Soviet efforts to befriend Pakistan):

> Each of the High Contracting Parties solemnly declares that it shall not undertake any commitment, secret or open, with regard to one or more states incompatible with the present Treaty. Each of the High Contracting Parties declares further that it has no commitments towards any other state or states and shall not undertake any commitments that may cause military damage to the other Party.

Finally, the second part of Article Nine constitutes the other half of the core of the treaty relationship. It guarantees that if either of the Parties "is attacked or threatened with attack," then India and the Soviet Union "will immediately start mutual consultations with a view to eliminating this threat and taking appropriate effective measures, to ensure peace and security for their countries." Thus, New Delhi and Moscow had agreed not to undertake any agreement with or give any assistance to a state the other is in conflict with and to undertake "immediate consultations" with one another if either becomes involved in a conflict. The message to Pakistan and China, as well as to the United States, seemed clear.

The message of the treaty—Soviet support for India was certainly clear to most in India. Although the country's constitution did not require it, Swaran Singh presented it immediately to the Lok Sabha. He was received with cheering and for six hours the treaty was praised, with the Swatantra being the only party opposed to it, and the possible violation of nonalignment being the only major concern of others. The joint statement issued by the two countries at the conclusion of Gromyko's visit summed up the positions of both New Delhi and Moscow on the new agreement:

> Both sides believe that the conclusion of this treaty is an outstanding historic event for both countries. This treaty logically follows from the relations of sincere friendship, respect, mutual trust and comprehensive relations which have been established between the Soviet Union and India over many years and which have stood the test of time. It meets the basic interests of the Soviet and Indian peoples and opens up broad prospects for raising the fruitful cooperation between the U.S.S.R. and India to a still higher level. Apart from other points referring to bilateral Soviet-Indian relations, the treaty provides for maintaining regular

contacts by the two sides on major international problems and for holding mutual consultations in order to take appropriate effective steps to safeguard the peace and security of both countries.
The treaty between the U.S.S.R. and India is a genuine act of peace expressing the common policy and aspirations of the U.S.S.R. and India in the struggle for strengthening peace in Asia and the world and for insuring international security. All its provisions serve these aims. The treaty is not directed against anyone, but is called upon to become a factor for the development of friendship and good-neighbor relations in accordance with the principles of the U.N. Charter.
The governments of the U.S.S.R. and India are convinced that the conclusion of the Treaty of Peace, Friendship and Cooperation will meet with full approval from all who are genuinely interested in the preservation of peace in Asia and the entire world, and from the governments of all peace-loving states.[54]

Although the treaty seemed to point to a new era in Indo-Soviet relations, a more accurate reading of the relationship was available in the joint statement that was particularly notable for its restraint. Once again an Indian leader was described as having had to explain to the Soviets the burden the refugees were placing on India. Apparently the Soviet leaders still did not fully appreciate this nor, therefore—and this is the crux—did they agree with India's perception of the imminent need to take action against Pakistan that would alleviate the growing refugee crisis. This explains also why it took "a detailed discussion" to reiterate the two sides' "firm conviction that there can be no military solution of this problem"— that is, not by Pakistan *nor* by India—and also the reference to the views of the two being "identical or *very close.*"[55]

THE APPROACHING CONFLICT

This interpretation that the treaty had *not* indicated a qualitative change in Soviet policy toward India and the civil war in East Pakistan seems borne out by Moscow's subsequent behavior. In the United Nations, a good deal more Soviet support for India was forthcoming. Pakistan, which had been mounting a campaign to obtain U.N. intervention in the crisis, ran into a Soviet roadblock after the August treaty. The Soviets also proceeded to postpone the visit to Moscow of the Pakistani foreign secretary. At the same time, however, Soviet action was focussed on providing reassurance to Pakistan. Soviet-Pakistani friendship would not suffer because of the treaty, Moscow said, and Soviet economic assistance to Islamabad would continue. Moreover, Soviet refusal to recognize Bangladesh was maintained. In sum, despite Moscow's behavior at the

United Nations, USSR policy showed the Soviet Union basically stood for stability. As New Delhi's *Statesman* later remarked, "The burden of Soviet comment is that the vital issue is not independence but the preservation of peace in the sub-continent."[56]

The September visits of the Pakistani foreign secretary and of Prime Minister Gandhi to Moscow shed further light on the Soviet Union's careful policy. After having his visit postponed in August, Foreign Secretary Sultan Mohammed Khan finally arrived in Moscow on September 4. His visit was seen by the Pakistani government as a test of "the true nature of the Soviet government's claim that the Indo-Soviet treaty is not directed against any country with which Moscow maintains friendly relations...." Khan held talks with Gromyko and Firyubin. Although details of the talks were not made public, Khan returned to Pakistan reporting that they had been "timely and useful." The Soviets supported peace on the subcontinent, the "unity" (obviously a key word for Islamabad) and "integrity" of Pakistan, and the government's handling of its own internal affairs. While no Soviet commentary stated the Kremlin's support for Pakistan's unity, Firyubin did term the "exchange of views"—that is, differences of opinion—a "positive development" and "fruitful."[57]

Mrs. Gandhi's visit later in the month was clearly more successful although still disappointing to many Indians, presumably including the prime minister herself. On September 28 Mrs. Gandhi held three hours of talks with the Soviet triumvirate—Brezhnev, Kosygin, and Podgorny—which was an indication of the importance to Moscow of its relations with India and of the present crisis. She held further talks with other top Soviet leaders and was met at the airport by a delegation that included Soviet Defense Minister Grechko; this latter fact underlined the military aspects of the Indo-Soviet relationship since the treaty. To a large extent, the two sides did not directly address the issues during the summit. The entire Soviet thrust continued to be on peace and on preventing war. Kosygin, for example, at a luncheon in honor of Mrs. Gandhi, condemned the actions of the Pakistani authorities in East Pakistan but then reiterated that the "Soviet Union is doing and will continue to do everything possible on its part to maintain peace in this region and to prevent the outbreak of an armed conflict."[58] The reference in the very next sentence to an "exchange of opinions... with you, Mrs. Prime Minister, on the question" indicates that Mrs. Gandhi was hardly so sanguine about a peaceful solution. According to one Indian analyst, "The Russians were tireless in trying to persuade Mrs. Gandhi out of any intention to intervene militarily."[59] The Soviet leadership stressed the uncertainty of the risks, especially the possible U.S. and Chinese roles.

The joint statement also revealed this difference.[60] Once again India "informed the Soviet side that the presence in India of over nine million refugees from East Pakistan had engendered serious social, economic and political tensions in India." Moscow was also forced to "take into account" the prime minister's statement:

> ... that the government of India is fully determined to take all necessary measures to stop the inflow of refugees from East Pakistan to India and to ensure that those refugees who are already in India return to their homeland without delay.

Rather than indicate any new Soviet policy, however, the statement then said that the "Soviet side reaffirmed its position" as set forth in Podgorny's letter of April 2. Thus, Moscow was still calling for peace. At the same time, the joint statement seemed to reveal a stronger stand than previously expressed. For the first time, the Soviets stated that they "highly appreciated" India's policy and "understood" the "difficulties confronting friendly India in connection with the mass inflow of refugees."

Mrs. Gandhi's visit seems to have moved Indo-Soviet relations on the Bangladesh question a notch closer. The statement reflects a Soviet perception that had grown closer to India's. Mrs. Gandhi may well have convinced the Soviet leaders of certain realities about East Pakistan—the degree of the people's commitment to independence and of Mujib's popular support—and that India had the right to adopt whatever means it thought necessary for resolving the crisis. Yet, in the end, Soviet policy did not change. A symbol of Moscow's continuing equivocation toward India's position is to be found in differences in terminology in the communiqué: although the Indian version referred to "East Bengal," the precursor to "Bangladesh," which obviously signified independence from Pakistan, the Soviet version retained the conventional "East Pakistan."

The early part of October appears to have been the time of Moscow's last desperate attempts to maintain this policy and make it work in the direction of a resolution to the crisis. President Podgorny, on his way to Hanoi, accompanied Mrs. Gandhi on her return to New Delhi in order "to pick up the thread of the friendly exchange and to continue contacts with the Indian leaders, this time on their native soil." There only for a day, Podgorny went so far as to offer "all possible assistance" to a settlement "in the spirit of the existing friendly relations with India." Yet, once again, the Soviet position was grounded on the need to avoid a military conflict: "We consider that the further sliding towards a military conflict must be prevented and that the tension there should be removed by means of an equitable political settlement with due account for the legitimate rights and interests of the people in that region."[61] What, in fact, Moscow was seeking to do was to get New Delhi to broaden its definition of a political solution that would be acceptable. Momentarily, at least, Moscow appears to have exercised influence successfully, for, on October 8, Swaran Singh publicly backed away from India's previous position that independence for Bangladesh was the only solution. Provincial autonomy or even reintegration might be acceptable, he said, as long as Dacca's elected representatives approved it.

At the same time, Moscow sought to persuade Pakistan of its support and its interest in peace. The most significant Soviet step in this direction came during Kosygin's state visit to Algeria, where he and Algerian President Boumedienne signed a joint communiqué that called for "respect for the national unity and territorial integrity of Pakistan."[62] Never before had Moscow (or Peking) referred to Pakistan's unity or its territorial integrity, previously confining itself to reference to "national independence" and "sovereignty." Although the Soviets explained to Prime Minister Gandhi that the Algerians had threatened to issue a far stronger statement unilaterally, the uproar in India was immediate. On October 13 the *Times of India* editorialized:

> The joint statement... enhances the doubts that have been increasingly felt recently about Moscow's attitude to the Bangla Desh struggle and its repercussions on relations between India and Pakistan. The doubts persisted after Mrs. Gandhi's visit to Moscow and the joint statement that was signed on that occasion, even though its language gave rise to hopes in India that Moscow was moving nearer New Delhi's standpoint. But these hopes have now been belied....

Regarding the treaty between the two countries, the editorial concluded, Kosygin's endorsement of the Algerian position:

> ... only provides further evidence that far from promoting the prospects of an independent Bangla Desh, the Indo-Soviet treaty is intended, at least by Moscow, to function as a brake.

Indian policy reaction was also swift. On October 14 Mrs. Gandhi announced that Foreign Minister Singh had been misquoted and that India saw independence as the only way out of the crisis in East Bengal. To complete the failure of Moscow's efforts to bring India and Pakistan together, President Yahya, on October 12, publicly rebuffed Soviet (and Indian) calls to negotiate with Mujibur Rahman and other elected Awami League leaders.

Moscow was now faced with a discouraging, yet clarified, situation. Neither India nor Pakistan was about to compromise even as skirmishes between them increased and tension mounted; the Soviets had been unsuccessful in applying influence to either state. The USSR response to this situation came quickly. On October 21 Soviet Deputy Foreign Minister Firyubin arrived in New Delhi, once again on a hastily arranged visit. The short notice of the trip was partially due to the deteriorating conditions in the region, but more directly to Mrs. Gandhi's imminent departure on a trip to Western capitals. Firyubin arrived in time to have talks with the prime minister the day before she departed and then had further talks with Swaran Singh, Indian Defense Secretary K.B. Lall, T.N. Kaul, D.P. Dhar (now head of Policy Planning), Giri, and other officials of the External Affairs Ministry. While the meetings were at first described as "routine bilateral consultations," this pretense was soon dropped and the importance of the talks were admitted. An Indian Foreign Ministry spokesman revealed that the talks were held under Article Nine of the Indo-Soviet treaty, which was the provision that calls for immediate mutual consultation "with a view to eliminating" an attack or threat of attack and to taking "appropriate effective measures to ensure peace and security for their countries."[63] These consultations "were held in connection with the tense situation that has taken shape on the Hindustan Peninsula and which is threatening the cause of peace in that area," wrote *Pravda* on October 28.

Even more significantly, for the first time since the conflict in East Pakistan had begun in March, Moscow came out in full agreement with India. In the words of the joint press release, "Both sides agreed completely in their assessment of the present situation."[64] No longer did the Soviets need to have India inform them or explain the situation to them. While Firyubin may still have counseled restraint to New Delhi, his mission clearly was intended to reassure the Indians, and particularly Mrs. Gandhi before she left for the West, that Soviet support would be forthcoming for India should a conflict ensue. Military discussions were reportedly an important part of the agenda. The October 29 issue of the Indian *Hindu* was quick to contrast Moscow's promise of support with the situation in 1965 when India had been hamstrung because Britain had denied India spare parts for its weapons.

By virtue of Firyubin's visit taking place under the provisions of Article Nine of the treaty, the Soviet Union thus became a formal party to the crisis. Although still not anxious for war, Moscow fully supported New Delhi. The atmosphere in the talks of "sincere friendship, mutual trust and mutual understanding"—the reference to mutual trust, which had been partially lacking during the year, is particularly significant— "demonstrated a coincidence of views on the questions discussed."[65] These shared perceptions were given further substance when it was announced during Firyubin's stay that Soviet Air Marshal Pavel Kutakhov, commander in chief of the Air Force, would follow Firyubin to New Delhi within the week. The nature of the tightening Indo-Soviet relationship and especially its growing military aspect were symbolized by this goodwill visit. The conditions were now set for the final, inevitable steps to war in the subcontinent.

WAR AND INFLUENCE

As the situation between India and Pakistan raced toward a climax following the visits of Firyubin and Kutakhov to New Delhi, the roles of the major powers became crystallized. Soviet support for India in the United Nations continued and Soviet demands on Pakistan for a political settlement with Awami League leaders intensified. In the meantime, Mrs. Gandhi journeyed to Washington where she held talks with Nixon and Kissinger. Although she reported that the two sides understood each other's position better after the talks, it is clear that differences between them predominated. The United States contended that although East Pakistan's autonomy was inevitable, it was on a longer timetable than New Delhi sought. Nixon and Kissinger refused to agree to put pressure on Yahya to bow, in Kissinger's words, to "India's determination to establish its preeminence on the subcontinent." In Kissinger's analysis, the two meetings Mrs. Gandhi had with the U.S. president were "the two most unfortunate meetings Nixon had with any foreign leader...."[66]

As Mrs. Gandhi was undertaking these fruitless meetings in Washington, President Yahya's personal emissary, Z.A. Bhutto, was leading a high-powered Pakistani delegation to Peking. While Mrs. Gandhi did not accomplish much in Washington, she did get a U.S. promise to hold back weapons to Pakistan already "in the pipeline," no indication that the United States would intervene in a clash in South Asia, and a U.S. analysis that China probably would not either. Bhutto, however, did not come back with much more from his trip. Nevertheless, he returned to Pakistan saying he was "more than satisfied" with the result of his visit, and Yahya disregarded public statements by Peking and claimed that China would intervene if Pakistan were attacked. More is revealed about Bhutto's trip, however, by what was *not* said. First of all, the two sides produced no joint communiqué, which is usually a sign of fundamental disagreement. China provided no specific assurances to Pakistan whatsoever regarding any PRC intervention. Moreover, there was no expression of support for Pakistan's *unity* or its *territorial integrity*. Indeed, one cannot find such a pledge in any Chinese statement during 1971. The evidence would seem to indicate that China was distressed by the situation all along and perceived a "mounting disaster." To support the "state sovereignty and national independence" of Pakistan is far from committing oneself to preventing the dismemberment of that state.[67]

On the night of December 3, the seemingly inevitable (at least given Yahya's handling of the whole affair) conflict broke out with a Pakistani attack on India in the West. Moscow quickly moved along three diplomatic lines in an effort to keep the conflict localized and enable India to bring it to a swift conclusion.[68] First, *TASS* issued a strong statement on December 5 blaming Islamabad for the war and warning all outside powers to stay out of the conflict. Secondly, Ambassador Pegov became almost a constant visitor to Indian government offices where he assured India that if any outside powers intervened the Soviet Union would aid India. Finally, the Soviets brought the issue before the United Nations, particularly the Security Council, and defended India's position. It was here that Moscow had its most public successes. On December 5, 6, and 13, the Soviet Union cast vetoes of a United States-backed resolution that supported Pakistan by calling for a ceasefire and the withdrawal of troops.

There is little doubt that Moscow's support of India in the United Nations provided India with the time it needed to complete the "liberation" of Bangladesh. Soviet pledges of assistance should China intervene were also comforting to New Delhi, as were Soviet naval deployments in response to Washington's dispatching the carrier "Enterprise" and a task force from the Seventh Fleet into the Bay of Bengal. The substantial increase in Soviet arms deliveries, dating from August, also greatly added to India's advantage over Pakistan. Nevertheless, there is a large amount of evidence of Soviet counsel of restraint even during the war. The *Statesman* reported on December 12 that Moscow had asked New Delhi after the beginning of the war to conclude its military operations in East Bengal within one week. As the time approached with no sign of an imminent end to the fighting, the Soviets proposed sending a high-level delegation to New Delhi "to coordinate strategies." Indira Gandhi declined unless an official of comparable status was also in Moscow. Once this was agreed upon, D.P. Dhar was dispatched to Moscow on December 11 and First Deputy Foreign Minister V.V. Kuznetsov arrived in New Delhi the next day. Expressing concern first at the slow pace of India's progress in the East, Kuznetsov secondly warned Mrs. Gandhi soon after arrival that although Washington and Peking would probably not intervene in the East, they might be forced to come to Pakistan's assistance if the integrity of *West* Pakistan was threatened. Kuznetsov reportedly pointed out that "Soviet opposition to a ceasefire became more untenable the longer the war goes on in the east."[69] It seems clear from this visit, which was extended twice (from two days to three and then to four), that India did not have *carte blanche*. Moreover, there do not need to be meetings "to avoid unnecessary delays in spelling out their respective approaches to the problem of peace and stability in the region" if the two sides are agreed on a single approach.[70]

On December 16, the West Pakistani forces in the East surrendered, and on the next day Mrs. Gandhi declared a unilateral ceasefire (which was accepted by Pakistan a day later) in the West. Bangladesh was now an independent state and Pakistan had been dismembered. India was the clear winner and Pakistan the loser with the Soviet on the former side and the United States and China on the latter. Moscow had prevented United States action, deterred the U.S. Seventh Fleet from intervening, and threatened China with diversionary action in Sinkiang should it intervene.

As one Soviet official at the United Nations exulted, "This is the first time in history that the United States and China have been defeated together."[71]

Concerning Soviet motivations throughout the crisis, the record indicates that U.S. and Pakistani accusations that Moscow's "encouragement of regional tensions between India and Pakistan" brought on a war that "might have been avoided" were inaccurate.[72] Certainly Moscow sought to use its relationships with India and Pakistan against China (and, secondarily, the United States); and India sought to use its ties with the Soviet Union vis-à-vis Pakistan. As one scholar has written, "the two entered into a coalition-type relationship in which collaboration for the attainment of shared objectives did not preclude efforts by each to influence the other for the pursuit of its own strategic interests."[73] Indeed, these differences in strategic objectives is what kept the two from complete agreement on the East Pakistan issue during 1971. Both sought to influence the other. Until mid-October, Moscow had slightly predominated in preventing further Indian action. Then, however, the Soviets evidently concluded that, given the circumstances, their interests would be better served by bowing to India's objectives. The treaty in August represented no change in the influence relationship, but the degree of Soviet support commencing with Firyubin's October visit did. India did exercise influence and Soviet policy was completely supportive of New Delhi until about the midway point of the war. At that time, Moscow again urged (demanded?) restraint.

The policies of all the three outside major powers in the South Asian crisis were reactive. The mutual influence relationship between Moscow and New Delhi was complex, but India clearly was the initiator. The actual exercise of influence, in terms of leverage, appears limited. In the end, there was mutual influence with perhaps India slightly the "winner." In any case, the exercise of influence in these cases seemed actually to depend on perceptions of interest. And if views or perceptions are identical, can one side be said to be exercising influence?

NOTES

1. *Pravda*, September 4, 1970; cited in Richard B. Remnek, *Soviet Scholars and Soviet Foreign Policy: A Case Study in Soviet Policy Towards India* (Durham, N.C.: Carolina Academic Press, 1975,) pp. 73-74.
2. Remnek, *Soviet Scholars*, p. 74.
3. See Dilip Mukerjee, "Gandhi Past and Present," *Far Eastern Economic Review* (hereafter cited as *FEER*), January 22, 1970, pp. 19-20.
4. *The Hindu*, January 23, 1970.
5. *Statesman* (New Delhi), February 12, 1970.
6. See *Statesman*, February 17 and 21, 1970.
7. *Statesman*, June 2, 1970.
8. Ibid.
9. See the analysis in Ramesh Thakur, "India's Vietnam Policy, 1946-1979," *Asian Survey*, October 1979, p. 965.
10. *Hindustan Times*, June 2, 1970. Emphasis added.
11. See *Statesman*, March 26, 1970; and Dilip Mukerjee, "The Appeal of Moscow," *FEER*, April 16, 1970, p. 13.
12. For example, see "Inviting Contempt," in *Statesman*, June 1, 1970; and also *Hindustan Times*, June 2, 1970.
13. *Statesman*, June 28, 1970.
14. Kapitsa's discussion is analyzed in Vijay Sen Budhraj, *Soviet Russia and the Hindustan Subcontinent* (Bombay: Somaiya Publications, 1973), pp. 203–04.
15. G.W. Choudhury, *India, Pakistan, Bangladesh, and the Major Powers* (New York: Free Press, 1975), pp. 67-68.
16. For coverage of the visit, see *Pravda*, June 24, 1970; *Morning News*, June 27, 1970; and Werner Adam, "What Did Yahya Get?" *FEER*, July 16, 1970, p.18.
17. *Pravda*, June 26, 1970.
18. See *The Times* (London), July 13, 1970; and *Statesman*, July 12, 1970.
19. See *New York Times*, July 15, 1970; and *Statesman*, July 12, 1970.
20. *Statesman* on July 18, 1970 reported that the External Affairs Ministry had decided: (1) to await clear signals from Peking; and (2) that the Chinese "have not quite got to the point of deciding how far they should go in promoting friendlier relations with India."
21. *Statesman*, July 14, 1970.
22. *Statesman*, June 27, 1970.
23. *Statesman*, September 11, 1970. See also *New York Times*, September 13, 1970. For the joint communiqué, see *Pravda*, October 1, 1970.
24. *Statesman*, October 21, 1970.
25. E. Bragina, "India-1970," *Mezhdunarodny. Ezhegodni Politika i Ekonomike 1971*, Moscow, 1971, pp. 250–57: reprinted in Zafar Imam, *Soviet View of India, 1957–75*, (Delhi: Kalyani Publishers, 1977), p. 144.
26. *Statesman*, October 26, 1970. Emphasis added.
27. *Statesman*, October 26, 1970. Also see the September 11 issue.
28. *Statesman*, October 21, 1970.
29. See *New York Times*, October 26, 1970. See also the analysis in *FEER*, October 24, 1970, pp. 6-7.
30. *New York Times*, November 12, 1970.
31. See Choudhury, *India, Pakistan, Bangladesh*, p. 195. The text of the joint communiqué. was carried in *Morning News*, November 15, 1970.
32. See Werner Adam, "Behind a Smile," *FEER*, October 17, 1970, p. 17. Significantly, Mrs. Gandhi made another public gesture toward better relations with China on November

13 in Paris, at the same time that Yahya was in Peking. See also *New York Times*, November 12, 1970.
33. *People's Daily*, November 9, 1970.
34. Banquet speeches were carried in *Morning News*, November 12, 1970.
35. Remnek. *Soviet Scholars*, p. 97. See also *FEER*, January 16, 1971, p. 57.
36. See B. Kalyagin, "Defeat for Indian Reaction," *New Times*, no. 12, March 1971, pp. 6–7.
37. *Pravda*, March 31, 1971. In his report to the Twenty-third Congress in 1966, Brezhnev had cited improved relations with Pakistan and made a milder reference to India; see *Pravda*, March 29, 1966.
38. See, for example, P. Viktorov, "India: Problems and Prospects," *New Times*, no. 26, June 1971, pp. 12-13. See also the analysis in Robert H. Donaldson, *Soviet Policy Towards India: Ideology and Strategy* (Cambridge, Mass.: Harvard University Press, 1974), pp. 242-44.
39. Pran Chopra, in his *India's Second Liberation* (Cambridge, Mass.: M.I.T. Press,1974), pp. 74-75, discusses the efforts of the Soviet Ambassador in New Delhi and the Foreign Ministry in Moscow in this regard; there were acrimonious discussions in the Kremlim with the Indian ambassador, he reports, and "Moscow was ultimately forced to convey its helplessness to Pakistan."
40. The text is reprinted in J.A. Naik, *India, Russia, China and Bangla Desh* (New Delhi: S. Chand, 1972), pp. 133-34.
41. See the discussion in Robert C. Horn, "Sino-Soviet Relations in an Era of Detente," *Asian Affairs*, May-June 1976, pp. 287-304.
42. Reprinted in Naik, *India, Russia, China and Bangla Desh*.
43. Bhabani Sen Gupta, "South Asia and the Great Powers," in William E. Griffith, ed., *The World and the Great Power Triangles* (Cambridge, Mass.: M.I.T. Press, 1975), p. 187.
44. Reprinted in Robert Jackson, *South Asian Crisis: India, Pakistan and Bangla Desh* (New York: Praeger, 1975), p. 172.
45. *Pravda*, June 9, 1971.
46. Ibid.
47. Chopra, *India's Second Liberation*, p. 84.
48. *Times of India*, July 8, 1971.
49. Chopra, *India's Second Revolution*, p. 84; and Choudhury, *India, Pakistan, Bangladesh*, p. 206.
50. Mohan Ram, "Ram and the Dragon," *FEER*, August 7, 1971, p. 15.
51. *Los Angeles Times*, August 9, 1971; and *Hindustan Times*, August 9, 1971.
52. The text of the treaty can be found in *New Times*, no. 33, August 1971, pp. 4–5. For a discussion of the treaty and a comparison to the similar Soviet-Egyptian one signed in May, see Naik, *India, Russia, China and Bangla Desh*, pp. 73–77, and Jackson, *South Asian Crisis*, p. 72.
53. *New Times*, August 1971, pp. 4-5.
54. *Izvestia*, August 13, 1971. See also the article in *Pravda* on August 10 and the editorial, "In the Interests of Peace and Good-Neighborliness," on August 11.
55. *Pravda*, August 12, 1971. Emphasis added.
56. Cited in A. Hariharan, "India: Bosom Friends," *FEER*, October 9, 1971, p. 14.
57. See *Morning News*, September 4 and 10, 1971.
58. *Pravda*, September 29, 1971.
59. Chopra, *India's Second Liberation*, p. 90. According to Chopra, the Indians were particularly disappointed that Brezhnev sided with Kosygin, who, as the "author" of the Tashkent agreement, had been seen as committed to a balanced policy between India and Pakistan. Mrs. Gandhi had the dates of her trip and of Brezhnev's European trip adjusted so that he would be present for the discussions because he was perceived by

New Delhi as "the least inclined to tolerate China's influence in Pakistan and in the present crisis was more fully alive to the danger India faced and the bonus China would get if Pakistan succeeded in imposing the burden of its own problems upon India" (pp. 90-91).

60. *Pravda*, September 30, 1971. The Indian "version" is in Naik, *India, Russia, China and Bangla Desh*, pp. 150–54.
61. *Times of India*, October 2, 1971.
62. *Dawn*, October 13, 1971.
63. *New York Times*, October 28, 1971.
64. *Izvestia*, October 28, 1971.
65. *Pravda*, October 28, 1971.
66. Henry Kissinger, *White House Years* (Boston: Little, Brown, 1979), p. 878. See also *Statesman*, November 5, 6, 7, 1971; and Christopher Van Hollen, "The Tilt Policy Revisited: Nixon-Kissinger Geopolitics and South Asia," *Asian Survey*, April 1980, pp. 339-61.
67. See *Statesman*, November 9, 1971.
68. See Choudhury, *India, Pakistan, Bangladesh*, p. 212.
69. See Vijay Sen Budhraj, "Moscow and the Birth of Bangladesh," *Asian Survey*, May 1972, p. 493.
70. See *Statesman*, December 12, 1971, and *The Times*, December 15, 1971. Jack Anderson reported in the *Washington Post* (December 21, 1971) that "Kuznetsov... told Indian officials that the Kremlin was 'impatient' with the Indian armed forces for their inability to liberate Bangladesh within the ten-day time-frame mentioned before the outbreak of hostilities."
71. *Hindu*, December 13, 1971.
72. *New York Times*, December 20, 1971; cited in Donaldson. *Soviet Policy Toward India*, p. 237. See also Dmitry Volsky, "The India-Pakistan Conflict and American-Chinese Collusion," *New Times*, no. 51, December 1971, pp. 7-9.
73. Bhabani Sen Gupta, "The Soviet Union and South Asia," in Roger E. Kanet, ed., *The Soviet Union and the Developing Nations* (Baltimore: Johns Hopkins Press, 1974), p. 132.

4

THE CONFLICT'S AFTERMATH: "THE ARITHMETICS OF SUPER POWER INFLUENCE"

The regional framework for the Indo-Soviet relationship was irrevocably altered by India's conclusive victory over Pakistan in the Bangladesh struggle. India was now the unchallenged indigenous power in South Asia. Pakistan was not only split in two but a large percentage of its army was in captivity, and critical internal issues could hardly be ignored; the Pakistani military threat to India appeared to be largely eliminated. Among the external powers, only the Soviet Union could claim to have backed the "winner," while China's relationship with India continued to be greatly strained, and Indo-United States ties were in a state of considerable disarray. The international context of relations between Moscow and New Delhi was also undergoing change. Detente between the Soviet Union and the United States was being furthered, which was symbolized by President Nixon's visit to Moscow in May, 1972. Moreover, Nixon's historic journey to China early in 1972 gave substance to the beginning of the far-reaching Sino-United States normalization process.

In order to understand the evolution of the Indo-Soviet influence relationship in the period following the war, we need to examine the attitudes of both states on relations within the subcontinent and on the roles and interrelationships of China and the United States. India's economic needs and the economic relationship with the Soviet Union continued to be a major issue. Moreover, it was in this period that Moscow gave new emphasis to its Asian collective security idea, that superpower involvement in the Indian Ocean emerged as a large issue in New Delhi's perception, and that India detonated a nuclear device. Finally, it was a period in which Indian domestic politics and issues became increasingly

---

The phrase "The Arithmetics of Super Power Influence," is borrowed from J. A. Naik.[1]

prominent and demanded more of Mrs. Gandhi's government attention, which culminated in the declaration of a state of emergency in June, 1975. Given the new circumstances in South Asia and in the Soviet-Indian relationship since the beginning of 1972, was either Moscow or New Delhi able to develop greater influence over the other? Did the relationship change to fit the new circumstances or not? Given, too, the many assumptions made and expectations held for a growth in Soviet influence in particular, this would appear to be a most fruitful period in which to gather data on the "arithmetics" of superpower influence.

INDIAN AND SOVIET PERSPECTIVES

The Indian victory in the war with Pakistan greatly strengthened Mrs. Gandhi's political position at home. She sought swiftly to capitalize on her enhanced personal stature by going ahead with midterm elections to eight state legislatures. Her ruling Congress won all of these by overwhelming majorities. India seemed to have regained political stability and to have been on the threshold of a new political era. At the same time, however, negative indicators were also beginning to accumulate. Factionalism continued to divide the Congress and regionalism to divide the country. Radical reforms and promises, such as the land reform of 1972 failed to fulfill expectations. There was a disastrous crop of failure in 1972, forcing the government to purchase expensive food grains on the world market. Industrial growth slowed down and urban unrest grew. Mrs. Gandhi's earlier campaign pledge to "Remove Poverty" was regarded with increasing cynicism. The already escalating prices and inflation rate were soon to be exacerbated by the international oil crisis.

In foreign policy also, 1972 began bright with expectations and opportunities for India, but with serious question marks as well. The victory over Pakistan had undeniably left India in a position of primacy in the region and had created an entirely new situation there. It had done even more, however, symbolizing a "resurgence of national self-respect" and "an assertion of independence in the conduct of foreign policy."[2] The question for Indira Gandhi and for India was how to translate victory in the war into regional power while gaining recognition as a major power in world politics. On the regional level, the situation called for Indian policies to focus on solidifying ties with the new state of Bangladesh and normalizing ties with a greatly weakened Pakistan. Efforts in these areas, particularly vis-à-vis Pakistan, dominated Indian foreign policy in the immediate aftermath of the war. Gradual progress toward normalization was made, with the biggest step coming at the Simla summit in July 1972 between President Bhutto and Prime Minister Gandhi. There Pakistan made a major concession on Kashmir in return for an Indian agreement to withdraw from Pakistani territory taken during the war. Although Islamabad refused to recognize Bangladesh for two years and although relations between New Delhi and Dacca grew closer in the first months after the war, before the end of the period all these relationships were to shift. For each of the three states, policies toward the other two were to be a vacillating mixture of distrust and recognition of the need for some degree of cooperation.

The postwar period witnessed an increased tempo of high-level exchanges in Soviet-Indian relations, an accelerated rate of cooperation in cultural and aid programs, expanded trade, and warmer references to one another in each country's press. Yet, below this surface of closer relations ran the current of an intensified Indian desire not to get too burdened with Soviet friendship or too dependent on Soviet ties. There were no dramatic new programs and India even turned down a Soviet offer to mediate, as in Tashkent, between New Delhi and Islamabad. Despite the Indo-Soviet treaty and the crucial Soviet backing during the 1971 war, there was still significant economic and political differences. One of the most revealing commentaries on the "new" Indo-Soviet relationship was contained in Mrs. Gandhi's interview with C.L. Sulzberger of the *New York Times* early in 1972.[3] Responding to a question regarding relations with the Soviet Union in light of Moscow's strong political and military support in the war, Mrs. Gandhi asserted that "we are unable to display gratitude in any tangible sense for anything." She added that "countries help one another because they need one another" and maintained that Indian foreign policy was still based on nonalignment despite the treaty with Moscow. Mrs. Gandhi clearly recognized that a major force pushing India closer to the Soviet Union was New Delhi's very poor relations with both Washington and Peking, and she indicated that she desired to improve ties with both the United States and China.

It is hardly surprising that at this point India's relations with the United States were at a new low. The U.S. shift toward Pakistan in the months preceding and during the war was a culmination of a decade of weakening relations. The ultimate blow, in India's perception, was the sending of the U.S. Seventh Fleet into the Bay of Bengal; one newsman reported that this action:

> ... left the Indians hugely angry. I have never seen such bitterness and fury directed by Asians against Americans—and that's saying a great deal. They used the most abusive language in referring to the Americans and their contempt for Nixon was almost unbelievably intense.[4]

Moreover, Washington seemed uninterested in trying to revive its waning role in South Asia generally or in India in particular. No new U.S. aid proposals were forthcoming and Nixon, in his February 1972 foreign policy report to Congress, stated that Pakistan's well-being and security were still of concern to the United States and implied that Washington would not compete for influence in the region with Moscow.[5]

Although Mrs. Gandhi was largely correct when, in the Sulzberger interview, she asserted that relations with the People's Republic of China "are not really any worse today than they were before," Peking's rhetoric had become more anti-Indian than it had been previously. The Chinese leaders may well have concluded that "India had become an even more helpless tool than before for Soviet expansionism and an instrument in the Soviet-led 'encirclement' of China."[6] At the end of January, moreover, new Pakistani President Bhutto journeyed to Peking, where he received promises of free military and interest-free economic aid in talks with Chou En-lai and Mao Tse-tung. At the welcoming banquet, Chou En-lai attacked the Indian government, "relying on the support of social-imperialism" (the Soviet Union), for having "grossly interfered in Pakistan's internal affairs."[7] The joint communiqué signed at the conclusion of Bhutto's visit condemned India's "naked aggression... against Pakistan and the occupation of Pakistan's territory by her in blatant defiance of international law," went on to call for the withdrawal of all Indian forces from East Pakistan and Kashmir, and continued to endorse Islamabad's position on the Kashmir issue, supporting the "just struggle" there for "the right of self-determination." Although there were some apparent differences between the two states, New Delhi clearly was concerned to see that Peking was "not averse to propping up Pakistan's belligerent anti-Indian postures."[8]

What completed the perceived external threat to India's interests was the linkage between the United States and the Chinese-Pakistan relationship. Coinciding with Bhutto's journey to Peking, U.S. Senator Edward Kennedy disclosed that the U.S. administration intended to continue to supply arms to Pakistan. New Delhi announced that it had already warned Nixon that additional arms would worsen Indo-United States relations, further increase tension in the subcontinent, and make a durable peace in the region difficult.[9] A source of at least as great apprehension for New Delhi was Nixon's long-awaited visit to China. India watched the Sino-U.S. summit very closely and, since it coincided with an Indian election campaign, it also often became a major topic in campaign speeches by Mrs. Gandhi and others. Mrs. Gandhi's position was that while a Sino-United States rapprochement was natural and to be welcomed in the interests of a more stable world, the crucial test would be the future "uses" of this friendship. Peace and tranquillity in Asia "would be endangered," the prime minister said, if the United States tried to "befriend China at the cost of enmity with India..."[10] The final communiqué signed in Shanghai was greeted with considerable relief in India, for it contained no explicitly anti-Soviet passages and showed that "fears of a new power bloc" had at least been premature.

New Delhi's satisfaction with the outcome of the talks on the broad scale was offset, however, by its discomfiture regarding the summit's impact on issues closer to home. One reason was that there was the reference in the communiqué to the Chinese side's support for "the people of Jammu and Kashmir in their struggle for the right of self-determination." Second, each side, separately but in almost identical language, called for Pakistan and India to withdraw their military forces to within their own territories and to their own sides of the ceasefire line in Jammu and Kashmir. Mrs. Gandhi and the Indian press denounced these provisions as "blatant interference in India's internal affairs."[11] Another of New Delhi's responses was to dispatch diplomatic troubleshooter and chairman of the Policy Planning Committee of the External Affairs Ministry, D. P. Dhar, to Paris, London, and, not surprisingly, Moscow. While in the Soviet capital, Dhar had talks with Deputy Foreign Minister Firyubin and a three-hour session with Kosygin. Although there was little information on the talks, Dhar and the Soviet premier were "believed to have assessed the developments in Asia and the prospect of Sino-American rapprochement. . . . " The talks were reported to have taken place in a "warm and friendly atmosphere" and to have resulted in a "complete identity of views on topics covered."[12] This was far from the first time that India and the Soviets had hastened to consult with one another in response to potentially threatening policy moves by their great-power adversaries in Washington and, especially, in Peking.

One impact of the Soviet Union's steadfast support for India throughout the 1971 crisis was a broadening of Indian support for close ties with the Soviet Union. Both sides seemed convinced that they had "a broad range of interests in common and they know how to work together successfully to achieve their aims—as well as how to keep their differences from getting out of hand."[13] Yet, as will be seen, on many specific political issues Moscow's greater prestige and close ties did not seem to equate with influence. For the most part, this nonaccretion of influence is traceable to India's long-standing sensitivity to its independence, its newly heightened sense of national self-respect and sovereignty regionally, and its unwillingness to express gratitude for USSR assistance. In addition, however, the Soviet Union also returned to its earlier posture of promoting South Asian stability. For Moscow the basic goal continued to be the limitation of China's role and influence in the region. In the pursuit of this objective, the Soviets would put greater emphasis on relations with India, but Moscow would again seek to develop sound relations with Pakistan as well.

The visit of President Bhutto to the Soviet Union early in 1972 clearly illustrates this hedging in Soviet policy. On the one hand, the fact that Bhutto was invited at all and so soon after the war is indicative of the Soviet desire for a stable South Asia and a secure Pakistan that was not in need of Chinese backing. On the bilateral level, moreover, the visit was successful. Trade was to be immediately resumed. Scientific, technological, and other relations disrupted in 1971 were to be restored. The Soviets were to resume assistance in geological prospecting, power engineering, and in building a metallurgical works in Karachi. Bhutto returned apparently satisfied that relations had been restored to the level that had existed prior to the war, and the joint communiqué asserted that "the viewpoints of the governments of the Soviet Union and Pakistan on the majority of current international problems coincide or are similar."[14] On the other hand, it was apparent that the talks were not completely successful. There was no movement on the resolution of Indo-Pakistani problems, and Bhutto was unable to gain Soviet support for the release of Pakistani POWs held in India or the return of territory in West Pakistan. Kosygin, who held most of the crucial talks with Bhutto, was blunt in his assessment of Islamabad's responsibility for the conflict and in calling for Pakistan to adopt a "realistic approach" to the "normalization of the situation in Hindustan."[15] The joint communiqué failed to mention most of Pakistan's specific concerns for a resolution of the conflict and characterized the talks as "a frank and useful exchange of opinions," thus implying that serious differences existed.[16]

Bhutto's visit showed that Moscow was anxious to restore its relationship with Islamabad and to bring stability to the region, but that it would in no way jeopardize, as it had in 1968, its more important relationship with New Delhi in pursuit of these goals. One knowledgeable Indian journalist met with Bhutto on his return from Moscow and reported that "the impression he gave me was of one who tried to wean Russia away from India and had failed."[17] However, the Soviets also failed in their attempt to pull Pakistan away from China. Another analyst:

> ... learned from authentic Pakistani sources that Kosygin tried hard to win Bhutto away from China and offered substantial economic assistance if he would reduce the relations of Pakistan with Peking.[18]

Indeed, Bhutto had dashed Soviet hopes on this score shortly after his arrival when he stated pointedly that "friendly relations between us should not be constructed at the expense of our friendly relations with other countries."[19] In short, as Pakistan and the Soviet Union probed each other, neither was willing to forego its primary relationship, those with China and India respectively. The interrelationships among these four states, with the United States sometimes involved but often only on the periphery, were to provide the major threads of the Soviet-Indian relationship from 1972 onward, just as they had prior to the 1971 crisis.

VISITS AND ISSUES

Immediately following Bhutto's visit to Moscow, another South Asian statesman, Indian External Affairs Minister Swaran Singh, arrived. This visit symbolized the differences between India and Pakistan's relationships with the Soviet Union and also highlighted the issues dominating ties between New Delhi and Moscow. On the symbolic side, Singh's reception was far warmer than that accorded Bhutto. He had two long, separate meetings with Brezhnev and Kosygin and all his talks were said to have proceeded "in a warm and cordial atmosphere" and "confirmed the identity of stands taken by the USSR and India on a wide range of international problems."[20] Substantively, Singh's visit was significant for two reasons. First, he sought to be reassured regarding Soviet support for India and that there had been no appreciable change in Soviet-Pakistan relations. Second, once that was clarified, Singh discussed specific issues regarding Moscow's visions of a settlement and normalization in South Asia. New Delhi had become particularly sensitive to hints from Kosygin and other Soviet officials that Moscow was interested in mediating the India-Pakistan problem in the form of a "second Tashkent." This was adamantly opposed by New Delhi and Singh was successful in obtaining unequivocal Soviet support for, in the words of the joint statement, a peaceful settlement "through direct negotiations between the governments of India, Bangladesh and Pakistan."[21] Although Bhutto had opposed "another Tashkent," as had Mujibur Rahman in his Moscow visit prior to Bhutto's, it was the explicit Indian opposition that had altered Moscow's stance. Singh's talks marked the end of this Soviet attempt at influencing Indian policy; no longer would Moscow seek a mediatory role or push as hard to affect Indian behavior on the issue.

Kaul and the Chinese Question

In early September, India and the Soviet Union began their most significant talks since Singh's visit when Foreign Secretary T. N. Kaul arrived in Moscow. Billed as the annual foreign office consultative meeting, and thus the first since the previous October, Kaul's talks with Kosygin and Firyubin took place in an "atmosphere of utmost cordiality and warmth" and the Soviet leaders showed "full understanding and appreciation of India's efforts to consolidate peace and promote good-neighborly relations." Firyubin was "understood to have expressed appreciation of the wisdom and farsightedness of Prime Minister Indira Gandhi and the policies of the Government of India."[22] Since the primary focus of the discussions concerned developments in South Asia—negotiations between Pakistan and India had produced the Simla Agreement but other obstacles remained, such as the precise line of control in Kashmir, Pakistani POWs, and Pakistan-Bangladesh relations—it is apparent that Moscow gave its full support to India's positions and policies.

Perhaps the major item on Kaul's agenda, however, was China's role in South Asia and Indo-Soviet relations. His visit came immediately after China's veto of the admission of Bangladesh to the United Nations and in the midst of PRC attacks in the United Nations and elsewhere on India and the Soviet Union—accusing Moscow of trying to "legalize its aggression" in the subcontinent and of "insolently" seeking Dacca's admission to the United Nations through "power politics"[23]—and a supportive visit to Pakistan by the Chinese vice foreign minister, Chiao Kuan-hua. Given this context, the timing of the Kaul visit is hardly surprising nor is the apparent high degree of agreement between India and the Soviet Union on the "Chinese challenge."

Nevertheless, almost immediately after confirming Indo-Soviet solidarity against PRC policy, India began probing China regarding some improvement in their bilateral relationship. During October and November there were reports of Indian overtures for normalization. Despite Indian reports of improved relations, there was no response from China and little change in Sino-Indian relations other than a slight softening in China's attitude toward Bangladesh. The point, however, is that India was seeking to play its "China card." From New Delhi's point of view such a gambit was intended to help normalize the situation in South Asia as well as enhance its own diplomatic "elbow room" and its bargaining leverage with Moscow. Even if it did not succeed in leading to normalized relations with Peking, it would, hopefully, force Moscow to be more forthcoming in some area of support for India. This leads to the second important aspect of this Indian maneuver: Moscow seems clearly to have been influenced by New Delhi's efforts. The major Soviet response came in the form of a lengthy study of Chinese policy toward the Indian subcontinent published in the new and limited circulation quarterly journal *Problemy Dalnego Vostoka* (*Problems of the Far East*), which appeared in December.[24] Entitled "Peking's Political Machinations on the Indian Subcontinent," the article was unprecedented in two ways. First, it represented Moscow's most detailed public denunciation of Chinese policies in South Asia in the 1950s and 1960s. Second, for the first time, Moscow acknowledged that India's position on the territorial question with China was correct, and the Soviets aligned themselves with it: the author points out that Peking was claiming about 33,000 square kilometers of Indian territory in the west, 2,500 in the central area, and 90,000 in the east. As recently as the previous May, the Soviet stance on the Sino-Indian border question had again precipitated a heated debate in the Lok Sabha. At a time when reports of rapprochement between India and China were particularly rife, however, Moscow had felt compelled to make a significant gesture to India on a long-standing issue. Nevertheless, the Soviets still did not revise their official maps to coincide with Indian claims or with their own rhetoric; the most the Soviets have done is either to mark disputed territory "undecided" or to have deleted it altogether from their maps. Thus, while the Soviets have made a significant concession to India, they have still retained some bargaining power for themselves.

Dhar and Economic Ties

Within less than two weeks after Kaul's departure from Moscow, Planning Minister D. P. Dhar arrived at the head of an important economic delegation. Dhar, former Indian ambassador to the Soviet Union, met with S. A. Skachkov, chairman of the State Committee for External Economic Relations, and N. K. Baibakov, chairman of the State Planning Committee, on economic matters, as well as with Firyubin and Kosygin on political ones. The talks appeared to have been highly successful. Dhar himself remarked that even though the Soviets had been given short notice on some of the "urgent problems" facing India, an understanding had been reached quickly. "This was a task which would ordinarily have taken several months or a year." He returned to New Delhi pronouncing himself "highly satisfied" with the "extremely fruitful" talks in Moscow.[25]

The major accomplishment of his visit was the signing of an agreement formally establishing an Inter-Governmental Soviet-Indian Commission on Economic, Scientific, and Technical Cooperation. This commission had been decided upon during Indira Gandhi's 1971 visit to the Soviet Union. It would meet yearly beginning early in 1973 in New Delhi and its principal task would be to work out the means of further expansion of Indo-Soviet cooperation. The planning for joint production projects represented a major, yet partial, Soviet effort to deal with one of India's most chronic economic problems: the underutilization of much of its industrial capacity, particularly many Soviet-built projects, due to the small size of the Indian market. In these joint production projects, the Soviets would export raw materials, such as cotton or steel, to India, where these would be converted into finished goods, such as textiles or cutlery, and reexported for the Soviet market. Discussion also led to a Soviet agreement to extend technical cooperation for the development of Indian metallurgical industries, petroleum refining, fertilizer output, electronic industries, and atomic and space research. As a direct outcome of Dhar's meeting, the Indo-Soviet Commission met in New Delhi and, on February 17, 1973, signed a detailed protocol covering numerous areas of Soviet economic and technical assistance and Indo-Soviet cooperation.[26] In addition to the complex joint projects and plans for dovetailing of the two countries' five-year plans, the most significant aspect of this new step in economic collaboration was the agreement for USSR assistance to India's fifth five-year plan, which was set to begin in 1974. The Soviets agreed to aid India in a variety of areas, including steel, nonferrous metals, oil refining and exploration, chemicals, power generation, shipping and transport, and electronics.

The area of Indo-Soviet trade was also discussed during Dhar's meetings with Kremlin leaders. Due to the war, it was not until May that Indian Foreign Trade Minister Mishra had gone to Moscow to sign a trade protocol for 1972. This agreement foresaw a substantial increase and diversification in trade. The only disappointment to India was the Soviet refusal to include crude oil in its exports. Nevertheless, the protocol was of benefit since the Soviet Union would sell a number of items previously obtained from the United States under the now suspended aid program. In November the two states signed a protocol for 1973 that envisioned a 15 percent increase in Indian exports and a total trade turnover midway between the $435 million transacted in 1970 and the apparently unrealistic $670 million projected for 1972.[27]

Ram, Arms, and the United States

While Dhar's visit was primarily concerned with economic matters, it is known that he discussed political questions with Firyubin and Kosygin. With the latter, the talk focused on the progress of Indo-Pakistani relations at Simla and changes that had occurred since then. With Firyubin, the focus was on the United States, its role in Vietnam, and the developing Soviet-United States detente.[28] Henry Kissinger had been in Moscow less than ten days before, and New Delhi was anxious to have the Soviets reaffirm that no superpower "collusion" was likely to threaten Indian interests. Whereas the Soviets were often concerned that Sino-Indian or United States-Indian relations might "develop to the detriment of Soviet-Indian ties" (that is, to the detriment of Soviet interests), so too was India concerned that a United States-Soviet rapprochement could be to the detriment of *its* interests. In any case, Soviet assurances were apparently satisfactory to Dhar and, indeed, there was little substance in the Moscow-Washington relationship to lead him to think otherwise.

Progress in relations between India and the United States was moving even more slowly. New Delhi continued to be wary of the new United States-Chinese relationship fearing that "from the one extreme of unremitting and senseless hostility to China, the United States may swing to the other extreme of ignoring the legitimate interests of others."[29] In her own lengthy discussion of Indian foreign policy in the U.S. journal *Foreign Affairs* in late 1972, Mrs. Gandhi analyzed the irony of recent developments in Indo-United States relations:

> The original misunderstanding with the United States had arisen because of our contacts with China, the Soviet Union and Eastern Europe. We find it difficult to understand why, when the U.S. policy toward these countries changed, the resentment against us increased.[30]

India was aware of President Nixon's continued anti-Indian attitudes, and such developments in Indian policy as the harsher anti-United States tone on the Vietnam war, diplomatic recognition of East Germany, and the severe curtailment on visits to India by U.S. scholars only further embittered relations.

The signing of the Vietnam peace accords in Paris in January, however, removed a major obstacle to better relations. Moreover, the new U.S. ambassador to India, Daniel Patrick Moynihan, seemed to symbolize a new U.S. approach to the subcontinent when he asserted that U.S. policy was to be based on three foundations: a recognition of changed realities (that is, a recognition of India's new status and role); a refusal to grant or sell lethal weapons to any state in the region; and a desire to build "realistic and pragmatic new relations with India based on mutual interests."[31] The release of frozen aid to India and the beginning of talks on the disposal of PL-480 wheat loan funds indicated a discernible improvement in relations. In March there was a temporary resurgence of Indian hostility toward the United States when Washington announced it would sell to Pakistan about $14.1 million worth of military equipment, which had been ordered and partially paid for before the war. Prior to his scheduled trip to Washington in July, President Bhutto was explicit in stating he would seek resumption of full-scale U.S. military aid "to attain parity with India."[32] Despite such repeated assertions, it was a measure of India's growing confidence in U.S. policies and the changed nature of the United States-Pakistani relationship that New Delhi reacted with only mild concern. After the visit's postponement (due to Nixon's illness), the *Statesman* correctly stated that there had been no indication "that Mr. Bhutto's plea for a resumption of arms aid would be favorably considered."[33]

The visit of the Indian defense minister, Jagjivan Ram, to Moscow in early July thus took place at a time when India was making some progress toward an agreement with Pakistan and when Washington appeared to be sticking to its March policy statement of not supplying lethal weapons to Pakistan. *Pravda* on July 17 reported that in Ram's talks with Kosygin "there was an exchange of opinions on questions of further development of Soviet-Indian cooperation in the spirit of the Soviet-Indian Treaty...." After Ram reported on "the steps taken by India in the interests of normalizing the situation on the South Asian subcontinent," Kosygin replied by "declaring the Soviet Union's unfailing support for the efforts directed toward strengthening peace in this area and in Asia as a whole." The talks were described as having been held in "a warm, friendly atmosphere."

What was the significance of Ram's visit and what does it say about the nature of Indo-Soviet relations at this point? Since the meeting had only limited substance, it is possible that Ram's visit was mostly ceremonial, that is, a continuation of high-level political and military contacts, and perhaps signified a reciprocation of Admiral Gorshkov's visit to India in April 1972. Moreover, as Gorshkov had encouraged India to develop a strong naval fleet, and Ram discussed the Indian Ocean situation with the Soviets, it may be that he was seeking further USSR aid in this area. It is known that sometime in the year the Soviets did agree to provide one more frigate for the Indian navy.[34] If Ram was seeking more aid, that meager response would explain the phrase "exchange of opinions" in the Ram-Kosygin talks. The postponement of the Bhutto visit to the United States also removed that possible incentive for a new round of acquisition of USSR arms.

The crux of the talks most likely related to regional trends that both India and the Soviet Union found to be unsettling. One issue was that Pakistan was in the process of obtaining about 30 Mirage fighter bombers sold by France in 1971 and was still receiving previously promised Chinese assistance. Moreover, at least as disturbing to New Delhi and Moscow, was the rapidly escalating arms buildup by Iran. Fears were growing in the Indian government that, with the active backing of Washington and Peking, Iran and Pakistan were seeking to form a new axis in South and Southwest Asia to the detriment of India's interests. It is known that Defense Minister Ram did discuss the acquisition of military hardware by Pakistan and Iran during his visit to Moscow. According to his own report, the only one available, "the appreciations of India and the Soviet Union are identical."[35] Yet their agreement—or their concern—was apparently not substantial enough to respond with a new military aid program. Kosygin also had specifically not said that Moscow supported all of India's moves in the region but rather it only supported "efforts directed toward strengthening peace...."; that is, India's policies had the Soviets' "unfailing support" to the extent that they worked toward the USSR position on peace. This clearly was an effort to keep Soviet options open, particularly in regard to Iran, whose Shah the Soviets had begun a substantial effort to befriend.

This fluid regional situation was to be almost immediately complicated when, shortly after Ram left Moscow, a coup led by Mohammed Daud ousted the king and took over power in Kabul. Although the new regime immediately asserted its neutrality, there was just as quickly speculation regarding USSR influence over it. While the Soviets were enthusiastic and India seemed relatively undisturbed, it was Iran and, particularly, Pakistan, that felt threatened by the coup and the new regime's relationship with Moscow. Although the uneasiness surrounding the coup would eventually dissipate, it was clear, and the involved states certainly perceived this, that this new development would add a complicating element to the regional picture. It would have been difficult for any of them, however, to have predicted the magnitude that the Afghan issue was to reach in December 1979 and thereafter.

"INDIA WELCOMES A GOOD AND TRUSTED FRIEND"

The long-expected announcement, in early October, that CPSU General Secretary Leonid Brezhnev would be arriving in New Delhi on November 26 precipitated a publicity campaign of unprecedented magnitude in Indo-Soviet relations. One correspondent in Moscow reported that:

> hardly a day has been allowed to elapse without the Soviet papers publishing stories, mostly under Indian datelines, describing in glowing terms the eagerness and anticipation of the Indians.
> Superlatives such as: "An occurrence of tremendous importance," "An event of immense significance," "A major historic milestone," "India hails Brezhnev visit with its whole heart," have been regularly used.[36]

Much of Brezhnev's visit, including the arrival and departure, was televised live back to the Soviet Union via a newly launched communications satellite. The Soviet leader was seen off and met on his return by virtually the entire Politburo. In short, the Soviets did all they could to play up the visit. For its part, India was more subdued but still contributed significantly to the publicity given to the visit, including billboards and posters, articles in the press, special programs on All India Radio for several days prior to the visit, and live local television and national radio coverage of his arrival and welcome. One of the more circumspect evaluations of the results of

---

The phrase, "India Welcomes a Good and Trusted Friend," is borrowed from Drieberg, Malik, and Joshi.[37]

the visit, which provides a perspective on most of the rest of the commentary, appeared in the Soviet-Indian joint declaration issued at the end of Brezhnev's stay:

> Everywhere they went, the General Secretary of the CPSU Central Committee and those accompanying him were given a cordial reception, testifying to the Indian people's feeling of sincere friendship and respect for the Soviet people and the leaders of the Soviet Union. L. I. Brezhnev's visit to India was a vivid demonstration of strengthening Soviet-Indian friendship.[38]

It is apparent that the Soviets did not intend for this to be a working meeting as much as a demonstration of Soviet-Indian friendship. This demonstration was vital for the Soviets given their recurrent fears of a Sino-Indian rapprochement and their perception of their role as the major ally of the nonaligned movement and the Third World in general. Brezhnev's theme in his first talks with Mrs. Gandhi was that the friendship and cooperation between India and the Soviet Union were a "model of relations between states of different social systems" and "at the same time can serve as an example of how relations between socialist countries and young national states should be arranged and developed."[39] Such an approach and a sensitivity to avoiding any hint of imposition of views was intended not only to strengthen Soviet-Indian relations but also to counter Chinese efforts to discredit the Soviet image among the states of the nonaligned movement. This theme of Indo-Soviet friendship dominated Brezhnev's speeches as well as the final declaration.

A second important aspect of Brezhnev's visit was his revival of the Asian collective security idea. In his second round of talks with Mrs. Gandhi, this proposal was apparently a major theme although Soviet spokesman Zamyatin contended it was not directly discussed. (Zamyatin also misleadingly contended throughout the summit that China was not a subject of the talks.) When Brezhnev addressed a joint meeting of the two houses of the Indian Parliament, there was complete candor.[40] His major theme was the need for a "thorough and comprehensive discussion of the idea of collective security in Asia." The Indians, continuing to fear that the plan was simply an anti-Chinese scheme and wanting to keep open the option of better relations with Peking, resisted Brezhnev's pleas, however, and the phrase "Asian collective security" was not found in the final declaration at all. As far as the Indian side would go was to cite a number of general principles that should govern relations between states and to call for Asia to be turned into a "continent of lasting peace, stability, and good cooperation...."

Establishing the Indian Ocean as a "zone of peace," with no military presence of either superpower, was a foreign policy theme that had been gaining in prominence in New Delhi; this was another item in the Brezhnev-Gandhi talks. The Soviets had been noticeably cool to any such proposal and, in his parliamentary address, Brezhnev seemed to advance the Soviet position only slightly. The audience was responsive when he consolidated the Indian Ocean "zone of peace" idea with the neutralization of Southeast Asia proposal and formulas for cooperation in South Asia as "interesting initiatives inspired by concern for the peaceful future of Asia. . . ." The formulation in the joint statement represented a compromise. India, rather than just calling for the ocean to become a zone of peace, as it had in Indira Gandhi's September 1971 visit to the Soviet Union, agreed to talks with other states while the Soviets subscribed to more positive language than previously. "The two sides," read the statement, "reaffirm their readiness to take part together with all interested states on an equal basis, in the search for the favorable solution to the question of turning the Indian Ocean region into a zone of peace."[41]

A fourth major theme of Brezhnev's visit was the Indian economy and future Soviet economic assistance. (Soviet military assistance was apparently not discussed despite the regional arms buildup. There was no military adviser in Brezhnev's delegation and no reference to defense issues in speeches or the final declaration.) The advance party, which preceded Brezhnev in New Delhi by one week, was led by Baibakov and Skachkov. Subgroups were formed to deal with various aspects of Indo-Soviet economic cooperation and thus to "prepare the ground for the full-scale talks" after Brezhnev's arrival. During Brezhnev's talks with Mrs. Gandhi, there were parallel economic talks. Among the several economic agreements produced by these negotiations, two stand out as particularly significant in the evolution of the Indo-Soviet economic relationship.[42] One was the "Agreement on Cooperation Between the USSR State Planning Committee and the Indian Planning Commission." It established a joint research group on cooperation in planning within the framework of the Soviet-Indian Commission. The other was the "Agreement on the Further Development of Economic and Trade Cooperation." This agreement was to remain in force for 15 years and pledged the two states to "continue [to] develop and strengthen economic and technical cooperation and trade" in the fields of industry, power engineering, agriculture, geological prospecting, "the training of cadres," "as well as in all other branches of the two countries' economies in which their distinctive economic preconditions present favorable opportunities for rapid development." The pact listed a few specific projects and fewer specific targets, stating that the amounts and terms of Soviet credits would be covered by separate agreements. In the joint communiqué, the two sides did pledge their efforts to ensure a 50 to 100 percent increase in trade before 1980.

Just how significantly these economic agreements would contribute to a stronger Soviet-Indian relationship would have to await the specifics of implementation. Mrs. Gandhi's government was immediately under attack from opposition parties for having, on the one hand, "sold out our self-reliance" for the "apron-strings" of the Soviet Union and, on the other, for settling for USSR commitments that were "disappointingly slight."[43] Despite these future uncertainties, problems on some specifics, and crosscutting attacks, the new agreement did point to an intensified level of economic cooperation and Soviet assistance in many areas of critical need for India.

The final item on the agenda of the summit in New Delhi was the nature of United States-Soviet detente. Mrs. Gandhi had repeatedly expressed India's concern that such a superpower arrangement could serve as a cover for carving the world into spheres of influence. In his talks with Mrs. Gandhi and in his speeches, Brezhnev went to great lengths to justify this detente as easing world tension and to reassure India that its interests would in no way be sacrificed. However, New Delhi resisted Soviet pleadings on this point by responding only that India "noted" the Soviet position that detente recognized "in a binding State-law form" peaceful coexistence as the basis of Soviet-United States relations. The Soviets were dissatisfied and urged India to demonstrate greater support. The joint declaration does indicate a small capitulation by India on this: "The Indian Prime Minister welcomed the relaxation of tension between the USSR and the USA, since the step facilitates the easing of world tensions."[44] Despite this compromise, it is clear that New Delhi continued to maintain its reservations and its suspicions about detente.

In sum, it would appear that the Brezhnev visit did advance the Indo-Soviet relationship but not nearly as much as New Delhi and, particularly, Moscow sought to portray.[45] The close relationship was symbolized by Brezhnev's reception (he was received as a head of state rather than a party leader), the economic agreements, and the many areas of similar or identical views—such as on the Middle East—as expressed in the final declaration. Yet, India strongly resisted the Soviets on collective security, continued to pressure Moscow on the Indian Ocean, and maintained reservations on detente. For its part, Moscow kept military issues out of the talks (at least publicly), presented its side of the above issues, and did gain a certain Indian concession in the joint declaration's reference to the 1971 treaty as signifying "a new stage," which was a phrase India had previously avoided using—"in strengthening the two countries' traditional friendship." It is apparent that both sides wanted to keep some distance in the relationship. That is, Moscow was once again seeking to appeal also to Islamabad and sought to avoid gratuitously offending Pakistan. (This may explain the lack of public reference to Soviet military aid to India). For its part, India wanted to keep its options vis-à-vis China open. This made the idea of collective security particularly unacceptable. Neither side seems to have wielded appreciable influence here. On balance, perhaps India's maintenance of its positions is more impressive. At the same time, Brezhnev was careful to avoid putting pressure on India and seemed to be indicating that, while Moscow would continue to try to change India's views on certain issues, these differences should not be allowed to affect their friendship.

COLLECTIVE SECURITY, THE INDIAN OCEAN, AND INDIA'S NUCLEAR DETONATION

Brezhnev's forceful presentation of the USSR proposal for the establishment of a collective security system for Asia marked another revival of this still obscure idea. The proposal had been shelved shortly after its introduction in 1969 and it was not until the fall of 1971 that the Soviets revived it. This resurrection may well have been prodded by the new United States-China contacts and the potential threat they represented to Soviet interests in Asia and may also have been related to the growing possibility of war in South Asia, the Indo-Soviet treaty, and Moscow's continuing desire to prevent a conflict in the region.[46] As in 1969, however, the proposal failed to separate Pakistan from China or prevent an Indo-Pakistani conflict. From mid-1972 until mid-1973, the proposal was rarely mentioned. In the summer of 1973, the plan enjoyed another resurgence. Along with a spate of articles in Soviet publications, Brezhnev again addressed the issue, more forcefully in New Delhi than anywhere else. Although India resisted the Soviet leader's urgings, Brezhnev was able to get Mrs. Gandhi's consent to a paragraph in the joint declaration on principles for the relations between all states. This paragraph repeated almost verbatim Brezhnev's list of principles for Asian collective security.[47] Still, India refused its explicit endorsement.

Despite returning virtually empty-handed, Brezhnev and the Soviet media maintained their effort to obtain Indian support by continuing to blame China for Asia's security problems and, implicitly, by reminding India of the Chinese "threat."[48] Through 1974 and into 1975, Moscow continued to push its proposal, although with less intensity, to Asian countries in general and specifically toward India. Nevertheless, New Delhi's desire to avoid what seemed to be an anti-Chinese alliance and to avoid bringing an outside power into the region permanently led it to be no more forthcoming. In fact, in Mrs. Gandhi's visit to Moscow in 1976 and Morarji Desai's in 1977 and 1979, the Indians, if anything, backed further away from Moscow's proposal.

New Delhi's concern with any policy that might underline the Soviet Union's regional role to the possible long-term detriment of India's role and interests helps to explain the differences between the two countries not only on the collective security idea but also on the question of the Indian Ocean. Soviet and Indian goals were slightly at variance on both of these issues. On the one hand, Moscow sought in the collective security proposal to contain China while its policy in terms of the Indian Ocean was to reduce the U.S. role and expand that of the Soviet Union. New Delhi, on the other hand, sought first to keep its options open with regard to China, and thus was wary of the collective security approach, and second, aimed to reduce the role of *both* superpowers in the Indian Ocean. India's frequently stated objectives included the defense of the freedom of navigation, and the assured maintenance of the ocean as an area of peace, which would be free from nuclear weapons. Moreover, while India needed the Soviet Union as an ally, it had no desire to blindly support Soviet policies that might lead to a situation wherein Moscow would become the exclusive superpower in South Asia or the Indian Ocean. Such an eventuality, however distant, would jeopardize India's vision of its own interests and its predominant role in the region.

Before the Soviets accelerated their own buildup of naval strength there in the 1970s, a concerted effort by a large number of nonaligned states, including India, was begun to create a zone of peace in the Indian Ocean and deny warships access to it. These states passed a resolution calling for the creation of a peace zone at the Third Nonaligned Summit at Lusak, Zambia in September 1970. One year later, with Sri Lanka in the lead, the issue was placed on the agenda of the U.N. General Assembly. The First Committee passed a resolution in December that called for:

> ... eliminating from the Indian Ocean all bases, military installations, logistical supply facilities, the disposition of nuclear weapons and weapons of mass destruction and any manifestation of great power military presence in the Indian Ocean conceived in the context of great power rivalry.

The measure further called upon the great powers to enter into immediate consultations with the littoral states in order to implement the declaration. The resolution passed the General Assembly by a vote of 61 in favor, zero opposed, and 55 abstentions. Among the abstainers were a few of the littoral states, the United States and the Western bloc, and the Soviet Union and its East European allies.[49]

India's displeasure with Moscow's abstention on a resolution that New Delhi was enthusiastically supporting was quickly tempered by superpower behavior in the Indo-Pakistani conflict. As part of its support for India in the conflict, the Soviets had added to their naval presence in the

Indian Ocean and this was increased when Nixon ordered the dispatch to the Bay of Bengal of the U.S. naval task force. As a result, the Soviets were encouraged to accelerate their involvement in the Indian Ocean in order to play a more significant naval role there. India, too, became more interested in a more active role in the region for its navy. The war's major effect on India was to force New Delhi to be acutely aware of the important Soviet role in deterring or counterbalancing other powers, particularly the naval capability of the United States.

Since the Bangladesh war, Indo-Soviet relations over questions regarding the Indian Ocean have followed a similar pattern. There have been yearly resolutions in the General Assembly, which have all passed by a large positive vote and no negative votes. Yet the Soviet Union and the Eastern bloc (and the United States and its allies) have always been among the abstainers. An ad hoc committee was set up in 1972 and held numerous meetings over the next several years but received very little cooperation from the major powers.[50] At the same time, there was a gradual trend of escalation in the United States-Soviet rivalry in the area. Both states courted potential regional allies, searched for bases, and denounced the other's military buildup. The Soviet deployment of a vastly increased fleet of warships at the time of the October 1973 Arab-Israeli war and the beginnings of the United States development of the communications facilities on the island of Diego Garcia into a major military base were among the significant steps in this escalation.

In response to the continuing calls of India and other states for the major powers to begin consultations to work toward the establishment of the Indian Ocean as a zone of peace, Moscow responded that it wholeheartedly supported the idea and was prepared to negotiate, on equal footing, as soon as the other side agreed. Indeed, Brezhnev had agreed to such a proposal in the joint declaration signed at the end of his 1973 visit to India. Moreover, said the Soviets, it was the United States that was undertaking an arms race in the region and threatening peace. Finally, Moscow sought to justify the Soviet presence in the Indian Ocean beyond just meeting the United States challenge, thus laying claim to a permanent and major role in the region. The USSR permanent representative to the United Nations responded to a report by the ad hoc committee by explaining that:

> The Soviet Union has never had, has not established, and is not now establishing any military or naval bases in the Indian Ocean region. Soviet ships and vessels have never posed a threat to anyone in that region. In accordance with the existing rules of international law and with universally recognized international practice they are engaged in training cruises and in the search and recovery of Soviet spacecraft that splash

down in the Indian Ocean. It must also be borne in mind that transit routes from the European parts of the USSR to the Soviet Far East pass through the Indian Ocean and that accordingly, in order to ensure the safe passage of ships and vessels, the Soviet Union is conducting scientific investigation in the region.[51]

India has continued to urge that the support of the international community be mobilized for concrete action to implement the original declaration. New Delhi has been particularly concerned with military bases, which focuses attention mostly on the United States regarding Diego Garcia, and also the trend of escalating great-power rivalry, which implicates both superpowers. The Indian government would hardly be willing to be too adamant on the issue with Moscow given the strained state of its own relations with Washington and Peking, and it has seemingly been far more concerned not with what the Soviets may do but rather with what the United States has already done in establishing its presence. This cautious, yet firm, approach in advocating a zone of peace serves two purposes: one, it does not overly alienate the Soviets, and two, it recognizes that (at least in New Delhi's perception) the only way to curtail greater Soviet involvement and a superpower arms race is to get the United States to decrease its own activity. In any case, the Indian Ocean has remained an issue on which New Delhi and Moscow share similar, but far from identical, views.

On May 18, 1974, in the Rajasthan desert, India took the step that many outsiders had been predicting yet hardly expected to happen so soon: it detonated a nuclear device. The underground blast was welcomed with enthusiasm "by Indian scientists, politicians and the majority of the population as a morale booster and as a demonstration of their country's technological expertise."[52] Mrs. Gandhi and other Indian officials were quick to reassure other states that the explosion was for peaceful purposes and that India was not about to manufacture nuclear weapons.

There had been periodic speculation for many years that the country was about to embark on a nuclear program. Most analysts have pointed to the program's origins as developing from the mid-1960s when the conflicts with China and Pakistan as well as Nehru's death shattered Indian confidence about its long-term security. The Soviet Union's attempt, moreover, to adopt a balanced position between India and Pakistan pushed New Delhi further toward a reassessment and a development of options. The best indication of India's evolving position was its refusal to sign the Nuclear Non-Proliferation Treaty (NPT) of 1968. Despite guarantees in the treaty and repeated assurances from these three powers separately that they would guarantee India's security, New Delhi refused to sign and there was a rapid increase in India's public discussion of becoming a nuclear power. The Soviet offer of arms to Pakistan only accelerated this discussion. Perhaps the final series of external events that provided incentive for a nuclear test occurred with the Bangladesh war and the subsequent shifts in the interrelationships among the major powers. With the Nixon-Chou summit early in 1972, New Delhi saw the increasing possibility of greater Sino-United States support for Pakistan and against India on issues such as Kashmir. Moreover, with the further development of the United States-Soviet detente, many in India began to worry about Moscow's long-term commitment as New Delhi's "protector."

It seems likely that all of these threads combined with others to lead Mrs. Gandhi to the decision to test a nuclear device. For one, the symbolic value of the explosion would enhance India's stature as a leader in Asia, the Third World, and the nonaligned movement. To the extent that China was recognized as a great power based on its nuclear program, which was a perception shared by many inside and outside India, the Indian action would offset it. Nuclear blackmail and greater relative prestige would both be denied to Peking. Furthermore, the device would signal that India had options in its foreign policy beyond its relationship to the Soviet Union. That is, the United States-Soviet detente and United States-Chinese rapprochement could not serve to deny India its legitimate interests; India's goals were not going to be sacrificed to the furtherance of any normalization among the external powers. Thus, New Delhi was at least symbolically demonstrating its continued independence, even from Moscow. India would not be dependent on major powers—against a Chinese attack, to be shielded from other threats, as in the Bangladesh war, or while big deals went on at the superpower summit level.[53] Finally, it may also have been hoped by Mrs. Gandhi that the wave of national pride that followed the event would serve to unify her people, decrease internal tensions, add to her prestige, and at least give her some time to deal with mounting internal difficulties.

The detonation greatly increased tensions on the subcontinent and complicated India's relations with the major powers. As will be seen, Islamabad's reaction was particularly vehement and Peking and Washington also expressed considerable concern. Moscow said very little about the explosion, beyond reporting it very routinely and frequently reiterating India's claim that it was related to peaceful purposes. The Kremlin's distinctly unenthusiastic response, and even its reported pique including the temporary recall of the Soviet ambassador from New Delhi for "consultations,"[54] revealed Moscow's dilemma in the face of India becoming a nuclear power. Moscow could hardly be pleased with the development since it symbolized even less Indian dependence on the

Soviet Union, and would hinder Indo-Pakistani relations and thus Soviet ministrations to Pakistan. In addition, it represented a further proliferation of nuclear weapons to which the Soviets had long been opposed. On the other hand, India's nuclear capability was for the visible future only symbolic and seemed directed more against China than any other state. Thus for the Soviets, the Indian test had a benefit that partially compensated for the costs. In any case, the issue did not appear to Moscow at that time worth the risk of disrupting its ties with New Delhi.

REGIONAL AFFAIRS AND OUTSIDE POWERS

By the time of the Indian detonation, regional affairs had grown significantly more complex. In Bangladesh, the Awami League's support continued to decline and there seemed to be a growing disenchantment with both India and the Soviet Union. Meanwhile, Bhutto's Pakistan, to China's applause, had finally taken the step of recognizing Bangladesh and this led to a foreign ministers' meeting in April at which India, Pakistan, and Bangladesh resolved a number of outstanding issues between them. Pakistan's growing ties with the Arab world, including reports of a joint Pakistani-French-Arab arms-producing scheme, and Moscow's continued courting of the Arab states added to the evolving picture. Finally, early 1974 saw fresh Soviet propaganda broadsides against China in which the Soviets, in broadcasts directed to India and the rest of South and Southeast Asia, charged that China was "an imperialist power, ambitious for hegemony in Asia, acting in collusion with Japanese and United States militarists in its expansion, and striving to subvert the independence of Asian nations by supporting insurgents."[55] These warnings of Chinese expansionism and support for guerrillas were not missed by an India concurrently faced with reports of Peking's military buildup in Tibet and continuing assistance to the local Naga rebels (as well as the reality of its military clash with Vietnam over the Paracel Islands).

Amid this swirl of events and changing relationships, President Bhutto journeyed to China in May. The warmth and scale of Bhutto's reception in addition to the substantive accomplishments may well have represented China's response to Brezhnev's reception in India.[56] Bhutto met with ailing Chou En-lai, who left the hospital for two rounds of talks, and had an unusually long discussion with Chairman Mao. Economic relations were discussed and, although details were not made public, it was known that China agreed to provide about $100 million in aid immediately. "The defense needs of Pakistan were discussed in depth" but these were shrouded in even greater secrecy.[57] The joint communiqué[58] confirmed that "both sides expressed full satisfaction with the results of the talks." As least as significant as these results were the political themes of the talks. Vice-Premier Teng Hsiao-ping in his speech at the welcoming banquet emphasized PRC support for Pakistan's position on Kashmir and the final communiqué reiterated China's "firm support" of "the people of Jammu and Kashmir in their just struggle for the right of self-determination." Teng's remarks at the banquet led to another walkout by the Indian chargé d'affaires, which in turn prompted Bhutto to depart from his prepared remarks and instead spend most of his banquet speech criticizing Indian behavior. Saying that he was "really baffled and puzzled" by the walkout, Bhutto went on to defend China's and Pakistan's position on Kashmir as "not a new development," to remind India that "peace cannot be a one-sided effort, friendship cannot be a unilateral endeavor," and to accuse India of "an intemperate and rather irresponsible attitude."[59]

Moreover, China and Pakistan made their objections clear to Indian policy and to India's close ties with the Soviet Union by repeatedly hammering at the danger of "expansion and hegemonism," the former referring particularly to India and the latter being Peking's newest code word for the Soviet Union. This theme was repeated half a dozen times in Teng's speech, once by Bhutto, and appeared no less than six times in the joint communiqué. Islamabad and Peking seemed to be staking out a continued opposition to New Delhi and Moscow and their joint or individual ambitions for regional supremacy. To those who might level such charges at the Sino-Pakistani relationship, Karachi's *Morning News* responded on May 14 that "it is strange logic indeed that India should be free to have a defense agreement with a superpower, but no country should be allowed to make any friendly gestures to Pakistan which has faced agression more than once."

Bhutto had barely returned to Pakistan when the Indian nuclear test triggered a new decline in bilateral relations. The next two or three months "witnessed one of the most virulent spurts of anti-Indian propaganda by Pakistan."[60] The Indian test was perceived by Pakistan as upsetting the emerging military balance between the two countries and as threatening Pakistan's security. Although the Pakistani reaction was to fade considerably by August, Bhutto did send his foreign minister to China in early June. China, which had not openly protested the explosion, responded by pledging its "full and resolute support [to Pakistan] in its just struggle in defense of its national independence and sovereignty against foreign aggression and interference *including that against nuclear threat and nuclear blackmail.*"[61]

Meanwhile, in the face of these greater tensions with Pakistan and China and a cooling relationship with Bangladesh, New Delhi had also been growing somewhat apprehensive about the constancy of its Soviet ally. Moscow's desire to rebuild its relationship with Pakistan after the 1971 war had been apparent. Moreover, the Indian nuclear explosion had not pleased Moscow. In August, the Soviet Union, the United States, and Great Britain agreed to place an embargo on the supply of fissionable material and specialized equipment to India in an effort to halt its nuclear program. Moreover, the proposal by Pakistan and Sri Lanka for denuclearization of South Asia, which was naturally opposed by India, was received with enough interest by Moscow to send a special emissary to Islamabad to study it. On the question of Kashmir, too, New Delhi perceived a change in the Soviet attitude. As the *Statesman* editorialized on September 7:

> Apparently Mr. Brezhnev's Kremlin does not hold the view, as the late Mr. Krushchev did, that Kashmir is an integral part of India. But this is not surprising. The Soviet Union has been temporizing on the Kashmir question for quite some time. What is perhaps seen by New Delhi as a tilt in favor of Pakistan may be no more than *a reminder that Moscow has kept and is keeping an open mind* on Kashmir. [Emphasis added]

The editorial pointed out that while such efforts to reestablish a good relationship with Pakistan did not necessarily mean that "Moscow's interest in India has diminished," it did go on to cite "cutbacks in the supply of spares and hardware to India" and little progress in "production cooperation" and elsewhere in the economic field. Such developments "have been causing New Delhi some anxiety."

It was in this context that Foreign Minister Swaran Singh went to Moscow early in September. Billed only as a routine review of bilateral relations and other matters, both India and Pakistan were still watching the visit closely. The Pakistani press rather gleefully headlined "Indo-Soviet ties strained"[62] while in India the *Statesman* on September 5 candidly admitted that India was "interested in finding out the present state of Pak-Soviet relations" (while, of course, "conceding a country's right to have any form of relations with a third country . . . "). The results of the visit, while somewhat ambiguous, seemed to provide more reassurance to India than to Pakistan. In the joint communiqué both sides expressed their "deep satisfaction" that their friendship and cooperation in political, economic, scientific, technological, and other fields were expanding.[63] In addition, specific mention was made of both sides' "complete satisfaction" with the progress in the economic field, and Planning Minister D.P. Dhar followed Swaran to Moscow by a few days to hold the second meeting of the Indo-Soviet Inter-Governmental Commission.

While Singh returned home apparently satisfied, Bhutto could take solace in what was *not* said in the communiqué and other reports. That there was no mention of Kashmir or of the denuclearization idea held out hope that Islamabad could garner Soviet support on those issues. Moreover, Moscow's vagueness on issues of the subcontinent seemed to indicate that the Soviets still hoped to strengthen ties with Pakistan. A primary Soviet evaluation of the visit for external audiences emphatically pointed out that the significance of the visit was not to be seen in "the framework of bilateral Soviet-Indian relations"; rather, it was important in indicating that "the positive trends in the situation in Asia, and particularly on the Indian subcontinent, are growing stronger." Soviet-Indian friendship was depicted as a contributor to a normalized political climate in South Asia and to world peace.[64]

In October Prime Minister Bhutto journeyed to Moscow to put to the test his hopes for strenthening Soviet-Pakistani relations and aiding in the decline of Soviet-Indian ties. The visit, reportedly postponed twice by the Soviet government, had several additional purposes for Bhutto. One was to enlist the Soviets to restrain Afghan leader Daud from pressing Kabul's claim to large sections of Pakistan. Another was to try to obtain Soviet endorsement of the plan to denuclearize South Asia. Bhutto may have been seeking further economic assistance and arms aid as well. Finally, it is clear that he sought to improve the atmosphere of Soviet-Pakistani relations as a further proof to his domestic audience and to the world that Pakistan had fully recuperated from the debacle of 1971.

It was in this last vague area where Soviet purposes most closely coincided with Pakistan's. For the Kremlin, the visit represented another step in the effort to rebuild relations with Islamabad. Not surprisingly, this was the area, too, where the visit seemed to be the most successful. At the dinner honoring Bhutto, Premier Kosygin spoke enthusiastically about the visit, calling it an "important new step in the continuation of our joint cause aimed at strengthening good-neighbor relations...."[65] The joint communiqué[66] commended the steps toward normalization in the subcontinent, cited "the identity or proximity of positions" on a number of international issues, and:

> ... confirmed their conviction that the development of friendly, good-neighborly relations between the USSR and Pakistan on the basis of the principle of peaceful coexistence of states with different social systems meets the interests of the Soviet and Pakistan people and serves the causes of strengthening peace and security in Asia and throughout the world.

Bhutto left Moscow expressing satisfaction with the talks and "hoping" that "opportunities have been created for further improving Soviet-Pakistani relations."[67]

That Bhutto was "hoping" for better relations rather than being convinced of them was an indication that he did not get all that he came for. While overall relations progressed by the visit—the Brezhnev-Bhutto talks were classified by Soviet sources the "highest stage of all negotiations" ever held between the two countries—the picture was more mixed on the specifics. On the Afghan issue, Bhutto got as much from the Soviets as he could reasonably expect; the joint communiqué "expressed the hope that the differences between Pakistan and Afghanistan will be settled by peaceful means through negotiations on the basis of the principles of peaceful coexistence." On the economic front, Bhutto did less well; he was able to obtain Soviet agreement to conclude a new trade agreement but no more. Elsewhere, the Pakistani prime minister was shut out and the reference in the communiqué to an atmosphere of "frankness"—i.e., disagreement—in the talks underlines this. Moscow was not at all forthcoming on arms if in fact that was even a subject of the talks. Such Soviet disinterest is hardly surprising given the Indian reaction to the 1968 Soviet-Pakistan arms deal.

It was on the issue of the denuclearization of South Asia that Soviet-Pakistani differences showed most clearly. At the dinner in his honor, Bhutto focused a significant portion of his speech on the question of nuclear weapons. After hailing various arms-control agreements, even including the NPT that Pakistan had not signed, he moved to an impassioned presentation of his concern that India was developing nuclear weapons:

> Unfortunately, there has recently been a setback to this evolution [of control of nuclear weapons] in our region. This is a matter of profound concern not for Pakistan only but for the entire world community. Unless nuclear proliferation is effectively checked, the barrier to the spread of nuclear weapons will be broken.

He then moved on to the denuclearization proposal:

> In Pakistan's view such a development [proliferation] would be ruinous, particularly for the developing countries. Pakistan has, therefore, consciously and deliberately opted for a political alternative. We have taken concrete initiatives, such as the proposal for the declaration of South Asia as a nuclear-free zone. We believe it will contribute to the achievement of the objective of non-proliferation.[68]

The Soviet leadership failed, however, to endorse either Bhutto's fears of India's nuclear capacity or his nuclear-free zone proposal. What they did, moreover, was to go another step. *TASS* in its published text and *Pravda* in its article on Bhutto's speech deleted the entire sections above[69] and there was no reference to either theme in the final communiqué.

Indian officials must have breathed a sigh of relief when they saw what the Soviet-Pakistani joint communique did *not* say. Either Swaran Singh's visit had been successful or, perhaps more likely, Indian fears had been exaggerated. In any case, significant Soviet-Pakistani differences still remained, and Moscow was willing to draw the line in India's favor in its pursuit of a balanced policy in South Asia. Nevertheless, the Soviets' sustained efforts to improve ties with Pakistan and their ongoing differences of varying significance in Indo-Soviet relations inclined New Delhi to keep a careful eye on Soviet behavior. The Soviets, on the other hand, were keeping a close watch on any developments in India's relations with the other two major powers, the United States and China.

The slow, halting process of improved relations between India and the United States had continued. Clearly India's economic needs, especially for credits and food, were a major motivating factor for New Delhi. It is also likely that Mrs. Gandhi hoped that this gradual "normalization" would enhance India's independence and flexibility in foreign policy. Washington, while evincing little desire to compete actively once again with the Soviet Union, certainly was interested in the possibility of helping to erode, even if slightly, the Indo-Soviet relationship. In 1973, the U.S. government reactivated a project to construct a radar and communications network along India's border with China. This project, worth about $20 million, had been suspended in 1971. At the end of that year, Indian Finance Minister Chavan was finally able to reach agreement with U.S. officials on the disposition of the enormous rupee holdings in India. The accord removed what both sides called "a major irritant" in bilateral relations. U.S. Ambassador Moynihan said that the door was then open for new talks on U.S. economic assistance to India. Indeed, in mid-1974 Washington agreed to participate again, as it had prior to 1971, in the Aid India Consortium. Richard Nixon's resignation in August 1974 removed the figure most closely associated with the pro-Pakistan shift of 1971. In the first meeting of a U.S. president and a high Indian official since 1971, Foreign Minister Singh met Gerald Ford in the White House in September and had "positive and helpful talks."[70] On the Indian side, Mrs. Gandhi shuffled her cabinet in October, moving Swaran Singh to defense and Chavan into external affairs. While these and other changes were primarily related to internal issues or needs, their significance for foreign policy should not be overlooked. Chavan's success in negotiating the rupee agreement with the United States and his economic expertise, at a time when economic needs were becoming ever more apparent and predominant in Indian foreign policy, may well have been a signal to explore Indo-United States relations further.

The main event through which the two sides hoped to develop a better understanding with one another was United States Secretary of State Henry Kissinger's visit to New Delhi at the end of October. At the banquet he hosted for Kissinger, Chavan praised the improvement in relations over the past year or two but reminded his listeners that "it would be idle to pretend that there are no differences between us." Kissinger responded by saying that his visit was designed "to renew longstanding friendship, remove old misunderstandings and to build a new and mature relationship."[71] In separate talks between Kissinger and Chavan and Mrs. Gandhi the next day, the two sides sought to put past mistakes and misunderstandings behind them. Significantly, the secretary of state implicitly gave recognition to India's leadership role in South Asia and acknowledged India's claim to the status of a major power. Kissinger promised desperately needed food aid; quantities were to be determined after the World Food Conference due to begin in Rome one week later. In the most concrete outcome of the visit, Kissinger reached agreement with Indian officials on the establishment of an Indo-United States Joint Commission for Economic, Commercial, Scientific, Technological, Educational, and Cultural Cooperation. This commission, much like the Indo-Soviet one, was to meet annually and create subcommissions in an effort to further cooperation in all the above areas.

The joint communiqué described the discussion as both "cordial" and "frank."[72] The issues that led to the latter characterization included the Indian Ocean, India's nuclear program, and the possibility of U.S. arms going to Pakistan. The Indians kept the first issue largely in the background, although they continued to argue against Diego Garcia. On nuclear matters, Kissinger expressed Washington's "concern over the implications for regional and global stability of nuclear proliferation." He then "welcomed" India's "affirmation" that it would not develop nuclear weapons and hoped it would not export nuclear technology or raw materials. (That the United States was not going to let this issue stand in the way of improving relations was seen in an earlier decision by the U.S. Atomic Energy Commission to proceed with a scheduled shipment of uranium ore to India's Tarapur plant under the provisions of a 30-year agreement.) Finally, the Indians expressed their continuing concern about the possibility of an end to the embargo of U.S. arms to Pakistan. Kissinger responded evasively that "the USA had no intention of encouraging an arms race in the subcontinent" and that it "did not favor the policy of equating Pakistan and India in terms of military strength."[73]

Moscow must have had quite mixed reactions as it viewed Kissinger's visit to New Delhi. United States-Indian detente could hardly be opposed by the Soviet Union, which was pursuing its own detente with the United States. Moreover, the Soviets saw clearly that the United States and India had serious differences; indeed, Indo-United States differences over the Indian Ocean and Pakistan were far more substantial than Indo-Soviet differences on the same issues. Nevertheless, the Soviets could not feel comfortable with the very positive reaction in India to the visit. The assertion in the joint communiqué that the two sides have "no conflict of national interests," the statements by Indian leaders that they had been "reassured" by Kissinger's visit, and Chavan's contention that the way had now been paved for "a mature relationshiup based on mutuality and equality"[74] all made the Soviets ponder their own relationship with India and status in the subcontinent.

Kissinger's subsequent 24-hour stop in Pakistan undoubtedly added to Moscow's discomfort. Contrasting starkly with talks that had just concluded between Bhutto and Soviet leaders in Moscow, the Bhutto-Kissinger meeting was described as an "orgy of mutual admiration."[75] The cordial United States-Pakistan relationship was underscored, Kissinger reiterated U.S. interest in a secure, unified, independent, and sovereign Pakistan, and Bhutto declared the talks "fully satisfying." There was nothing in the brief meeting that threatened building a new Indo-United States relationship; indeed, Kissinger again resisted Pakistani entreaties for a resumption of military supplies. For the Soviets, however, Kissinger's whirlwind South Asian tour must have made them wonder if Washington was not in the process of accomplishing what Moscow had been intending to do, that is, achieve a strong position in *both* India and Pakistan.

Prime Minister Bhutto's trip to Washington for talks with President Ford in February 1975 appeared likely to be one more step in this dynamic U.S. policy. Moreover, Chavan was to lead the Indian delegation to Washington in March for the second session of the Indo-U.S. Joint Commission and Ford was to visit India that same spring. On his visit, Bhutto cited threats to Pakistan's security—including India's nuclear developments, Indian designs in Kashmir, and Afghan hostility—as justification for military assistance from Washington. By the end of the meeting, the United States had agreed to food aid, had reaffirmed its support for "the independence and territorial integrity of Pakistan," had committed itself along with Pakistan to strengthen their mutual relations but had not agreed to lift the arms embargo. Ford did, however, consent to open up the subject and give it "active consideration."

Bhutto left Washington amid a rash of reports, in New Delhi and in Washington, that the arms embargo was on the verge of being lifted. And, indeed, barely two and a half weeks later the State Department formally announced the end of the embargo. A spokesman said that the United States did not intend to upset the strategic balance in the subcontinent, to stimulate the arms race, or to disrupt moves for reconciliation between India and Pakistan. He added that "we presently enjoy very good relations with both India and Pakistan and we see no reason why this should not continue to be the case."[76] The Indian reaction was swift. Ambassador to the United States, T.N. Kaul, who had warned Kissinger that such a move would hinder Indo-United States bilateral relations as well as the process of normalization in the subcontinent, called a press conference to announce that India had lodged "a strong protest" against the U.S. action. "We do not accept or agree," he added, "that the lifting of the arms embargo will not lead to an arms race or hinder the process of normalization." New Delhi was hardly mollified by the State Department's assurances that the sales would be in cash only or that a number of considerations would be weighed before agreeing to any sales:

> ...including the high importance we attach to continued progress toward India-Pakistan normalization, the effect of any particular sale on the outlook for regional peace and stability, the relationship between United States sales and those of other external arms suppliers, and, of course, the relationship of the request to legitimate defense requirements and the level of armaments in the region.[77]

Mrs. Gandhi described the action as a "reopening of old wounds" and announced that Foreign Minister Chavan's trip to the United States for the Joint Commission meeting had been postponed. In June this meeting was postponed again by India. New Delhi's recent cirumspection on the U.S. role in Vietnam was promptly jettisoned and Indian gratification over the increasing communist victories in Indochina led Washington in April to announce the cancellation of Ford's trip to India. A front-page cartoon in the *Statesman* showed this linkage between Pakistan and Indochina in the India perception: a one-legged, wounded, and hobbling South Vietnam is pictured telling Bhutto, who is beating a war drum, "I was America's ally, too."[78] Clearly, the new and delicate fabric of an improving United States-Indian relationship had been ripped apart. Moscow's obvious relief at the rupture in Indo-United States relations was only partially offset by its concern at the setback to regional normalization which was still part of the USSR strategy in South Asia.[79]

Sino-Indian relations had continued through 1973 and 1974 to exhibit the same tendencies as previous years: hints toward normalization were countered either by the eruption of conflictive issues or simply the lack of any real change. The result was a continuing stalemate. The major item of friction through the period was the gradual absorption into the Indian Union of the state of Sikkim. With the adoption by the Lok Sabha in August 1974 of the draft law incorporating Sikkim as an "associate state," China escalated its denunciations of India's "flagrant act of colonial expansionism." Peking accused India of "regarding itself as a sub-superpower" with dreams of lording it over South Asia: "Nehru and his daughter have always acted in this way and Indira Gandhi has gone further." A major theme in this verbal assault on India was the link between the Soviet Union and the Indian action:

Facts have shown once again that Soviet revisionist social-imperialism and Indian expansionism constitute a serious threat to the independence and sovereignty of the South Asian countries and are the main cause of the unstable situation in the South Asian subcontinent.[80]

India was portrayed as the "junior member" of the club striving for hegemony and led by the Soviet Union. Peking made the analogy to the Soviet-led invasion of Czechoslovakia in 1968 calling the Indian action a "mini-Czechoslovakian incident." Both were depicted as the products of power politics, of bigger countries bullying smaller ones.[81]

To what extent India was justified in its action in Sikkim was debated even in India but is not our concern here. What is of concern is the perception China had of the changed geopolitical relationship between India and China. While Peking may well have exaggerated its response for effect, Sikkim is part of a strategic buffer of states between China and India. Moreover, the Soviets' close ties with India and support for the annexation of Sikkim very conveniently fit China's fears of Moscow's hegemonistic efforts to encircle and contain China. Adding to the credibility of Peking's perception of a growing threat from India and the Soviet Union were a number of anti-Chinese broadsides that had emanated recently from Moscow. One was an article, in the March issue of *Problemy Dalnego Vostoka*, that refuted China's claims on the Sino-Indian border dispute point by point.[82] It marked the second major endorsement by the Soviets of India's position on the border. This time, the Soviet move seemed intended not to prevent any Sino-Indian normalization but rather to strengthen New Delhi's resolve against Peking and offset the latter's attacks on the Sikkim issue. The Soviets continued in this vein and sought also to offset the turmoil over India's nuclear explosion with a constant barrage through 1974 of warnings of a Chinese missile buildup in Tibet and of a nuclear threat to India from China.

New Delhi seemed to hold out only slight hopes for any improvement in ties with Peking. There were certain feelers from Peking, which included the visit of a Chinese table-tennis team led by a vice-minister, who was the first political functionary to visit India since Chou En-lai had come for border talks in 1960. Despite this event and various Chinese statements calling for normalization, New Delhi perceived no concrete evidence of a new PRC policy. The skeptical Indian attitude was only substantiated by Chinese Vice-Premier Li Hsien-nien's visit to Pakistan from April 20–25. The arrival of a man thought to be China's top economist and Chou En-lai's right-hand man was of great symbolic significance to Islamabad. Arriving to a warm welcome, Li repeatedly engaged in glowing rhetoric as he described Sino-Pakistani ties as a "genuine friendship which no force on earth could undermine," expressed China's resolute support for Pakistan, and attacked a wide variety of

Indian policies.[83] In his thorough endorsement of the Pakistani side of many Indo-Pakistani differences, Li hammered away at "hegemonism and expansionism." Specifically, he reiterated Chinese support to the people of Sikkim "against naked annexation by the Indian expansionists." Li reaffirmed Peking's support for the right of self-determination for Kashmir's people and denounced, in a speech that was televised live in India, New Delhi's strengthening of its stranglehold there. He endorsed Pakistan's proposal to establish a nuclear-free zone in South Asia, as well as Sri Lanka's proposal for declaring the Indian Ocean a zone of peace, and offered Pakistan a wide range of textile machinery and cement-making plants on very favorable terms.

Overall, there was little of comfort for India in the meeting. Although specific deals were few and there was apparently no military aspect to the talks, Li's visit represented a ringing reaffirmation of Sino-Pakistani opposition to India on a wide range of regional issues. (The one exception was the Indian Ocean as a zone of peace proposal where China's and India's positions were quite close.) Whatever regional aspirations India possessed, it was obvious that China, through its friendship with Pakistan, meant to continue to challenge them.

As 1974 was drawing to a close, moreover, there was increasing evidence that the more significant aspects of Indo-Soviet relations supposedly ushered in by Brezhnev's visit had not come to fruition. The period after the visit had begun auspiciously with the signing in January of a trade protocol for 1974. Negotiated by a 12-member USSR delegation led to New Delhi by I.T. Grishin, deputy minister for foreign trade, the new accord called for a substantial increase in trade in 1974. Significantly, the Soviets demonstrated a willingness to aid India in three critical areas of need in the Indian economy through increased exports of kerosene, fertilizers, and newsprint. Nevertheless, the *Statesman* quickly pointed out that a large share of the increase in trade was in the form of higher prices. Kerosene and fertilizers were double the price of a year earlier. In addition, "Soviet prices of commodities which have a ready market in hard currency areas are invariably higher than prevailing world prices...."[84] In May there were reports, uncharacteristic of the Soviet approach since the Skachkov visit of 1968, that a Soviet Embassy spokesman had been quite frank in his assessment of India's efforts to raise steel production: the delays in the expansion of Bhilai and Bokaro were said to be India's fault, through late deliveries, unavailability of raw materials, and chronic labor trouble.[85] A deepening newsprint shortage led to charges of Soviet "newsprint blackmail" when expected Soviet shipments did not arrive.[86] This flap coincided with the release of a Reserve Bank of India report that questioned the benefits of trade with Eastern Europe in general. Directly contradicting a World Bank study completed in April, the Indian study asserted that India has often had to pay higher import prices and has received lower export prices. It also criticized the prevalence of "switch trading," whereby the East European countries reexported Indian goods to hard-currency areas.[87] Near the end of the year, Moscow turned down an Indian request for a loan of 3 million metric tons of wheat. (A Soviet loan of 2 million tons in mid-1973 had helped set the stage for Brezhnev's enthusiastic welcome in New Delhi.) Finally, the Soviets began a move to revalue the ruble against the rupee. Amid growing concern of the impact of such a change on India's trade and repayments to the Soviet Union, the two states held inconclusive talks in New Delhi.

A major item of Indian concern to which the Soviets were only partially responsive was the staggering increase in oil prices. This increase began in 1970 and took a quadruple jump with the Middle East war of October 1973. By the end of 1974, about 70 percent of India's oil requirements were met by imports and this figure was still rising. Prices of petroleum products jumped, and budget cutbacks had to be made due to the increasing drain on the country's foreign exchange. India became active in "oil diplomacy" as it searched for assured supplies of crude and long-term credits on good terms to finance its purchases. Although most of India's attention was thus focused on the Persian Gulf and Middle East oil producers, New Delhi also sought assistance from the Soviet Union. The topic was brought up during Brezhnev's visit but the Indians were turned down. The request was made again in the trade talks with Grishin and the results were similar. At the same time, however, the Soviets quickly pointed out that they were supplying finished petroleum products such as kerosene and fertilizer. Moreover, the Soviets dispatched their minister for oil to New Delhi prior to the Grishin visit. Those talks led to a protocol in which Moscow agreed to collaborate with India in oil exploration and production. The Soviets were to supply specialists and equipment including three drilling rigs.

During 1974 there was even some evidence of a cooling in the military sphere of the Indo-Soviet relationship. India was repeatedly reported to be seeking to reduce its arms dependence on the Soviet Union by manufacturing more on its own or by seeking weapons from such Western countries as France, Britain, and Canada. It is likely that the spate of reports of India's dissatisfaction represented at least partly an attempt by New Delhi to pry further commitments from the Soviets. The fear of becoming too dependent on Moscow militarily was, however, a real one and had been expressed before and would be again in the future. In fact, the joint communiqué had pledged the United States to "give careful consideration to Pakistan's additional requirements" and New Delhi seemed increasingly convinced that Washington would eventually lift the embargo. In addition, Pakistan, with obvious U.S. endorsement, had hosted naval forces from Great Britain, Iran, and Turkey in November for CENTO "Midlink" naval exercises. Undoubtedly, Moscow shared New Delhi's anxieties and India may have hoped to prod Moscow, by its hints, into new commitments. If so, it seems to have had some success for, in November, the Soviets hosted an Indian military mission and reached agreement to dispatch a delegation under Defense Minister Grechko to India in 1975.

Grechko's mission was a very significant one, at least in symbolic terms. Grechko was not only minister of defense but he also sat on the CPSU Politburo. Moreover, included in his delegation were the naval chief, Admiral Sergei Gorshkov who had last been in India early in 1972, and the air force chief, Marshal Pavel Kutakhov, whose visit in October 1971 had helped to solidify Indo-Soviet military ties just prior to the war with Pakistan. Such a group represented one of the most powerful military delegations ever to visit any country, and the Indian press enjoyed pointing this out.[88] The delegation carried on "marathon sessions" with Defense Minister Swaran Singh with talks focussing on "various aspects of [the] military and logistics situation connected with India's security" and "the latest developments in the region, including the growing military build-up in the Persian Gulf area and Pakistan."[89] Grechko and the others also met with Mrs. Gandhi and discussed "political relations in addition to defense and security problems of India."[90] The concrete results of the meeting are not completely known. The joint communiqué[91] indicated that the Soviet Union had agreed to expand the area of cooperation with India in the field of defense production. Reports revealed that India was to be provided with more advanced Soviet technical knowledge in order to produce an improved version of the MiG. (India was already producing at least two improved versions of the MiG-21 under licenses granted by the Soviets in 1964, 1972, and 1974.)[92] This assistance was consistent with India's desire for further "indigenization" of its defense. The Indian navy was also thought to have benefitted, since naval expansion was known to have been discussed. Later evidence revealed that this meeting either finalized or came close to finalizing two agreements: India would purchase four Il-38 "May" antisubmarine aircraft and eight "Nanuchka" missile patrol boats.[93] It thus appears that New Delhi had finally acquiesced to Soviet efforts to sell its antisubmarine warfare (ASW) aircraft to India; indeed, there were reports that India had decided to coordinate its ASW forces with those of the Soviet Union in detecting U.S. submarines in the Arabian Sea and the Bay of Bengal.[94] There was no evidence of an agreement involving assistance for the Indian air force, despite Kutahkov's presence in the delegation. Thus, the trend of allocating most Soviet aid since 1971 to the Indian navy—with tanks and armored personnel carriers for the army—and none to the air force continued (other than the MiGs produced under license and with a growing percentage of indigenous parts and materials).

From what is known, then, the substantive results of Grechko's mission in terms of new military assistance, while not insignificant, did not represent a major arms deal or a new stage in military relations. In any case, the symbolic and political aspects of the meeting were of far greater importance. One reason was that Grechko's visit was apparently intended to ease the tension caused by the various differences that had arisen between the two sides. Grechko delivered a letter from Brezhnev to Prime Minister Gandhi undoubtedly to this effect. Moreover, in his address at the banquet in his honor on February 25, the Soviet leader asserted that "*no trials* could ever undermine the stability of the deep-rooted friendship between the two countries."[95] This was probably both an offer to resolve differences as well as a reminder to India not to allow irritants to affect the overall relationship. A further symbolic aspect of the meeting was that Grechko's arrival coincided with Washington's announcement that it was lifting the embargo on arms sales to South Asia, i.e., Pakistan. The juxtaposition of Indian denunciations of this "destabilizing step" toward "imperialism in new form" and Grechko's glowing praises for growing Indo-Soviet cooperation and their friendship being of a "substantial importance for peace and security in Asia and all over the world" could not have been more stark. In this context, Grechko's confidence that "our talks with Indian leaders on problems of mutual interest, our talks with the leadership of the Defense Ministry and armed forces, will promote further strengthening of friendship and all-around cooperation between our peoples and armed forces in the name of progress" took on additional meaning. In the final communiqué the two sides expressed "grave anxiety at the actions taken by certain quarters to step up [the] arms race" in the region.[96]

Grechko's mission certainly did not resolve all differences between Moscow and New Delhi. There was still no Indian endorsement of the collective security scheme, slightly different perceptions of the treaty were expressed, differences remained on the Indian Ocean question and detente, and some disharmony remained regarding economic and military ties. Grechko's mission was intended to give the relationship a boost; the lifting of the U.S. embargo and the consequent strengthening of United States-Pakistani ties made this more significant as New Delhi and Moscow suffered a jolt in their efforts to explore closer ties with Washington and Islamabad. Was this "renewal" of the relationship more in the nature of a temporary restrengthening of it, or did it suggest, as the February 28 *Statesman* speculated, that "military relations with the Soviet Union will be far closer and—on New Delhi's part—more dependent than the country has so far been led to believe?"

THE POSTWAR PERIOD: LITTLE IN THE WAY OF SPOILS

The period from the end of the Bangladesh war to the declaration of the state of emergency does indeed represent what one analyst has aptly termed "a search for the spoils that go with victory."[97] The promise of influence that the post-1971 situation seemed to hold did not come to fruition. India had not been disposed "to display gratitude in any tangible sense" to the Soviet Union for its support in the war. India's increased status as a regional power was of greater significance than the "arithmetics of super power influence in the region." Mrs. Gandhi's statement to Brezhnev in 1973 that "in all these years Soviet leaders have never put pressure on us, never dictated conditions to us, never imposed their will on us"[98] was intended as praise for Soviet policy as well as a warning to Moscow for the future. The record of this period indicates that, despite instances of frustration, the Soviets adhered to this admonition.

The crux of the relationship, however, was that since Indian and Soviet perceptions of the world largely coincided, there were relatively few situations where one or the other might need to "impose its will." The hardening Indian position in 1972 on the U.S. role in the Vietnam war, for example, seems to be an instance of shifting Indian views rather than Soviet influence, although Moscow was clearly pleased with this policy alteration.[99] The key to the level of Soviet-Indian ties remained the degree of coincidence of their respective views of the United States, China, and Pakistan. During 1974, in particular, the tentative efforts by New Delhi and Moscow to explore better relations with Washington and Islamabad somewhat strained the Indo-Soviet relationship. These efforts were aborted by the lifting of the U.S. arms embargo and China's seemingly unqualified endorsement of Pakistan's policies and opposition to both India and the Soviet Union in South Asia. Thus, in many ways the interrelationships between the regional states and the external powers had come back to those prevailing in 1972 but without the intensity of the immediate postwar period. The Soviet Union was indeed the strongest external power in South Asia. Its relationship with India was relatively stable, and cooperation and coincidence of views were substantial. Yet Moscow knew, and so did New Delhi, that this situation had not provided the Soviet Union with significant leverage or influence over Indian policy.

NOTES

1. J. A. Naik, *India, Russia, China and Bangladesh* (New Delhi: S. Chand, 1972), p. 102.
2. Ramashray Roy, "India 1972: Fissure in the Fortress," *Asian Survey*, February 1973, pp. 231–45.

3. *New York Times*, February 17, 1972.
4. Olle Tolgraven, "Classical Warfare," *Far Eastern Economic Review* (hereafter cited as *FEER*), January 1, 1972, p. 9. Another analyst concurred later, saying: "All President Nixon's efforts to tilt the Administration in favor of Pakistan would not have mattered but for this last provocation, which brought Indo-American relations to their lowest watermark since independence," A Hariharan, "Low Watermark," *FEER*, July 1, 1972, p. 33.
5. *New York Times*, February 10, 1972.
6. Bhabani Sen Gupta, *Soviet-Asian Relations in the 1970s and Beyond* (New York: Praeger, 1976), p. 152.
7. *Peking Review*, no. 5, February 9, 1972, p. 5; the communiqué is on pp. 7–8.
8. See *Statesman*, February 5, 1972.
9. *Statesman*, February 4, 1972.
10. *Statesman*, February 27, 1972.
11. Mrs. Gandhi in a campaign speech; *Statesman*, March 3, 1972. See *Peking Review*, no. 9, March 3, 1972, pp 4–5 for the text of the communique.
12. *Statesman*, February 25, 1972.
13. William J. Barnds, "Moscow and South Asia," *Problems of Communism*, May-June 1972, p. 27.
14. *Pravda*, March 19, 1972.
15. *Pravda*, March 18, 1972.
16. *Izvestia*, March 19, 1972.
17. Kuldip Nayar, *Distant Neighbors. A Tale of the Subcontinent* (Delhi: Vikas Publishing House, 1972), p. 213.
18. Sen Gupta, *Soviet-Asian Relations*, p. 100. Nayar reported (p. 213) that whenever he "mentioned Pakistan's close relations with China" during his talk with Bhutto, the Pakistani president responded by saying, "You have a treaty with the Soviet Union."
19. *Pravda*, March 18, 1972.
20. From the joint statement; *Pravda*, April 7, 1972.
21. Ibid.
22. *Statesman*, September 7, 1972.
23. *People's Daily*, August 28, 1972.
24. See *FEER*, June 17, 1974, pp. 31–32.
25. See *Statesman*, September 23, 1972; and *Indian Express*, October 2, 1972.
26. See R. V. R. Chandrasekhara Rao, "Indo-Soviet Economic Relations," *Asian Survey*, August 1973, pp. 793–801.
27. *Hindu*, November 26, 1972. See also *FEER*, May 20, 1972, pp. 34, 37.
28. *Tribune*, September 24, 1972.
29. *The Times of India*, March 3, 1972.
30. Indira Gandhi, "India and the World," *Foreign Affairs*, October 1972, pp. 65–77.
31. See Bhabani Sen Gupta, "South Asia and the Great Powers," in William E. Griffith, ed., *The World and the Great Power Triangles* (Cambridge, Mass.: M.I.T. Press, 1975), p. 252.
32. *Statesman*, July 7, 1973.
33. *Statesman*, July 17, 1973.
34. *The Military Balance, 1974–1975* (London: International Institute for Strategic Studies, 1974) p. 91.
35. *Statesman*, July 23, 1973.
36. Edmund Stevens in *The Times* (London), November 23, 1973. Interestingly, this article was reprinted in Karachi's *Morning News* on November 27.
37. Taken from the title of Part One of Trevor Drieberg, Harji Malik, and D. K. Joshi, *Towards Closer Indo-Soviet Cooperation* (Delhi: Vikas Publications, 1974). This volume contains complete texts of speeches and documents from the visit.

38. *Pravda*, December 1, 1973.
39. Sh. Sanakoyev, "A New Phase in Soviet-Indian Relations," *International Affairs*, no. 2, February 1974, p. 15. See also *Statesman* November 28, and December 4, 1973.
40. The full text can be found in Drieberg, Malik and Joshi, *Closer Indo-Soviet Cooperation*, pp. 109–21. For those who are statistically inclined, Brezhnev received six "Applause" marks, two "Prolonged Applause," one "Stormy Applause," and two "Stormy, Prolonged Applause"; see *Pravda*, November 30, 1973.
41. *Pravda*, December 1, 1973.
42. See *Izvestia*, December 1, 1973 for the complete texts. See also *Statesman*, November 19 and 21, 1973.
43. For example, see *Statesman*, December 3, 1973, and *The Times*, December 6, 1973.
44. *Pravda*, December 1, 1973.
45. *Pravda*, December 4, 1973.
46. See O. Borisov, "For Peace and Security in Asia," *New Times*, no. 39, September 1971, pp. 10–11.
47. Compare the joint declaration with Brezhnev's address to the Fifteenth Congress of Trade Unions of the USSR in *Pravda*, March 21, 1972.
48. For example, see V. Kudryavtsev, "The Problems of Collective Security in Asia," *International Affairs*, no. 12, December 1973.
49. See K. R. Singh, *The Indian Ocean: Big Power Presence and Local Response* (New Delhi: South Asia Books, 1978), pp. 223–25.
50. See the excellent discussion in ibid., pp. 222–39.
51. Cited in ibid., pp. 232–33.
52. A. Hariharan, "India's 'peaceful' Atomic Bang," *FEER*, May 27, 1974, p. 14.
53. For one example of these arguments, see Subramanian Swamy, "The Case for India Acquiring Nuclear Weapons," *Los Angeles Times*, February 28, 1973.
54. See *FEER*, June 24, 1974, p. 5; and *Morning News*, September 10, 1974. See also *New Times*, no. 21, May 1974, pp. 13, 15.
55. Denzil Peiris, "Renewing the Verbal Offensive," *FEER*, March 25, 1974, p. 30.
56. On the visit, see Salamat Ali, "Ali Bhutto's Affair with Peking," *FEER*, May 20, 1974, p. 14.
57. *Morning News*, May 15, 1974.
58. *Peking Review*, no. 20, May 17, 1974, pp. 10–11.
59. Ibid., pp. 8–9.
60. Satish Kumar, "Major Developments in India's Foreign Policy and Relations, July–December 1974," *International Studies* (New Delhi), July–September 1975, p. 421.
61. *The Times*, June 26, 1974. Emphasis added.
62. *Morning News*, September 10, 1974.
63. See *Statesman*, September 12, 1974.
64. *New Times*, no. 38, September 1974, pp. 16–17.
65. *Pravda*, October 25, 1974.
66. Pravda, October 27, 1974.
67. *Morning News*, October 27, 1974.
68. For the texts of Bhutto's as well as Kosygin's speeches see *Morning News*, October 25, 1974.
69. *New York Times*, October 27, 1974; and *Pravda*, October 25, 1974.
70. See Kumar, "India's Foreign Policy," p. 430.
71. *Statesman*, October 28, 1974.
72. *Statesman*, October 30, 1974.
73. See Kuldip Nayar in *Statesman*, October 30, 1974.
74. *Statesman*, November 6, 1974.

75. *FEER*, November 15, 1974, p. 16. See also *Morning News*, November 1 and 2, 1974; and *Statesman*, November 1 and 7, 1974.
76. *New York Times*, February 25, 1975.
77. Ibid. See also *Times of India*, February 26, 1975; cited in Pushpesh Pant, "Major Developments in India's Foreign Policy and Relations, January-June 1975," *International Studies*, January-March 1976, p. 50.
78. Ramesh Thakur, "India's Vietnam Policy, 1946–1979," *Asian Survey*, October 1979, p. 969.
79. For example, see P. Mezentsev, "Normalization in South Asia and its Opponents," *New Times*, no. 29, July 1975, pp. 12–13.
80. *People's Daily*, September 3, 1974; cited in *China Quarterly*, December 1974, p. 840. For a detailed discussion of China's response to the various stages of Sikkim's annexation, see Nancy Jetly, *India-China Relations, 1947–1977: A Study of Parliament's Role in the Making of Foreign Policy* (Atlantic Highlands, N.J.: Humanities Press, 1979), pp. 281–85.
81. See Denzil Peiris, "A Dangerous Precipice," *FEER*, August 16, 1974, p. 24.
82. *FEER*, June 17, 1974, pp. 32–33.
83. See Salamat Ali, "Bhutto: Showing off a Powerful Friend," *FEER*, May 16, 1975, p. 34. See also the extensive front-page coverage in *Morning News*, April 20–25, 1975.
84. *Statesman*, January 22, 1974.
85. See *FEER*, May 27, 1974, pp. 45–46.
86. *FEER*, July 15, 1974, p. 42.
87. See *FEER*, April 22, 1974, p. 45, and July 15, 1974, p. 43.
88. *Statesman*, February 27, 1975.
89. *Statesman*, February 25, 1975.
90. *Statesman*, February 26, 1975.
91. *Statesman*, February 28, 1975. See also *New York Times*, February 25 and 26, 1975.
92. See Stockholm Peace Research Institute, *World Armaments and Disarmament: Yearbook 1975* (Stockholm: Almquist and Wiksell, 1975), 8A, p. 208. See also Rajan Menon, "India and the Soviet Union: A New Stage of Relations," *Asian Survey*, July 1978, pp. 731–50.
93. *The Military Balance, 1975–1976* (London: International Institute for Strategic Studies, 1975), p. 92. See also P. R. Chari, "Indo-Soviet Military Cooperation: A Review," *Asian Survey*, March 1979, p. 237.
94. Alexander O. Ghebhardt, "Soviet and US Interests in the Indian Ocean," *Asian Survey*, August 1975, p. 681. For the report of India's previous rejection of the Soviets' ASW aircraft, see *FEER*, October 18, 1974, p. 31.
95. *Statesman*, February 26, 1975. Emphasis added.
96. Ibid.
97. William J. Barnds, "Soviet Influence in India: A Search for the Spoils that Go with Victory," in Alvin Z. Rubinstein, ed., *Soviet and Chinese Influence in the Third World* (New York: Praeger, 1975), pp. 23–50.
98. *Pravda*, November 28, 1973.
99. See Thakur, "India's Vietnam Policy," pp. 966–68.

5
INDIA'S STATE OF EMERGENCY

On the morning of June 26, 1975, Indira Gandhi explained to her people in a radio broadcast that:

> The President has proclaimed an emergency. This is nothing to panic about. I am sure you are conscious of the deep and widespread conspiracy which has been brewing ever since I began to introduce certain progressive measures of benefit to the common man and woman of India. In the name of democracy it has been sought to negate the very functioning of democracy ... How can any government worth the name stand by and allow the country's stability to be imperilled?[1]

This declaration was accompanied by the jailing of several score of opposition leaders (including the future prime minister, Morarji Desai). For the next 18 months, India's democracy was in a state of suspension as widespread arrests followed by often lengthy detentions continued. Strict press censorship was imposed on the domestic media as well as on foreign correspondents. Constitutional provisions and amendments were passed by a pliant legislature, which gave further legal basis to the emergency and Mrs. Gandhi's increasing power. With the December 1975 decision to postpone the sixth general elections, scheduled for March 1976, the "temporary" emergency looked more and more permanent.

The factors and forces that led to the imposition of a state of emergency in India are complex.[2] Although India's economy, thought by many to be the most likely cause of a crisis, was much improved by early 1975, the escalating threat to law and order, the growing unity of the political opposition, the decline of Mrs. Gandhi's personal appeal as well as that of the Congress, and the legal challenges to the prime minister combined with other, less tangible factors to create a political crisis. Thus, while the conditions that led to Mrs. Gandhi's action were unrelated to foreign policy, and she contended that it signified absolutely no revision in India's foreign policy,[3] the concentration of India's energies on domestic issues meant that foreign policy would be at least overshadowed if not accorded a lower priority than before. Of course, a different dynamic might also be at work: Mrs. Gandhi, with her own power over Indian politics enhanced, might be able to initiate foreign policies that a more democratic system might have restricted. Across the board, then, India's foreign relations, including ties with the Soviet Union, while not dramatically changed were certainly to be influenced by this new situation in India.

Foreign reaction to the state of emergency was mixed. Near neighbors and Third World states tended to be either very quiet or generally approving. Despite official attempts in the United States to mute criticism of developments in India, there were enough subtle official comments of disapproval and more than enough of unofficial ones to put further strains on an Indo-United States relationship already burdened by the U.S. decision to lift the Pakistani arms embargo. It was from the Soviet Union and its allies in the Communist bloc that the most unequivocal statements of approval and support came.

Moscow's response to the developments in India was immediate and wholeheartedly supportive. At a public meeting in mid-July to mourn the death of D.P. Dhar, who had been ambassador to the Soviet Union since February, the Soviet ambassador to India stated that "the course of the Government of India aimed at the speediest solution of internal socioeconomic tasks received complete understanding and appreciation in the Soviet Union."[4] Professor R. A. Ulianovski wrote authoritatively in *Pravda* of this "unprecedented" step, which was "justified by the situation obtaining in the country."[5] Ulianovski was unstinting in his criticism of the "reactionary" opposition, which ranged from "profascist militarized organizations" to "vociferous pro-Peking extremist groupings." Significantly, Moscow utilized the opportunity to argue that Mrs. Gandhi's action had rescued not only "law and order" in India, but also the country's nonaligned foreign policy. China was singled out for having sought to benefit from the reactionaries' efforts and for having "interfered" in India's internal affairs through allying themselves with the reactionary forces; indeed, "in the vociferous anti-Indian campaign unleashed following the declaration of the state of emergency, the loudest voice is that of Peking."[6]

For Moscow, the choice to support Mrs. Gandhi in her declaration of emergency does not seem to have been a difficult one. She was a major architect of the close Indo-Soviet relationship and there was no indication that an increase in her personal power would change that. The opposition that she sought to stifle had never had any sympathy from Moscow, in any case; the Soviets had long been blatantly critical of the rightist parties as reactionaries and such leftists as the Communist Party of India—Marxist (CPI-M) as extremists. The Soviets had backed Mrs. Gandhi all along and her attempt to stabilize India was seen as beneficial to Soviet interests there. Moreover, unlike the United States, the Soviet leadership did not have to be concerned with the importance of India's democracy. From Moscow's point of view, Mrs. Gandhi's actions were supportable because she was supportable.

One further indication of Moscow's steadfast support for Mrs. Gandhi through these developments in 1975 was the role of the pro-Soviet Communist Party (CPI). Historically, the CPI had been dominated by Moscow and while Soviet control had lessened in the 1960s, Soviet influence over CPI policy was still substantial.[7] While the two pursued their own interests, the Soviets had maintained efforts to keep CPI-CPSU relations close; for example, during his 1973 visit to India, Brezhnev had met with the party leadership as had Grechko in 1975. Since the mid-1950s, the Soviets had worked to get the CPI to move out of opposition and to support the Indian government. While the Soviets thus saw the CPI as an instrument that might enhance the USSR role, they clearly did not put major emphasis on the party; ever since Stalin's death, the Kremlin sought to make certain that the CPI's behavior did not adversely affect its much more important concern of Soviet-Indian state relations. For example, during his visit in November 1973, Brezhnev demonstrated the Soviet Union's emphasis on ties with the Congress government. As Robert Donaldson has aptly summed it up:

> Brezhnev's direct praise of the Congress Party and its program during his 27 November 1973 speech at the Red Fort rally amounted to Soviet certification of the progressive credentials of Mrs. Gandhi's government. This endorsement diminished further the ability of the CPI to criticize as insufficiently radical the ruling party's policies. Brezhnev's statement left some Indian observers... concluding that the Soviet stake in Mrs. Gandhi's Congress had heightened, leaving the CPI as a redundant appendage in Indian politics.[8]

In any case, the party had stood solidly with Mrs. Gandhi ever since she had forced the split in the Congress in 1969. After her sweeping electoral triumph in 1971, she had needed the CPI's support less, but this had begun to reverse again as her popularity waned in 1974 and 1975.[9] Although the party's political role and significance would not be clear in an emergency situation, the CPI had no reason not to support Mrs. Gandhi, particularly given the threat from the opposition. Such continuing support was undoubtedly encouraged by Moscow, and seen as a positive development, albeit one that could be sacrificed, if necessary, for Soviet efforts in India.

REGIONAL AND EXTERNAL CONCERNS

Indian-Pakistani relations continued to be strained in the wake of the U.S. decision in February to lift the arms embargo. Although negotiations on outstanding issues were held, there was also a series of notes sent back and forth in which each protested the hostile propaganda of the other. Moreover, Islamabad evidenced concern about India's close collaboration with Pakistan's "Western antagonist," Afghanistan, and New Delhi was uneasy over reports that Pakistan was to receive ten more advanced Mirage III aircraft from France and that it had submitted to Washington a list of arms that Pakistan was interested in buying.[10]

These relatively normal Indo-Pakistani tensions, however, were completely overshadowed by the developments in Bangladesh. Within six weeks of the proclamation of the state of emergency in India, a violent coup took place in Dacca, in which President Mujibur Rahman was killed. Although the new regime immediately asserted that there would be no shift in Bangladesh's foreign policy, there were various reasons for New Delhi to be anxious. For one, Mujib had been held in high esteem in India, had been a champion of friendly ties between the two countries, and had had an excellent personal relationship with Mrs. Gandhi. The violence and bloodshed that accompanied the coup was also disturbing to New Delhi (perhaps especially in light of similar tendencies in India prior to the state of emergency). This coup, and a short-lived countercoup of four days in early November, suggested a renewed instability in the region that could not be viewed with equanimity by India.

Of perhaps greatest concern to India in the Dacca developments were the indications that Bangladesh's foreign policy was changing. The new leadership committed itself to emphasizing its identity as an Islamic country—its secularism under Mujib was thought to have been adopted particularly to please its Indian and Soviet supporters—and to building its ties with other Islamic countries. The new leaders were also perceived in India to be pro-Pakistan and resentment of India's large role in the country was known to have been a factor in moving against Mujib. Moreover, the new regime made it clear that it would seek to establish diplomatic relations with countries where it had no ties, including Pakistan and China. The immediate and favorable response in Islamabad and Peking to this policy change in Dacca greatly heightened India's anxiety. Both granted prompt recognition to the new regime and extended various forms of economic assistance. In early October both established diplomatic relations with Bangladesh. U.S. recognition also came quickly as did promises of substantial economic assistance.

These events in the subcontinent had two major effects on Indian foreign policy. First, New Delhi evidenced increasing concern about the involvement of "outside powers," meaning China, Pakistan, and the United States. As former Defense Minister Swaran Singh said:

> We have contributed to the freedom of Bangladesh. We will be happy to see it managing its own affairs. But we will not like any power, be it the United States, China or Pakistan, to make it a base for creating problems for India. Diego Garcia is thousands of miles away, but Bangladesh is next door. We have a long land border with it.[11]

The second impact was seen in the steady deterioration in bilateral relations between India and Bangladesh. Despite various negotiations and attempts to diminish hostile feelings, suspicion and distrust grew. India, and, by extension the Soviet Union, was implicated in the countercoup in November.[12] Clearly, political forces in South Asia were being realigned, which was a shift that was not in India's favor.

Indira Gandhi's declaration of emergency added one more issue to the suspicious and hostile relationship between China and India, which had recently been worsened by Indian actions in Sikkim. The *People's Daily* carried a signed article at the end of June entitled "Indira Gandhi's Government's Ferocious Features Fully Exposed," which attacked Mrs. Gandhi personally and also lambasted her policies and particularly her dependence on "Soviet revisionist social-imperialism."[13] China's reaction to, and possible involvement in, the developments in Bangladesh added another major irritant to Sino-Indian relations. Moreover, at a time when Sino-Soviet polemics were also intense in bilateral relations and in broader forums such as the United Nations, China and India engaged in a series of small-scale clashes along their disputed border. After repeated skirmishes in August, reportedly initiated by the Chinese side in an effort to dissuade India from intervening in post-Mujib Bangladesh,[14] the two sides engaged in their most serious clash since the mid-1960s, which left four Indian soldiers dead. New Delhi lodged a strong protest with the Chinese Embassy, and Peking countercharged that it was the Indians who had crossed into PRC territory. Although Mrs. Gandhi reacted by increasing Indian troop strength in border areas and by accusing China of hostile activities on India's border, she did not turn the clash into a major incident. Perhaps more significantly, China showed even greater restraint, returning the bodies promptly and treating the clash "as an isolated event rather than a portent of heightening tension."[15]

The effect of the state of emergency and events in Bangladesh had a negative impact on Indian-United States relations as well. When President

Ford again cancelled an anticipated visit to India in September, relations seemed headed even lower. Shortly after that, however, the Indo-United States Joint Commission had a successful meeting in Washington. Agreements were drawn up to increase trade, to encourage joint ventures between the United States and Indian firms in third countries, and to continue to work for further cooperation in agriculture, electronics, energy, environment, and education. When External Affairs Minister Chavan visited the United States in early October to open the joint commission meeting, he openly acknowledged problems in relations—particularly the U.S. attitude regarding Bangladesh, its supply of arms to Pakistan, and its building of a military base on Diego Garcia—and warned against "interference in internal matters" by "outside powers" but he also had cordial talks with Ford and Kissinger. He and his delegation left Washington believing that the United States genuinely desired better relations with India, India's economic development, and normalization in the subcontinent.

It was within this context of regional and great-power developments that Indian Foreign Secretary Kewal Singh traveled to Moscow in late November for the annual consultations between the two countries.[16] Singh had "detailed discussions" with Kosygin and Gromyko and also met briefly with Brezhnev. He also carried a personal message from Prime Minister Gandhi to Kosygin, which reportedly affirmed the importance that India attached to cooperation with the Soviet Union. The USSR leaders reiterated their support for Mrs. Gandhi's declaration of a state of emergency: they "expressed admiration for Mrs. Gandhi's handling of the difficult situation in the country and for introducing far-reaching socio-economic reforms." The Soviets also indicated that they were standing by India on the Bangladesh situation: the Soviets were said to "share" India's "concern at negative trends likely to affect the stability of the South Asia region." The talks also covered bilateral economic issues. The two sides agreed, again, to double their trade with one another by 1980, and the ground was prepared for the next meeting of the Indo-Soviet Joint Commission.

On these issues of critical importance to India, then, the Kewal Singh mission seems to have been a success. What is also of significance, however, is what was not mentioned or was referred to only slightly. In an interview with two *New Times'* correspondents, Kewal asserted that the meetings and discussions had been "extremely useful for understanding each other's points of view,"[17] which clearly indicated that differences remained. A clue about what one of these differences might have been is provided in a November 10 *Statesman* article, which had announced that the talks would focus on "the Soviet proposal for an Asian collective security arrangement" in the wake of the recent Helsinki accords that included collective security for Europe. However, there was no further mention of Asian collective security in any of the reports of the meeting except in Singh's interview with *New Times*. There, the foreign secretary was asked "How would you assess the significance of the Conference on Security and Cooperation in Europe for ensuring peace and security in other parts of the globe, notably Asia?" In his reply Singh devoted a lengthy paragraph to lauding Soviet efforts in Europe but related this to Asia only as a seeming afterthought:

> In our part of the world, in Asia, there is a lot of tension in different areas. But we nevertheless hope that the detente achieved in Europe, mainly thanks to the efforts of the Soviet leaders, will gradually extend to the Asian continent.

This is hardly a strong endorsement of the Soviet proposal; in fact, Singh did not even mention collective security at all. It appears that once again New Delhi had resisted Moscow's efforts to influence its behavior on this issue.

A second apparent major difference between the two sides is suggested by the *complete* lack of reference to China. A lengthy *New Times* article entitled "Peking Provocations against India" was published just prior to Singh's arrival.[18] Taking the Indian side, the article sought to undermine any possibility of a Sino-Indian rapprochement. It first linked Peking's "provocative and subversive actions" with "Indian Maoists and the Right-wing reactionaries in India." These were all "pursuing a common goal: . . . to undermine stability in the country, to plunge it in chaos, to divert it from giving effect to progressive reforms and pursuing a peaceable foreign policy." The authors also utilized quotations from Mrs. Gandhi herself, who had denounced Chinese interference along their common border. Finally, in what was the main message of the article, the authors asserted: "Evidently the shots fired by the Chinese troops on the parties were Peking's reply to India's desire to normalize relations with China." Given this Soviet position, it is remarkable that China was not even mentioned in any of the press reports. The likely explanation is that the Indians did not want to exacerbate relations with Peking, which itself had not played up the border incident. This may have been because President Ford's trip to China was just about to take place and New Delhi did not want to force the two together in an anti-Indian posture. In any event, this restrained Indian appraisal of the "threat from China," which diverged so from Moscow's perception, was followed by an equally restrained view of the Sino-United States summit and Ford's "Pacific Doctrine," where again New Delhi diverged from the Soviet position. Since the degree of similarity in attitude toward China had always been a fundamental indicator of the closeness of Indo-Soviet ties, Moscow must have been concerned with this evidence of substantial differences in approach.

INDIA'S CHINESE POLICY SHIFT

The early months of 1976 witnessed a further divergence in Indian and Soviet perceptions of China. India undertook several "gestures of good will" toward China. New Delhi concluded an agreement with Peking to install a general telex link with the Chinese Embassy on a reciprocal basis, invited China to participate in a regional UNESCO conference, and supported China's candidacy for the Asian Development Bank. Mrs. Gandhi signed the book of condolences in the Chinese Embassy after Chou En-lai's death; this prompted a large group of Chinese officials, up to the level of vice-minister for foreign affairs, to attend the Republic Day reception at the Indian Embassy in Peking. Although Indian officials refrained from being overly optimistic, it was apparent that there was some movement in Sino-Indian relations.[19]

On April 15 External Affairs Minister Chavan delivered a bombshell in the Lok Sabha when he announced that, after almost 15 years, India would restore the level of its diplomatic representation in Peking to the ambassadorial level. It was the government's understanding, he said, that India's initiative would be followed by a similar action by the PRC government. There were some questions raised about the effect of this move on Chinese "occupation of Indian territory" as well as cautions that:

> ... the actual normalization depends largely on China, on its shedding its suspicions about India, its suspicion that India has ganged up with Russia against it, its suspicion that India is out to challenge its position in South and South East Asia, and so on. ...[20]

Nevertheless, the policy initiative was generally hailed by Parliament, the press, and public opinion alike. In less than three months, K.R. Narayanan assumed his post as India's ambassador to China. China then named as its ambassador to India, Chen Chao-yuan, an experienced diplomat, who had served as counsellor at the embassy in New Delhi from 1963 to 1970 and had also been ambassador to Spain and Burma. Shortly after his arrival in September, Chen expressed Peking's position that "full normalization of Sino-Indian relations through joint efforts" was in the interests of the people of both countries and that China hoped that their friendship and relations would improve.[21]

There is little question of the potential value to India of this step, which would enhance New Delhi's options in foreign policy. Yet the question remains as to why the change was made at this particular time. Part of the explanation undoubtedly lies with PRC policy. There had been some change in Peking's attitudes toward India, as witnessed by the downplaying of the October border clash. The Chinese had also responded favorably to Indian gestures in early 1976, which was something

Indian leaders had complained Peking had not done in the past. Although Chinese motivations are not clear,[22] Peking may have been persuaded that India was not a USSR stooge due to the former's opposition to the Asian collective security idea and may also have wished to slow India's nuclear program by reducing Sino-Indian tensions.

It was not just a change in Chinese policy that explained this highly significant shift in India's policy toward the People's Republic, however. The negotiations that had been going on for three months by the time of Chavan's mid-April announcement had been on Indian initiative; moreover, the terms he announced represented a startling reversal of Mrs. Gandhi's tenaciously held policy that an Indian ambassador to Peking would be sent only *after* China sent its ambassador to New Delhi. One of the factors that may help to explain India's unexpected shift at this time was the regional situation India faced. India's relations with Pakistan had not improved substantially by early 1976. Chavan pointed out in mid-January that Pakistan was staging an anti-Indian propaganda campaign and also importing sophisticated weapons, and these were causing a setback to the process of normalization.[23] Morever, relations with Bangladesh were steadily deteriorating. The new regime in Dacca continued to assert its independence of India and to give vent to its suspicion and hostility toward its former "big brother." The growing dispute over India's diversion of the waters of the Ganges River, at Farakka, added new bitterness to the relationship. Thus, a move toward normalized relations with China, since it was the major ally of both Pakistan and Bangladesh, might well reduce the extent to which those states could threaten India; with their major ally not as committed as before, they might see the value in becoming more conciliatory. In the case of Pakistan, this may have worked. On May 14, one month after the announcement regarding China, India and Pakistan announced that they had agreed to restore diplomatic relations at the ambassadorial level (as well as to resume road links, rail and air traffic, and overflights). While problems remained, particularly over Kashmir, Indo-Pakistani relations were thus moving toward the normalization that India saw as being in its interests.

Meanwhile, the significance that Moscow attached to its relationship with New Delhi was underlined in February by the Twenty-fifth Congress of the Communist Party of the Soviet Union. Delivering the Central Committee report to the Congress, Brezhnev praised India to a degree unprecedented in this forum.[24] At one point in his address, Brezhnev saluted Mrs. Gandhi's regime for being among those that "proclaim socialist goals and are carrying out progressive transformations" in the face of "heavy pressure from domestic and foreign reaction." His major reference to India, however, was in the segment of his speech devoted to Soviet relations with noncommunist states. After discussing the multifaceted cooperation between the two countries, Brezhnev pointedly said "we attach special importance to friendship with this great country." Referring to the treaty signed in 1971, the CPSU leader asserted that "during the past five year period Soviet-Indian relations rose to a new level."

> In even this brief time, its enormous importance for our bilateral ties and its role as a stabilizing factor in South Asia and on the continent as a whole have been clearly demonstrated.
> Close political and economic cooperation with the Republic of India is on steady course. Soviet people are sympathetic toward—more than that, they feel solidarity with—India's peace-loving foreign policy and the courageous struggle of that country's progressive forces to solve the difficult social and economic problems confronting it. We wish the people and government of India complete success in their struggle.

Brezhnev concluded this glowing evaluation of India and Indo-Soviet relations by looking at the region as a whole:

> The course of events has shown the correctness of the Soviet Union's approach to the problems of South Asia. We welcomed the end of the Indian-Pakistani military conflict in 1971 and the important changes that occurred then in the direction of the establishment of normal relations between the states in that part of the world. We note with satisfaction that to some extent we were able to contribute to this positive process.

Moreover, there is no doubt that the Soviets intended that the Indian leadership should grasp the significance of these statements. Soviet propaganda emphasized the "special importance" Brezhnev had attached to Soviet ties with India.[25] At the Congress itself, the CPI was treated as the CPSU's most important Asian ally and its leadership was given extensive opportunity to express support for the Soviet Union. In various addresses to the Congress and interviews on Moscow television and in the press, CPI Chairman Dange and General Secretary Rao also attacked China and "Maoism," clearly seeking to remind India of the importance of Indo-Soviet ties and of the dangers of dealing with Peking. Said Rao in an interview with Soviet journalists:

> The biggest enemy of peace is the Maoist leadership of China. This is being realized more and more by all well-meaning people in Asia.... Maoism is shamelessly collaborating with militarists, with enemies of detente in the West and with racists in South Africa and with fascists in Chile.[26]

The rather mysterious trip of Soviet Deputy Foreign Minister Firyubin to New Delhi may also have been part of the Soviet response to what it naturally regarded as an untoward normalization between China and India. Firuybin's visit, his first to India since 1971, was only announced in the Indian press on February 28, which was the day of his arrival. India seemed to make every effort to play down the visit, which stood in marked contrast to the enthusiasm Brezhnev expressed for India only a few days before. The articles in the *Statesman*, for example, on February 28 and March 2, 3, and 4 were extremely brief, not very descriptive, and usually "buried" somewhere in the middle of the paper. The only specific item that news reports "believed" Firyubin to have discussed with Indian leaders was the forthcoming nonaligned summit; Firyubin was said to have "expressed appreciation of the nonalignment policy (of India) and the role of the nonaligned countries in international forums."[27]

We should probably not place too much emphasis on this visit. Kewal Singh had been in Moscow in November, and Moscow naturally sought to maintain contacts with New Delhi. Moreover, the Soviets were quite concerned with the nonaligned summit and undoubtedly wished to be sure of India's intentions for it and to make clear to India the USSR preferences. Moreover, Firyubin went on to Pakistan, where he spent three days and had talks with Foreign Minister Aziz Ahmed, thus giving his trip all the appearances of a routine South Asian swing. However, India's restrained treatment, the paucity of details, and Firyubin's abnormally long stay in India—almost one week when he was expected only for a "few days"—suggest additional aspects. Given the growing divergence in Indian and Soviet perceptions of China, Firyubin, who had been a troubleshooter for the Soviets on previous visits to India (in March and September 1966, September 1968, July 1970, and October 1971), may well also have been there to further admonish India and discourage any additional divergence in view. As part of this mission, he may have sought a reassurance from India that any new ties with China would not be at the expense of Indo-Soviet relations; this reassurance would never completely satisfy Moscow but might serve to enhance India's sensitivity to its special relationship with the Soviet Union and that country's interests.

Moreover, it was at this time that reports appeared suggesting that Mrs. Gandhi was expected to visit the Soviet Union in the summer. Moscow had been pressing for the return of Mrs. Gandhi for some time, having renewed "again and again" the invitation extended to her (and which she accepted) during Brezhnev's visit in 1973.[28] Thus, it may have been that Firyubin, seeking assurances of India's good intentions in the face of its evolving policy change regarding China, was able to get Mrs. Gandhi to finally commit herself to visit Moscow. Since she had not visited the Soviet Union since prior to the 1971 war, such a visit would symbolize the continuing vitality of the Soviet-Indian relationship (or at least give the Soviets the opportunity to make a case for it) and demonstrate it to India and to the rest of the world. That it was difficult for Firyubin to get even this much of a commitment is testified to by the length of his stay. The paucity of details and India's low-key handling of the visit can likewise be explained by the fact that much of the negotiations was over sensitive, potentially divisive issues. That is, there were significant differences between the two but, given their still strong ties in other areas, neither side wished to broadcast or exaggerate irritants in the relationship.

There are two other indicatons that the Soviet Union was responding to India's changing policy and that Moscow was the supplicant in this situation. One was the report, which appeared at the beginning of May, that "after protracted negotiations," India had finally persuaded the Soviets to provide another advanced version of the MiG fighter plane.[29] This was designated the MiG-21 bis, apparently a step more advanced than the aircraft agreed to by Grechko in 1975, and was an aircraft the Indians had been seeking ever since the defense minister's visit. The planes were to be produced in India at Hindustan Aircraft Limited where the other MiGs were also produced. Thus, despite India's interest in aircraft from the West, the Soviets once again apparently offered New Delhi better terms than Western countries.[30] Moscow was anxious to maintain this link with India and utilized it at this particular time as a way of underlining and strengthening the Indo-Soviet relationship.

An additional Soviet response to India's changing relationship with China came in the economic area. In April the Third Session of the Intergovernmental Soviet-Indian Commission was held in Moscow and further progress was apparently made on a number of projects. Shortly after that, Soviet Deputy Premier Arkhipov traveled to India to head a Soviet delegation for the ceremonial opening of a hot-rolling mill at the Soviet-assisted Bokaro steel mill. Mrs. Gandhi was also present for the occasion and the Soviets enthusiastically repeated her comments regarding the significance of the Indo-Soviet friendship and the role of Soviet cooperation in India's economic development.[31]

The most significant development on the economic front was the signing in New Delhi of a new long-term trade agreement for 1976–80 in mid-April. Like the joint commission meeting and the Bokaro opening, the conclusion of this agreement was hardly a spontaneous response by the Soviets to India's changing relationship to China; indeed, the Indian press reported that talks had begun in 1974, there had been two rounds of discussions in 1975, and a Soviet trade delegation had worked on it in January and February 1976.[32] Yet it may have been the change in relations between India and China that gave the final impetus to complete the details that had been preventing the finalization of the accord. It is known that the two sides at this time finally reached an agreement on the method of India's repayment of the 1973 wheat loan. It was to be able to repay in goods rather than in wheat, thus allowing the country to build up its own grain reserves; this represented a significant Soviet concession. The trade agreement itself, to follow the five-year agreement signed in December 1970, called for a total trade turnover of Rs 935 Crores, a figure that, if achieved, would realize the goal set during Brezhnev's 1973 visit to India of doubling trade by 1980. The agreement provided for continued Indian importation of such critical items as kerosene, diesel oil, fertilizers, and newsprint. India would export to the Soviet Union both traditional and nontraditional goods. Both sides would continue work on finalizing plans to collaborate on production and on establishing arrangements with third countries for the supply of goods produced in India with Soviet help.

For Moscow, the significance of the agreement went beyond the specifics. The Soviets had been anxious to refute "ill-wishers' allegations" that Indo-Soviet cooperation as seen in trade had "reached its apogee and must now decline."[33] There was, in fact, something to such "allegations." In 1955–56, India's imports from the Soviet Union represented less than 1 percent of India's total imports. In 1974–75, the figure was almost 9 percent. India's exports to the Soviet Union in 1955–56 represented just over 0.5 percent of India's exports while for 1974–75 the figure was more than 12 percent. However, Indian exports to the Soviet Union had already peaked in 1972–73 (at 15.5 percent). While Indo-Soviet trade increased in absolute terms almost every year, partly due to rising prices, Moscow's percentage share of India's trade declined. The Soviet share of India's imports dropped to around 6 percent in 1975–76 and 1976–77 and its share of India's exports plummeted to 10.3 percent and then to 8.6 percent for those years. From being India's number-one export market in 1974–75, the Soviet Union slipped to fourth by 1976–77 (behind the United States, the United Kingdom, and Japan). In imports, the Soviet Union ranked fourth behind the United States, the United Kingdom, and Iran, and was also being pressed by West Germany and Japan. Moscow's 10-plus percent share of India's total trade was good for second place in 1974–75; in 1975–76 however, that share was less than 8 percent and the Soviets had dropped to third and by 1976–77 the figures were 7 percent and a fourth-place ranking.[34]

Soviet-Indian trade had been and remained significant. Growth in India's trade with the Soviet Union from the 1950s until the mid-1970s was the largest of India's trade with any country. The Soviets had provided new and assured markets for Indian goods that might not have been competitive on world markets. India had been able to save foreign exchange by repaying aid programs through increased exports. Trade with the Soviet Union had allowed India to reduce its economic dependence on the West. There were repeated accusations that the Soviets charged higher prices for its exports and lower prices for India's, that the Soviets "switch-traded" or "dumped" Indian goods by reselling them to hard-currency markets, which thus hurt other Indian sales, and that this trade was just a diversion from other markets.[35] However, there were even more studies, many of them by Indian scholars, that argued the opposite.[36] Yet, these criticisms drew attention to irritants in the economic relationship. Although the relative decline of Indian exports to the Soviet Union may have been partially explained by a decline in the rate of repayment for Soviet credits due to a slowdown in India's drawing on credits Moscow had extended, this was hardly comforting to the Soviets. (About $450 million of the USSR total of $1,943 billion in credits had not been utilized by India by the end of 1976, and New Delhi had been drawing on less than $25 million per year in recent years.)[37] Continuing disagreement over the ruble-rupee ratio as well as Moscow's ongoing reluctance to shift to program assistance, such as the raw materials and components desired by the Indians, did not augur well for Indo-Soviet trade relations. In the midst of all this, the trade agreement raised as many questions as it answered. Moreover, would it be sufficient to counterbalance changes in India's Chinese policy? In this context, Mrs. Gandhi's visit to Moscow appeared crucial.

MRS. GANDHI IN MOSCOW: "THE BEST OF FRIENDS"?

Before Mrs. Gandhi journeyed to the Soviet Union, Pakistani Prime Minister Bhutto headed for Peking. He sought the same thing from his visit that the Soviets sought from Mrs. Gandhi: reassurance. Ever since the announcement that India and China had agreed to raise their relations to the ambassador level, Islamabad had been noticeably nervous about the constancy of its Chinese ally. Pakistan stressed, with undisguised anxiety, that the foreign policies of Pakistan and China had converged as "a natural and expected phenomenon" and not due to "international exigencies or political expediency." Without even mentioning India, Mushtaq Ahmed in the May 26 edition of *Morning News* went on to conclude, with fervent hope, that the relationship between Islamabad and Peking "is based on sound principles and has, therefore, the quality of durability which will remain unaffected by Peking's diplomatic ties with any other country howsoever large or populous."

On his arrival in Peking, Bhutto was received almost as warmly as he had been two years earlier. At a banquet in his honor that night, new

---

The phrase, "The Best of Friends," is borrowed from the title of an article in *Far Eastern Economic Review*.[38]

Chinese Premier Hua Kuo-feng provided enormous relief to the concerned Bhutto by stating that Sino-Pakistani relations had "stood the test of time" as well as "the vagaries of political weather." He promised Chinese support "*in the future*, as in the past...."[39] Bhutto's relief could not have been expressed more clearly than in his speech at the banquet he gave for Hua at the end of his visit:

> We are going back to our country with *the renewed faith in the Sino-Pakistan friendship and solidarity which has withstood strains and weathered storms in the past*. We are confident that this friendship and cordiality will endure whatever vicissitudes or inclemencies of international political climate that the future event may bring about.
>
> Two decades of our close relations with the People's Republic of China vindicates the position of Pakistan that this relationship between the two Asian neighbors is of a positive character *and not directed against any country*.[40]

On specifics, Hua also was forthcoming with Chinese support for Pakistan. The Chinese government, he told Bhutto, was "ready to assume appropriate commitments" arising from Pakistan's proposal for a nuclear-free zone in South Asia, which India opposed. China agreed to aid Pakistan on no less than 15 economic projects, and although no new military agreements were made public, additional Pakistani military officials were summoned from home and the talks continued after Bhutto's departure under the auspices of a newly established Joint Military Committee. Moreover, at this time it became known that Bhutto had signed two protocols on defense collaboration during his 1974 trip; one covered Chinese supplies to all three of Pakistan's services and the other concerned collaboration in defense production.[41]

The only area in which there seemed to be any change in China's support of Pakistan was on the question of Kashmir. Bhutto made it a major theme of his comments, launching into it at the first opportunity in the opening night's banquet. There was no Chinese response at this time but Bhutto brought it up again in his talks with Hua on May 28. Again, Hua only acknowledged Pakistan's position. Finally, at the return banquet he hosted on the May 29, Bhutto made Kashmir the central focus of his speech. Defending Pakistan's position "on principle" he seemed clearly to be putting the Chinese leadership in the dilemma of having to choose between Pakistan and India. Normalization was fine, he stressed, but not at the sacrifice of "sovereignty and political independence."

> I am sure you will agree with me that normalization does not mean that one side must abandon its traditional support to the right of self-determination of the people of Jammu and Kashmir, that it resile from the

basic principles of its foreign policy or that it compromise its sovereignty and political independence.

Normalization means acceptance by both sides of the principle of reciprocity and admission of realities. Hence the path of normalization is a two way street. It is equally incumbent on the other side to accept the existence of the dispute and to acknowledge the necessity of its settlement on the basis of self-determination through negotiations on an equal footing.[42]

Bhutto's approach seems to have worked, for Premier Hua finally expressed Peking's support, although without elaboration, for Pakistan's stand in his speech at that banquet. Once again, the Indian chargé d'affaires and his wife walked out as they had in response to the same issue in 1974. The final communiqué, which reiterated the above areas of PRC support for Pakistan, also included Chinese backing on Kashmir.[43] This backing was somewhat more muted, however, than it had been before: the "just struggle" of the people of Jammu and Kashmir for the right of self-determination was reduced to "struggle." Despite Hua's reinsertion of the missing word in his farewell address to Bhutto, the consensus among analysts was that the Chinese preferred to deemphasize the Kashmir issue but had been forced to go along with Bhutto.[44]

Just more than a week after Bhutto returned to Pakistan from China, Prime Minister Gandhi left India for the Soviet Union. As Mrs. Gandhi left Palam airport in New Delhi, she had two major purposes in mind for her trip. One was to explain India's Chinese policy in a manner that would not threaten Indo-Soviet ties; the second was to further Soviet support for India in the form of new levels of economic cooperation. For the Soviet leaders, the purposes were similar, yet with a difference in emphasis. First, the Kremlin wanted reassurances from Mrs. Gandhi that the change regarding China would not affect Indo-Soviet relations. Second, the Soviets wanted to strengthen those relations, through closer economic cooperation, or better yet, through a diminution of Sino-Indian ties or even Indian adherence to the frequently proposed Asian collective security system. Finally, they hoped to be able to demonstrate to the world, especially to its Third World and nonaligned countries, that "Soviet-Indian cooperation furnishes a model" for relations among states where "peaceful cooperation, understanding, and good neighborliness" prevail.[45]

It was in this context of a changing regional situation and overlapping, but partially contradictory, objectives in their mutual relationship that Mrs. Gandhi landed in Moscow on June 8. Her visit had been given a lavish buildup in the Soviet media. Soviet correspondents interviewed Mrs. Gandhi, new Ambassador Gujral spoke on Radio Moscow, and Mrs. Gandhi was interviewed for Soviet television. She was greeted at the airport by virtually all of the top Soviet leadership, including Brezhnev, who was making his first such trip for a noncommunist visitor since French President Giscard d'Estaing's visit the previous October. After a wet yet colorful and enthusiastic welcome at the airport and a motorcade through flag-waving and cheering crowds, Mrs. Gandhi was ensconced in the Kremlin, an honor traditionally reserved for visiting heads of state. Over the next four days, there were talks with the top Soviet leadership, a private meeting with Brezhnev, various public functions, and two banquets.

It is likely that China was the primary topic in Prime Minister Gandhi's talks with the Soviet leaders. Although there is no mention of China in the joint declaration at the end of the visit,[46] press reports indicated that the subject had come up several times, including the first round of talks when India discussed it and in the second round when Brezhnev "summed up for the Indian delegation his own assessment of China's policies and its intentions."[47] At a press conference at the conclusion of the visit, Mrs. Gandhi stated that China was among a wide range of subjects discussed: "When we discuss the international situation we cannot leave out a country like China," she said. When she was asked if the Soviet leadership disapproved of the Indian decision to improve relations with China, she replied, "I don't think so because there is no question of this coming in the way of friendship with the Soviet Union. I think the Soviet leaders understand our position."[48] In spite of this and other reassurances that Mrs. Gandhi proffered to the Soviets, there was no indication that India had backed off from its policy change toward China nor that the Soviets were very pleased with this situation. In his welcoming speech for Mrs. Gandhi, for example, Brezhnev complained that "there are forces in Asia which, ignoring the rights and sovereignty of states, are striving to subordinate other people to their rule."[49] This was a typical Soviet way of implicitly asking India how it could possibly think of normalizing relations with a state that behaved in such a manner. In their second round of talks, Brezhnev is said to have told Mrs. Gandhi that the Soviet Union "regarded the Indo-Soviet friendship as a common treasure"—that is, in the interests of both states—and, in a thinly veiled warning, to have then said that this treasure must be "carefully guarded."[50] Finally, the Soviet side in the joint declaration expressed support for the "recent steps toward further normalization" in the subcontinent, such as the Indo-Pakistani agreement of May 14, but pointedly made no mention of the step toward Indo-Chinese normalization. The fact that India was maintaining its position is also clear in several of Mrs. Gandhi's statements. As a reminder to her Soviet hosts, she responded to Brezhnev's welcoming speech by praising the Soviet Union's "great foresight in accepting India's non-alignment" and said that "the acceptance of the right of other countries to live as they choose is the first essential of peace." Mrs. Gandhi's remark in her address at the banquet on the first night should be read not only in reference to Chinese propaganda but also in light of the Soviet denunciations of the "Maoist menace." She said:

> Darkness is not dispelled by cursing but by lighting lamps. Along with international efforts for peace, *each country must act on its own to reduce areas of suspicion and to enlarge areas of goodwill.*[51]

Finally, although the declaration called the atmosphere for the talks one of "trust, friendship and mutual understanding" (the same as in Brezhnev's 1973 visit except that then the word "mutual" was omitted), the Indian prime minister also was quoted as describing the talks as "candid and frank," that is, with significant differences among the agreements.[52]

One barometer of India's stand on the Chinese issue has always been available through its reaction to Soviet appeals for an Asian collective security system. The Soviets had once again been increasing their efforts to promote the idea at the time of Prime Minister Gandhi's visit.[53] Yet there was no explicit public mention of the idea during the visit, and the paragraph in the joint declaration that probably refers to it is innocuous and virtually identical to the one in the declaration after Brezhnev's visit. Indeed, Mrs. Gandhi had seemed to hinder the Soviets' opportunity for success on this issue a week *prior* to coming to Moscow. At that time, she told Soviet correspondents that the safest guarantee for peace and stability in Asia "is for every country to become economically strong and stable through a more equitable distribution of the product of labor." Emphasizing her point and making clear the gulf between her view and the Soviet one of laying the blame on China, she added that "we believe that the chief threat to stability in Asia is economic stagnation and social injustice."[54] This position was reiterated at the press conference in Moscow when Mrs. Gandhi was asked about a security system for Asia and she replied that "the way towards strengthening security in Asia . . . lay in strengthening the stability, interdependence and economic might of each individual country of the region . . . ." It would appear that China's *People's Daily,* which published a vehement attack on collective security the same day that Mrs. Gandhi arrived in Moscow, need not have bothered.

In the area of expanded economic cooperation there apears to have been a great deal of talk but few specific new developments. Before she left New Delhi, Prime Minister Gandhi had praised previous assistance and made clear that one of the major purposes of her trip was to "continue to look for new forms of cooperation to avoid any slackening of the pace of development of our relations."[55] In talks with her, Brezhnev was reported to have said that the Soviet Union was "ready to seek these new forms of economic cooperation," which he hoped would deepen Indo-Soviet relations.[56] The joint declaration asserted that the two sides recognized the need for "new areas and new modes of cooperation" in order to reach trade targets. The only specific agreements, however, were to expand collaboration in production in the fields of nonferrous metallurgy, textiles, electronics, and agriculture. Thus, despite emphasis by both sides on economic issues and despite the work of an economically oriented advance team, the details of expanded cooperation would have to await future implementation (or decision). Not even the ruble-rupee exchange-rate problem had been resolved, although it too had been discussed by the team sent ahead of Mrs. Gandhi.

An area where the Soviets expressed their continuing support was in defense of the state of emergency and Mrs. Gandhi's internal policies. At the Kremlin banquet on Mrs. Gandhi's first night in Moscow, Brezhnev "praised the policies of the Indian National Congress led by Mrs. Gandhi and reiterated this country's understanding of the measures taken in India against forces of internal and external reaction last year." The next day Brezhnev again expressed his pleasure with the stabilization in India, which was viewed as the result of Mrs. Gandhi's "firm and decisive steps," and his appreciation of the socioeconomic measures taken by the government "to serve the interests of the people." Mrs. Gandhi's frequent denunciations prior to and during her visit of Western criticisms of the state of emergency made it clear that she appreciated Soviet support. The joint declaration also reflected Soviet "understanding" of the situation in India.

On the question of the Indian Ocean, there was some change in the Soviet position but it seemed slight; the 1973 statement that the two states were ready "to take part ... in the search for a favorable solution to the question of turning the Indian Ocean region into a zone of peace" was prefaced in the 1976 version with joint support for "the desire of the peoples of the Indian Ocean area to prevent it from becoming an arena for the setting up of foreign military bases." Since the Soviet Union could be partly responsible for causing the area to become an arena with foreign bases, this was a small USSR concession to the Indian viewpoint. Yet, the Soviets had for years renounced any intention of setting up their own bases and had denounced the United States for its bases, particularly Diego Garcia. This Soviet position, plus the additional qualification added in 1976 that any solution had to be "in conformity with generally recognized rules of international law"—a Soviet defense of its naval activity in the area for some time—limited the significance of any "score" by India, as one Indian correspondent had claimed.[57] Moreover, Mrs. Gandhi evidenced greater opposition to U.S. activity in the area. There was a great difference, she told a Western correspondent in Moscow, between ships that passed by and those that were constantly there, "particularly if these latter were strengthened by military bases, especially nuclear ones."[58]

On the whole, then, one wonders whether the two sides attached as much importance to the meeting after it was held as they had claimed to prior to it. Actually, it is likely that neither side expected the meeting to produce sensational results or even important agreements. As *The Times* observed on June 9, it was "first and foremost a goodwill visit." Most differences were minor. Both sides had given and received reassurances on their mutual relations. Mrs. Gandhi said at the first banquet that "the foundation on which the edifice of Indo-Soviet cooperation was built remained solid and stable and India would continue to strengthen it." That and her statement at the press conference that the result of the visit "was both consolidation and extension of India's friendship and cooperation with the Soviet Union" were gratifying to the Soviets.[59] The economic negotiations, although they produced no new agreements during the summit, further reassured each side of the constancy of the relationship. Thus, India maintained its policy of independence vis-à-vis China but reassured the Soviets enough not to threaten the Indo-Soviet relationship. For the Soviets, the solidity of its bilteral relationship with India had been reaffirmed. Moreover, the image of this "model" relationship between the Soviet Union and a Third World and nonaligned state had not been tarnished. Still, the ultimate reassurance to Moscow would have been no change in New Delhi-Peking relations at all.

INDO-SOVIET RELATIONS AND INTERNATIONAL FORUMS

Further light was shed on the nature of the Indo-Soviet relationship at the nonaligned summit meeting in Colombo, Sri Lanka, in August 1976 and at the United Nations in the fall. Regarding the former, the Soviets even directly confronted the major issue of the contradiction that some perceived between India's claim to nonaligned status and its treaty with the Soviets. The Soviet Union utilized the occasion of the fifth anniversary of the treaty's signing in August, which was just a few days prior to the opening of the conference, to proclaim the value of Indo-Soviet relations for nonalignment, in general, and for South Asia's peace and stability, in particular. One *New Times* article argued that "in the past five years India's prestige as the largest nonaligned nation, a champion of peace, detente, independence and equality has been enhanced."[60] It continued:

This is particularly evident at the present moment, on the eve of the Fifth Summit Conference of the Non-aligned Nations. Representatives of many of these countries have visited Delhi to consult the Indian government on urgent problems in the nonaligned movement. It is largely thanks to the Indian government that imperialist and hegemonic forces have failed to undermine the efforts to strengthen the anti-imperialist foundation of the movement.

Regarding the subcontinent:

In the past five years since the conclusion of the Indian-Soviet Treaty the situation in South Asia has improved considerably even though the imperialists and the Peking leaders have not abandoned their plans to tip the balance of forces in their own favor.

On balance, the Soviets must have been disappointed with the outcome of the Colombo summit. The Soviets certainly could agree with the "normal" positions adopted by the Conference on Africa, the Middle East, and the establishment of a press agencies' pool. They could acknowledge, if not get enthusiastic, about the call for a new international economic order. However, the organization in general moved toward the center from the left-wing radicalism of the earlier Algiers summit. This new moderation showed in the relatively balanced treatment of the United States and the Soviet Union. Mrs. Gandhi's 20-minute address to the gathering was a typical example of the appeal for restraints and the need to avoid divisive issues.[61] A particular disappointment to the Soviets was the statement about the Indian Ocean in the final political document. Although the statement was along the lines of the United Nations resolution and put a great deal of emphasis on the need for a withdrawal from foreign bases in the region, it went further than Moscow had wanted. Despite intense Soviet lobbying through Cuba, Vietnam, Laos, and Jamaica, the conference deplored the "increasing development of foreign naval power" and opposed "any manifestation of Great Power military presence in the Indian Ocean conceived in the context of Great Power rivalries"; both charges embraced the Soviet Union as well as the United States. There is no evidence that India sought to push the Soviet viewpoint; indeed, that would have been extremely unlikely given the differences that existed between the two states on the issue. (Moreover, India was more immediately concerned with fighting off efforts by Bangladesh to include "powers in the region" as a potential threat to the area.) On the issue of detente, the Soviet position did not fare well, either. The word "detente," which the Soviets had sought, was not used. Instead, the reference was to "relaxation of tension between the Great Powers," which was viewed as "still limited in scope" and which was criticized for implying outworn practices such as "balance of power," "spheres of influence," military alliances, the arms race, and rivalry between power blocs. Once again, this formulation more closely corresponded to New Delhi's rather than Moscow's position.[62]

The Thirty-first General Assembly of the United Nations in the fall of 1976 provided another glimpse of Indian and Soviet views of broader issues. Disarmament was a major item for discussion and the Indians and Soviets were usually in agreement. India was particularly supportive of the Soviet proposal for a treaty on the nonuse of force in international relations. Much of India's efforts were also taken up with challenges from Pakistan, whose foreign minister raised the Kashmir question in his address, and from Bangladesh, which chose to bring the Farakka Barrage issue before the world body. There is no evidence of active USSR involvement in either of these issues; it is likely that the Soviets were happy not to get dragged into them.

At this General Assembly session, India continued its past pattern of voting with the Soviet Union far more often than it voted with the United States. This, of course, tells us nothing about influence; Moscow may have influenced New Delhi or vice versa, or each may have arrived at its position independently.[63] The voting records *do* illustrate the broad identity of views between India and the Soviet Union on a wide variety of world issues. For example, an examination of 20 important resolutions before the General Assembly reveals that India voted with the Soviet Union and against the United States seven times—mainly regarding Third World issues, the Middle East, and South Africa—while voting with the United States against the Soviet Union only once—on the integration of East Timor into Indonesia.[64] There are no issues that stand out here as possible tests of influence; that is, both India and the Soviet Union voted the way they would have been anticipated to vote. Nor do we have any evidence to indicate that either tried to influence the other on any of the votes. What is clear is that New Delhi's perception of the world, and hence its predisposition in policy, was much closer to that in Moscow than to the one prevailing in Washington.

EXPANDING ECONOMIC COOPERATION

Prime Minister Gandhi's visit to the Soviet Union in June had not led to the conclusion of new agreements that would expand Indo-Soviet economic cooperation or stimulate trade substantially. Despite all the rhetoric about "new forms" of economic cooperation during the visit and in the final declaration, the Soviets still found it difficult in August to deny what they called the "plateau theory" (invented, they said, by "the

Western and local Right-wing press") which "maintained that Soviet-Indian relations had reached a point of stagnation...."[65] Although an important shipping agreement was signed by the two countries in July, little else was accomplished until August when the long-awaited protocol that identified new areas of collaboration in third-country projects was signed. This had been discussed prior to, during, and since Mrs. Gandhi's visit, and it had taken a final week of negotiations in Moscow in August to conclude it. This agreement provided, for the first time, for India's entry into heavy industrial construction abroad. In September the two sides signed another agreement, one in which India agreed to supply steel plants in the Soviet Union with 30,000 tons of metallurgical equipment to be produced by the Heavy Engineering Corporation (HEC) at Ranchi, which was one of the major public-sector projects built with Soviet assistance. Together, these two agreements would aid in expanding Indo-Soviet cooperation and aid India by utilizing more of its public-sector production, which would enable these industries to produce at closer to full capacity.

Another important step came with Soviet Deputy Foreign Minister I.T. Grishin's visit to India in December. Grishin and his Indian counterparts drew up a trade protocol for 1977 that envisaged a trade turnover of Rs 900 Crores.[66] (Trade in 1975 was said to have reached Rs 775 Crores and was expected to be about Rs 827 Crores in 1976.) Moreover, Soviet imports were to include certain nontraditional Indian exports such as machinery from the HEC, freight containers, forklift trucks, and machine tools. India was to continue to import petroleum products, nonferrous metals, and engineering goods, among other items.

What made Grishin's visit and the agreement he negotiated so significant, however, was that for the first time the Soviets offered to sell crude oil to India. India had been seeking crude oil from the Soviet Union for years, but the Soviets had always turned New Delhi down, claiming that domestic and Eastern European (as well as hard-currency sales) needs took priority. In 1974, during the energy crisis, the Soviets had been willing to offer kerosene and diesel fuel but not crude oil, and they had continued that policy. Now, however, Grishin announced Moscow's willingness to consider a long-term deal of Soviet crude oil in exchange for Indian pig iron, which was currently in abundant supply in India. The Soviets offered 5.5 million metric tons of crude, 1 million of it in 1977, with 1.5 million coming in each of the next three years. Since one of the problems in Indo-Soviet trade had been the difficulty India had in finding Soviet goods to import, now trade could be expanded; there was some speculation that by adding the provision of oil for pig iron, bilateral trade might reach the 1980 target in 1977. Moreover, India would be getting between 7 and 10 percent of its crude oil imports from the Soviet Union at virtually no cost in foreign exchange.

Given India's ongoing requests for crude oil from the Soviets, Moscow's previous resistance, and the other demands on USSR supplies, the Soviet agreement to sell crude oil on the rupee or barter basis was significant and suggests the exercise of influence by India. It was not clear what India "traded" for this or even what prompted the Sovients finally to capitulate. There was some strain in their bilateral relations due to India's approach to China. If there was one step the Soviets could take to demonstrate to India and to third parties the importance Moscow attached to its relationship with New Delhi, the provision of crude oil was it.

Perhaps the only other step the Soviets could have taken with regard to India that could have had an impact (at least symbolic) on the scale of the crude oil deal was the area of nuclear fuel. India had been having a difficult time with fuel supplies following its peaceful nuclear explosion (PNE) in May 1974. Canada, which had supplied most of the heavy water for the research reactor CIRUS from which the plutonium for the test was derived, immediately suspended nuclear and all other forms of aid to India. Protracted negotiations over the next two years finally resulted in a decision by the Canadian government to terminate nuclear supplies to India. Earlier in the year, moreover, the major suppliers of nuclear equipment, including the Soviet Union, agreed to ban the sale of nuclear equipment to countries that had not signed the Nuclear Non-Proliferation Treaty. Finally, with revelations in the United States that some heavy water from the United States had been involved in producing the plutonium for India's "device," there was increasing pressure in Washington to stop shipments of low-enriched uranium, under a 30-year contract signed in 1963, to India's Tarapur Power Station near Bombay. Jimmy Carter's victory in the presidential election and his emphasis on steps the United States could take to ensure the nonproliferation of nuclear weapons did not augur well for the future of this aspect of Indo-United States relations.[67]

Into this situation stepped the Soviet Union again. In early December India informed the International Atomic Energy Agency that the Soviet Union had agreed to provide aid in the form of desperately needed fuel for its reactor in Rajasthan. The Soviets agreed to sell India between 200 and 240 tons of heavy water, one-quarter of it to be shipped immediately. In an effort to adhere to its stance on nonproliferation, Moscow sought to modify India's position on safeguards. Nevertheless, as one author has pointed out:

> In the end, however, the Soviets apparently had to compromise, managing to win Indian assent only to safeguards that were limited to the time and place that the Soviet heavy water was actually used.[68]

At least as significant as the fact that the Soviets tried to influence India's position on safeguards was, of course, that they largely failed. Yet they went ahead with the agreement for the supply of the fuel. Thus, this appears to be a case of a certain exercise of influence by India with the Soviets responding with support in an area of high visibility and great symbolic importance to India and to the world.

INDIA'S EXTERNAL AND INTERNAL ENVIRONMENTS: ELECTIONS AND INFLUENCE

By the early months of 1977, then, Soviet-Indian relations seemed to be regaining some of the momentum they had lost over the past year. Nevertheless, Moscow's major concern remained the possibility of normalization between India and China. The Soviets undoubtedly derived some comfort from the fact that there was very little substantive progress in relations between the two. Moreover, with Mao's death in September, Moscow had virtually ceased its polemics against China, apparently in the hope that such restraint might influence an outcome in the struggle for leadership that would be favorable to Soviet interests.[69] Still, any hint of rapprochement upset the Soviets, and Moscow still hoped in vain for Indian support on the idea of an anti-Chinese Asian collective security system.

Of particular concern to India in its relations with China was that country's potential for fomenting trouble between India and its neighbors. The visit of Bangladesh leader, Ziaur Rahman to Peking in January 1977 naturally heightened New Delhi's anxiety.[70] The Chinese used the meeting as a springboard for a highly polemical attack on Soviet policy in South Asia. As Chinese Vice-Premier Li Hsien-nien said at the banquet:

> The superpower that flaunts the title of the so-called "natural ally" of the third world is resorting to nice rhetoric and changeful deceptive tactics. But its sinister intention to control and enslave the South Asian countries has been seen through by more and more people.[71]

How much Ziaur's own reticence in this regard was due to the sudden and rather surprising pretrip visit to Dacca by Nikolai Firyubin is not known, although it is likely Firyubin urged Bangladesh not to side with the Chinese. In any case, Moscow was undoubtedly not comfortable having Ziaur "highly satisfied" with the visit when a major theme during it had been Chinese attacks on Soviet policy.[72] Another development of major significance was the lack of China's response to Zia's rather guarded reference to Bangladesh's problems with India over the border and the waters of the Ganges. The distinct message seemed to be that Peking wanted to be cautious about upsetting its delicate "new" relationship with India. Thus, while India could take some comfort in this visit, it served largely to heighten Soviet concerns.

India's relations with the United States had undergone gradual improvement since declining again with the U.S. announcement in February 1976 that it was cutting off talks on aid due to India's anti-United States statements and attitudes. Economic relations were improving through the year, and, in November when Kewal Singh presented his credentials to President Ford as the replacement to T.N. Kaul as ambassador, Ford seemed to point to a warmer relationship between New Delhi and Washington with his reference to U.S. support for "the special role of leadership and high responsibility...which India bears...."[73] There were also hints that the new Carter administration might accord the Third World and particularly India a somewhat higher priority. The rather strenuous U.S. pressure on France and Pakistan to cancel an agreement for Paris to sell nuclear reactors to Islamabad, which finally resulted in Bhutto's cancellation of the deal, was received enthusiastically in New Delhi. When it became known, however, that an apparent part of the tradeoff for the Pakistan cancellation was the sale of about 110 A-7 bombers by the United States to Pakistan, India was upset anew. All of the old Indian accusations about U.S. policy threatening stability and the normalization process in South Asia once again captured front-page headlines in the Indian press. Washington's continuing effort to develop Diego Garcia into a major military base also continued to provide a significant irritant to better relations—an irritant the Soviets did not hesitate to exploit.[74]

On the regional level, the major question marks for Indian and Soviet policy, beyond Pakistan and Bangladesh, were Afghanistan and Iran. Since Mohammed Daud had come to power in 1973 the question of the border between Afghanistan and Pakistan had become a contentious issue and the conflicting claims of Baluchi self-determination and of "Pakhtoonistan" rose to the fore. Many suspected Moscow's hand behind Kabul's revival of this old issue, but the Soviets seemed to be interested in stabilizing the situation. That had been their message to Bhutto when he was in Moscow in October 1974 and to the Afghan leaders during Podgorny's visit there in December 1975. Both Bhutto and Mrs. Gandhi visited Kabul in mid-1976, and it seemed that tension was considerably reduced. However, even after a return visit to Pakistan by Daud, it was evident that considerable friction existed on that fringe of the subcontinent. Morevoer, acting both in its own interests and on behalf of Washington, Iran still sought a major regional role. Thus, while old areas of instability seemed to be quieting down—such as India-Pakistan, India-China, Bangladesh-Pakistan, and Bangladesh-China—new ones were emerging—India-Bangladesh, Afghanistan-Pakistan, and Iranian ambitions. In addition, both Moscow and New Delhi had to ponder the future roles of Peking and Washington.

On January 19, Mrs. Gandhi announced that there would, in fact, be elections to the Lok Sabha in March. The repercussions of this unexpected announcement dominated India's next three months. New initiatives were not taken in foreign policy. At most, New Delhi sought to maintain continuity in its external relations, especially in its improving ties with neighboring countries.

By this time, the Soviet attitude toward Mrs. Gandhi's state of emergency had become somewhat more mixed. Although public support had continued, there were other hints of Soviet dissatisfaction. The meteoric rise of the prime minister's son, Sanjay Gandhi, was not greeted enthusiastically by the Soviets. He was openly contemptuous of the Communist Party and seen to be indifferent to socialism. Such traits marked him as a very different character from his mother with whom the Soviets indeed had comfortable relations of mutual understanding. To the CPI and undoubtedly to many in Moscow, Sanjay represented the reactionary right wing of the Congress. Mrs. Gandhi's own bitter denunciation of the CPI in late 1976 and various other programs favoring the private sector and "big business" in India certainly added to the consternation within the CPI and the CPSU.

When it came to the election campaign itself, however, the Soviets quickly decided to continue to support Mrs. Gandhi and the Congress. The main issues in the campaign revolved around domestic issues, mainly the state of emergency. The Soviets recognized that certain failures of Congress policy, such as in the "Down with Poverty" promise, tended to "complicate the position of the Congress Party and make its election campaign more difficult than in 1971." Nevertheless, the Soviets perceived the opposition, united under the label of Janata, as "zealous champions of the interests of the big landowners, usurers and local and foreign monopolists...." Their "true intentions... run counter to the vital interests of the people." Moscow was quick to denounce any thought of working against the INC. No matter how difficult, the CPI and other progressives had to view their main tasks as "warding off the Rightist threat... and to rebuff the power-seeking reaction."[75]

Even more significantly, Moscow was sensitive to the divergence in foreign policy perspectives between the Congress and the Janata. Although there was a broad consensus in foreign policy as expressed in the parties' election manifestoes, and although foreign policy was not a major issue in the campaign, there were two important areas of difference between the Congress and the Janata.[76] One regarded relations with neighboring countries and the degree of threat that came from those states. The other, though somewhat vague, was more central. While both parties pledged support for the policy of nonalignment, the Janata qualified its stance by calling for "genuine" and "honest" nonalignment. It criticized the Congress for deviating from true nonalignment by leaning too heavily on the Soviet Union, as seen in the 1971 treaty. The Janata leader, Morarji Desai, told one questioner that the treaty would "automatically go" if his party came to power. Mrs. Gandhi rejected the Janata charges explaining that "India does not seek any exclusive relationship, nor does it think that its relations with any one country should affect or be at the cost of its bilateral relations with other countries."[77]

This period of the state of emergency had not been nearly so conducive to Soviet influence as Moscow must have hoped. India had been somewhat stabilized and Indo-Soviet relations had remained strong. Yet, political differences between the two remained, new economic ties were developing only slowly, and the new "era" in military cooperation had not come about. Moreover, Mrs. Gandhi had used her power in the state of emergency to improve relations with China, which was the one development Moscow feared most. Yet, Mrs. Gandhi and the Congress were highly preferable to the other option emerging in Indian politics. The Congress was given high marks for its "fidelity to the policy of nonalignment," while the Janata was a group of "enemies of the peace-loving, anti-imperialist policy of India, of her friendship and cooperation with the socialist states...."[78]

The Soviets turned out to have understated the "complicated" and "difficult" nature of the election for Prime Minister Gandhi and her Congress Party. Indeed, few predicted accurately the outcome of the election. Nevertheless, this exercise in democracy, as with the one that just preceded it in neighboring Pakistan, was to have a profound impact on India, although an impact perhaps not quite so profound as the instability and eventual military takeover in Pakistan. Yet, it was an election with far-reaching significance for India domestically and in its foreign policy, especially in relations with the Soviet Union. The question of the nature of the Soviet-Indian influence relationship was about to be tested with a substantially different leadership at the helm in New Delhi.

NOTES

1. Cited in Norman H. Palmer, "India in 1975: Democracy in Eclipse," *Asian Survey*, February 1976, p. 100.
2. Immediate scholarly attempts to analyze the reasons for the state of emergency led to a symposium on the emergency in India at California State University, Northridge, which produced Ram M. Roy, ed., *Indian Democracy in Crisis* (Northridge: California State University Foundation, 1976); and the Fourth Wisconsin Conference on South Asia led

to another excellent collection of analyses in Henry C. Hart, ed., *Indira Gandhi's India: A Political System Reappraised* (Boulder, Colo.: Westview Press, 1976.)
3. See *The Times* (London), July 13, 1975; and also *Statesman*, June 29, 1975.
4. *Times of India*, July 13, 1975; cited in S.D. Muni, "Major Developments in India's Foreign Policy and Relations, July-December 1975," *International Studies* (New Delhi), July-September 1976, p. 404.
5. *Pravda*, August 15, 1975. See also V. Shurygin, "India: A Time of Important Decisions," *International Affairs*, no. 11, November 1975, pp. 55–62; and P. Mezentsev, "Normalization in South Asia and its Opponents," *New Times*, no. 29, July 1975, pp. 12-13.
6. Mezentsev, "Normalization in South Asia," pp. 12-13.
7. See Bhabani Sen Gupta, *Communism in Indian Politics* (New York: Columbia University Press, 1972); and William J. Barnds, "Soviet Influence in India: A Search for the Spoils that Go with Victory," in Alvin Z. Rubinstein, ed., *Soviet and Chinese Influence in the Third World* (New York: Praeger, 1975), pp. 32–36.
8. Robert H. Donaldson, *The Soviet-Indian Alignment: Quest for Influence* (Denver: University of Denver Monograph Series in World Affairs, 1979), pp. 18–19.
9. On the relationship with the Congress, see Ouseph Varkey, "The CPI–Congress Alliance in India," *Asian Survey*, September 1979, pp. 881–95. On the CPI's situation vis-à-vis the CPI (Marxist), which had split from the CPI in 1964, see Bhabani Sen Gupta, "Indian Politics and the Communist Party (Marxist)," *Problems of Communism*, September-October 1978, pp. 1–19.
10. See *Far Eastern Economic Review* (hereafter cited as *FEER*), October 10, 1975, pp. 5, 24.
11. *Times of India*, December 31, 1975; cited in Muni, "India's Foreign Policy," p. 402. Swaran had been replaced as defense minister on November 30.
12. For example, see Lawrence Lifschultz, "The Crisis Has Not Passed," *FEER*, December 5, 1975, pp. 25–34; and *FEER*, December 12, 1975, p. 5.
13. *NCNA*, June 30, 1975; cited in *China Quarterly*, September 1975, p. 592.
14. See *FEER*, October 31, 1975, p. 5.
15. *China Quarterly*, March 1976, pp. 183–84. See also Nancy Jetly, *India-China Relations, 1947-1977* (Atlantic Highlands, N.J.: Humanities Press, 1979), p. 288.
16. *Statesman*, November 30, 1975.
17. *New Times*, no. 49, December 1975, pp. 8–9.
18. Y. Gotlober and Y. Shtykanov, "Peking Provocations against India," *New Times*, no. 46, November 1975, pp. 12–13.
19. See Pushpesh Pant, "Major Developments in India's Foreign Policy and Relations, January-June 1976," *International Studies*, January-March 1977, pp. 51–52.
20. *Hindu*, April 7, 1976. See also *Hindustan Times*, May 15, 1976.
21. *Indian Express*, September 11, 1976.
22. See Shirin Tahir-Kheli, "Chinese Objectives in South Asia: 'Anti-Hegemony' vs. 'Collective Security,'" *Asian Survey*, October 1978, p. 1005.
23. *Times of India*, January 17, 1976.
24. The text of Brezhnev's lengthy address is found in *Pravda*, February 24, 1976. For its unprecedented nature, compare it to Brezhnev's remarks on India at the Twenty-fourth Congress in 1971 (*Pravda*, March 31, 1971) and the Twenty-third in 1966 (*Pravda*, March 29, 1966).
25. For example, see Victor Sidenko, "From the Indian Point of View," *New Times*, no. 11, March 1976, pp. 6–7.
26. See Miles Hanley, "India Takes the Lead in Moscow," *FEER*, March 19, 1976, pp. 22–23.
27. *Statesman*, March 4, 1976.
28. *Times* (London), March 15, 1976.
29. See *FEER*, May 7, 1976, p. 39.

30. The question of terms is a difficult one to clarify. Previous research by this author indicated that, in the case of Soviet arms aid to Indonesia, the Russians charged far less than world market prices; see Robert C. Horn, "Soviet-Indonesian Relations Since 1965," *Survey*, Winter 1971, pp. 216–32; and "The USSR and Southeast Asia: The Limits of Influence," in Roger E. Kanet and Donna Bahry, eds., *Soviet Economic and Political Relations with the Developing World* (New York: Praeger, 1975). Some sources (e.g., *FEER*, October 18, 1974, p. 30) assert that the Soviets have charged India a higher price than the "going world market rate." On the other hand, repayment terms (10 percent down and the remainder at 2 percent over nine or ten years, according to Donaldson, *Soviet-Indian Alignment* (p. 10), and the fact that this repayment could be paid through Indian exports rather than by scarce foreign exchange have presumably combined with availability to make the Soviet offer for military aid attractive to India. Other sources (e.g., *FEER*, May 7, 1976, p. 39) emphasize that India is "getting the best bargain out of the Soviets" and the Indian negotiators have been "shrewd bargainers."
31. For example, see V. Sidenko, "Strong as the Steel of Bokaro," *New Times*, no. 23, June 1976, pp. 8–9.
32. *Statesman*, April 12, 14, and 16, 1976.
33. *New Times*, no. 23, June 1976, p. 9.
34. See Annexure II in V.B. Singh, ed., *Indo-Soviet Relations, 1947–77* (New Delhi: Sterling Publishers, 1978); and *India: A Reference Annual 1977–78* (New Delhi: Ministry of Information and Broadcasting, 1978) pp. 327, 329.
35. For example, see Asha L. Datar, *India's Economic Relations with the USSR and Eastern Europe, 1953–1969* (Cambridge: Cambridge University Press, 1972); the Reserve Bank of India report, cited in *FEER*, April 22, 1974, pp. 42–43; and *Hindu*, June 23, 1969.
36. R.K. Sharma, ed., *The Economics of Indo-Soviet Trade* (New Delhi: Allied Publishers, 1979); World Bank Study, cited in *FEER*, April 22, 1974, p. 45; and Deepak Nayyar, ed., *Economic Relations Between Socialist Countries and the Third World* (Monclair, N.J.: Allanheld, Osmun, 1977), especially the chapters by Nayyar and Chaudhuri.
37. Donaldson, *Soviet-Indian Alignment*, p. 11.
38. From the title of a report on the visit in *FEER*, June 25, 1976, p. 14.
39. *Morning News*, May 26, 1976. Emphasis added.
40. *Morning News*, May 29, 1976. Emphasis added.
41. Salamat Ali, "Bhutto's Winning Ways," *FEER*, June 11, 1976, p. 33.
42. *Morning News*, May 29, 1976.
43. For the text, see *Peking Review*, no. 23, June 4, 1976, pp. 7–8.
44. See David Bonavia, "The Kashmir Test of Friendship," *FEER*, June 11, 1976, pp. 33–34; *China Quarterly*, September 1976, pp. 683–84; and *Peking Review*, June 4, p. 5.
45. Editorial, "A Valuable Asset," *New Times*, no. 25, June 1976, p. 1.
46. The text is in *Statesman*, June 14, 1976.
47. *Statesman*, June 10, 1976. See also June 9.
48. *Statesman*, June 12, 1976.
49. *New York Times*, June 9, 1976.
50. *Statesman*, June 10, 1976.
51. *Statesman*, June 9, 1976. Emphasis added.
52. *New York Times*, June 12, 1976.
53. See I. Kovalenko, *The Soviet Union Struggles for Peace and Collective Security in Asia* (Moscow: Nauka Publishers, 1976).
54. *Statesman*, June 1, 1976.
55. Ibid.
56. *Statesman*, June 10, 1976.
57. *Statesman*, June 14, 1976.
58. *FEER*, June 25, 1976, p. 14.

59. *Statesman,* June 12, 1976.
60. Victor Sidenko, "Soviet-Indian Treaty: Five Years," *New Times,* no. 32, August 1976, pp. 6–8.
61. See *Statesman,* August 18, 1976. See also *FEER,* August 20, 1976, p. 14; August 27, 1976, p. 14.
62. See *FEER,* September 3, 1976, pp. 12–13.
63. See the discussion and tables in Donaldson, *Soviet-Indian Alignment,* pp. 30, 32–34.
64. The data are drawn from Donald F. Keys, *The 31st General Assembly of the United Nations* (New York: The Institute for World Order, 1977),pp. 50–54.
65. *New Times,* no. 32, August 1976, p. 8.
66. See *Statesman,* December 21 and 29, 1976.
67. See the excellent article by Paul F. Power, "The Indo-American Nuclear Controversy," *Asian Survey,* June 1979, pp. 574–96.
68. Donaldson, *Soviet-Indian Alignment,* p. 57. He is drawing upon the analysis by Gloria Duffy, "Soviet Nuclear Experts," *International Security,* vol. 3, no. 1, 1978.
69. See Robert C. Horn, "China and Russia in 1977: Maoism without Mao," *Asian Survey,* October 1977, pp. 919–30.
70. For analysis and reports of the visit, see S. Kamaluddin, "Zia Walks the Water-front," *FEER,* January 21, 1977, pp. 20–22; David Majlis, "Dacca Plays the Peking Card," ibid., p. 22; and *New York Times,* January 3, 1977.
71. *Peking Review,* no. 2, January 7, 1977, p. 18.
72. *FEER,* January 21, 1977, p. 22.
73. *Hindu,* December 2, 1976. See also Abdul Q. Zia, "Revising U.S. Strategy Towards the Indian Subcontinent," *Asian Profile,* June 1978, pp. 269–79.
74. See A. Segeyev, "Political Realities and Security in Asia," *International Affairs,* no. 6, June 1976, p. 47; and A. Chernyshov, "Peace and Security for the Indian Ocean," *International Affairs,* no. 12, December 1976, pp. 42–50.
75. Pavel Victorov, "Pre-Election Scene," *New Times,* no. 10, March 1977, pp. 13–15. See also Mohan Ram "Congress Crumbs for the Communist Party," *FEER,* February 11, 1977, pp. 26–27.
76. The discussion that follows is based primarily on S.D. Muni, "Major Developments in India's Foreign Policy and Relations, January-June 1977," *International Studies,* January-March 1978, pp. 82–84.
77. *Indian Express,* January 21 and February 11, 1977.
78. See V. Tretyakov, "The Election Manifestoes," *New Times,* no. 11, March 1977, p. 5; and Victorov, "Pre-Election Scene," p. 13.

6

THE JANATA INTERREGNUM

The outcome of the March 1977 election was a shock to many, participants and observers alike. Mrs. Gandhi's Congress lost over 200 seats in the Lok Sabha, dropping from 363 to 153, while the Janata Party, which was an electoral front hastily put together just prior to the election, totalled 295 seats. For the first time in India's independent history, the Indian National Congress would not be forming the government. This would be the responsibility of the Janata; its task was made particularly difficult by the ideological and political diversity of the groups that comprised it. From this confusion, two of India's elder statesmen selected 81-year-old Morarji Desai to be India's fourth prime minister. Desai, from whom Mrs. Gandhi had split in 1969, had spent 19 months in jail during the state of emergency and promised an end to "tyranny" and a return to democracy in India.[1]

The election was fought and decided almost exclusively on domestic issues. Nevertheless, foreign policy also appeared likely to undergo some change under this new administration. As pointed out above, during the campaign the Janata had promised to return the country's foreign policy to one of "genuine" or "proper" nonalignment. The Indo-Soviet treaty was a prime focus of attention in this context and, although the new leaders backed off from campaign intimations that it would be scrapped, Desai did state in his first press conference that if the treaty "involved any want of friendship with others, it would have to be changed." Indo-Soviet friendship, he said, "must not come in the way of our friendship with any other state."[2] In debate in the Lok Sabha in June, new External Affairs Minister Atal Bihari Vajpayee, former leader of the often virulently anti-Soviet Jan Sangh, stated that:

One can very well ask why the Janata Party is so emphatic about nonalignment. My humble submission is that India should not only remain non-aligned but must also appear to be so. If anything that we say or do gives rise to the feeling that we have leaned towards a particular bloc and have surrendered our sovereign right of judging issues on their merits, it will be a deviation from the straight but difficult path of nonalignment. The Janata government would never allow this to happen.[3]

The implication that Mrs. Gandhi's government had leaned too heavily toward the Soviet Union and had thus compromised India's independence was clear.

The setting at the beginning of this period, then, provides an excellent background in which to evaluate the nature of the Soviet-Indian influence relationship. A whole series of questions can be examined: What was the impact of the political change in New Delhi on Indo-Soviet relations? Was either side's influence enhanced or decreased? What was the impact of personality on world politics? That is, how significant a role did Indira Gandhi play in relations between Moscow and New Delhi? How much did Indian foreign policy actually change? Finally, do the developments in this period give us any further insights into the *long-term* nature of this influence relationship?

MOSCOW'S INITIAL RESPONSES

The Kremlin's concern with this unexpected turn of events was substantial. The Soviet media had vilified Desai for more than a decade as reactionary and had continued this characterization right up until the election. The Soviets were well aware that Desai had favored outright condemnation of the Soviet Union after the invasion of Czechoslovakia in 1968 and had criticized the 1971 Indo-Soviet treaty at that time and since.[4] Moscow may well have feared a repetition of the events in Egypt that had resulted in Cairo's abrogation of its treaty with Moscow in 1976. Domestically, the Soviets had been, for the most part, enthusiastic supporters of the state of emergency, seeing Indira Gandhi as the leader of India's progressive forces that were committed to strengthening the public sector and opposing imperialism. Moreover, they were skeptical of the Janata's "right-wing" approach to economic and social issues within India.

The Soviets lost little time after the election in seeking to shore up their position in India. Soviet media abruptly halted criticism of the Janata with its victory. Without going into detail, *Izvestia's* postelection analysis attributed Mrs. Gandhi's defeat to "mistakes and exceeses" during the state of emergency. Other Soviet commentators quickly emphasized that foreign policy had not loomed very large in the election "because on this score there is general accord in the country."[5] Statements by Janata leaders such as Vajpayee that the new government would observe all the commitments undertaken by its predecessor were prominently displayed by the Soviet media. Before the end of March, the Soviet ambassador in New Delhi met with Vajpayee, and the Indian news agency, Samachar, reported that the meeting had confirmed the desire of *both* governments to strengthen relations of friendship and cooperation. The Soviets missed no opportunity to reiterate to New Delhi's new leaders their contention that "the continued promotion of the two countries' traditional friendship and cooperation accord with their long-term interests as well as with the interests of peace and security in Asia and elsewhere." Moscow's anxieties about the Janata's appreciation of this argument were only thinly concealed.

The Soviet Union's major step in its effort to mend relations with the new Indian regime came with the visit to New Delhi of Foreign Minister Andrei Gromyko. Gromyko arrived barely one month after the Janata's electoral triumph. In what was mainly a "damage-limiting" visit aimed at deemphasizing any negative reverberations of the USSR's partisan support for Mrs. Gandhi, Gromyko also sought to ensure the continuation of the development of Soviet-Indian relations. Upon his arrival at New Delhi's airport, the Soviet foreign minister immediately offset criticism of India's "Soviet connection" by asserting that the Soviet Union's friendship was never aimed against a third country: "It has never been our policy, it will never be," he added, reportedly "with much emphasis."[6] Gromyko proceeded to defend the Indo-Soviet treaty, saying it was in the interests of world peace and that "it was his hope that the Indian leaders would take a similar view of it." He repeatedly emphasized that the friendship between the two countries was long-standing and was not the product of "transient or momentary circumstances." The Soviet Union intended to promote this friendship and "fruitful" cooperation "steadfastly" and "hoped the Indian side would strive towards this as well." When Vajpayee responded positively to many of these sentiments at the airport welcoming ceremony, the meeting seemed for the Soviets to be headed in the right direction.

Indeed, the visit exhibited many indications that Soviet-Indian relations were continuing very much unchanged. Foreign Minister Vajpayee spoke enthusiastically about Soviet friendship at a luncheon he gave for Gromyko. Significantly, he also "set at rest all speculation about the Janata Government's attitude to India's ties to the Soviet Union," in the words of the *Statesman*, "when he said that *the bonds of friendship between the two countries were strong enough to survive the demands of divergent systems, the fate of an individual or the fortunes of a political party.*"[7] Vajpayee could not have provided a much more explicit reassurance to the Soviets, and Gromyko's sigh of relief must have been almost audible in the banquet hall. He responded to this by putting greater emphasis on the need to strengthen—i.e., not just maintain—Soviet-Indian ties and "raise them to a new level." The joint communiqué signed at the conclusion of the visit revealed the continuation of substantial areas of agreement on international issues.[8] The two sides agreed to further strengthen their "time-tested" friendship and cooperation "on the basis of the Soviet-Indian treaty...." Before he left, Gromyko and his delegation also signed several agreements with the Indian leaders. One was a trade agreement for 1977 that envisioned a substantial increase in trade turnover. The most important accord was the extension of a new 20-year credit of about $300–340 million. This substantial loan was on very favorable terms—repayable in 20 years, after a grace period of 3 years, and with an interest rate of only 2.5 percent annually—and was to be for the import of equipment for India's steel plants, coal mines, and other industries.

Nevertheless, there were several signs that relations were not precisely as close as they had been. One indication of this was in the tone of the joint communiqué. Although it referred to the atmostphere of the talks as being one of "cordiality and mutual understanding," it lacked the repeated expressions of Soviet-Indian friendship and cooperation seen in previous documents. The effusiveness present in the joint delegation from Mrs. Gandhi's visit less than one year earlier was lacking; the "cordiality" in Gromyko's visit was depicted in the far stronger terms of "trust" and "friendship" in Mrs. Gandhi's talks. Finally, whereas the two countries had seen the 1976 visit as a "new major contribution" to *friendship* and cooperation, they only saw the 1977 one as a "major contribution to mutual understanding and cooperation"; friendship implies a much closer relationship than does mutual understanding.

On balance, the Gromyko visit revealed that the Indo-Soviet relationship was now neither quite as warm as the Soviets asserted nor as cool as much Western commentary contended.[9] Two indications of the Soviets' willingness to adapt to the change in New Delhi and to seek to maintain Indo-Soviet friendship are that Moscow offered a new line of credit to New Delhi when large amounts of previous loans had not yet been drawn upon and on the *most favorable* terms the Soviet Union had ever offered India. In this sense, it serves as an example of Indian influence over Soviet behavior. The repeated emphasis on the close Indo-Soviet relationship by both Gromyko and the Soviet media thus should be read as expressing Moscow's *hopes*, rather than convictions, for the relationship.

For their part, what Desai and Vajpayee sought to do was to reassure the Soviets on the solidity of the Indo-Soviet relationship while making clear their intention to strengthen ties with the West at the same time. To

India's new leaders, this seemed not only reasonable but also feasible, but the Kremlin tended to think that any gain in India's ties with the United States and other Western states necessarily meant a diminution of India's ties with the Soviet Union. Hence, while assuring his hosts that the Indo-Soviet relationship was in no way directed against any other state, Gromyko missed no opportunity to warn that there can be no "weeds... on the soil of Soviet-Indian cooperation."[10]

It is undoubtedly on this issue of India's relations with other states that the two sides had some of the "frank exchanges" that Vajpayee referred to at the end of the visit. Yet, India needed the Soviet Union, and Vajpayee saw value in the meeting in "removing misunderstanding."[11] New Delhi's new leaders seemed to be shedding their "prejudices" and moving to a more accurate appreciation of the realities underlying the Indo-Soviet relationship. Given the tone and substance of Gromyko's visit and its agreements and final communiqué, it would appear that Moscow made more "adjustments" than did New Delhi. Thus it would seem that at this point, while each needed the other, Moscow's need for India was perhaps greater than India's for the Soviet Union.

Foreign Minister Vajpayee's testimony during Gromyko's visit that Indo-Soviet relations could withstand changes in "the fate of an individual or the fortunes of a political party" had greatly comforted Moscow. In this sense, Gromyko's trip had been a success. Yet, Soviet nervousness about India's reliability continued. In the economic realm, Soviet efforts to strengthen ties were substantial and New Delhi seemed highly interested. By the middle of the year, New Delhi had reversed its earlier stand of not wanting any further Soviet assistance in the steel industry. Moreover, the two countries signed an agreement for Soviet aid in an additional steel mill (at Visakhapatnam on India's east coast). Meanwhile, Indo-Soviet trade grew, boosted especially by Moscow's crude oil sales, to the point where India was the Soviet Union's primary trade partner among developing countries for 1977. The Indo-Soviet Joint Commission was upgraded to a higher level of representation: India would not be represented by its external affairs minister and the Soviet Union by a deputy prime minister.

Moscow also moved quickly to strengthen military ties with New Delhi. Shortly after the election, the Soviet defense minister told his new Indian counterpart, Jagjivan Ram, that he looked forward to "developing further" the military cooperation between the two countries.[12] Moscow's concern in this important area seemed justified. The rather steady talk in New Delhi that it was time for India to stop depending solely on the Soviet Union had accelerated after the Janata's victory, and there were increasing complaints regarding Soviet control of blueprints for advanced versions of weapons as well as Moscow's denial of sales to third countries of arms manufactured under Soviet license. The Egyptian experience of the USSR cutoff even of spare parts for MiGs after their quarrel was also unsettling to the Indians. In any case, shortly after Gromyko's departure, Soviet army chief Pavlovskiy arrived in India and, in July, Indian naval head Cursteji journeyed to Moscow. Although information on these visits is virtually nonexistent, it is known that sometime during 1977 the two countries concluded a number of significant, although not major, arms deals.[13] These agreements were likely concluded or at least furthered during these visits. One of the agreements was for India to purchase 70 T-72 medium tanks for the army. For the navy, the Soviets agreed to sell India two "Kashin" class destroyers, five Ka-25 helicopters, and two Il-38 maritime reconnaissance aircraft. This marked a significant continuation of the naval-weapons relationship and an important step forward with the army, which produced most of its own equipment indigenously, but was now shopping for new battle tanks to replace its British-based "Vijayanta" tanks. (The Indian army also had over 900 Soviet-supplied T-54 and T-55 tanks, among others.)

Perhaps the most critical service in India at this point was the air force. After a raging debate in military and political circles, the government, in mid-1977, chose a French air combat missile for the air force rather than a Soviet system, which the Soviets had tried to sell Mrs. Gandhi's regime as well as Desai's. Even more importantly, there was a growing debate in the air force over where to buy new aircraft; the "pro-Soviet" faction was actively pushing for an advanced version of the MiG, while the "anti-Soviet" group, arguing the need for options and that Moscow's deliveries of spare parts were slow, was seeking a deal for the Anglo-French Jaguar. Moscow was soon to join in this battle in a major way, and in 1978 the aircraft decision was to become a crucial test of the Janata regime's foreign policy outlook.

India's relation with China was clearly one of the areas of Moscow's greatest concern. By the end of April, the Soviets had lost their patience with the post-Mao leadership, and anti-Chinese polemics became the norm again in Sino-Soviet relations. At the same time, however, the Janata government was taking new initiatives to improve Sino-Indian ties. A representative was sent to the Canton Trade Fair in May and the modest deal he signed there marked the resumption of trade between India and China after a break of 15 years. Further Indian gestures to improve ties followed, such as allowing Indian ships to call at Chinese ports and the sending of an Indian journalist to China. Of some comfort to Moscow in all of this was India's frequently repeated insistence that real improvement in relations depended on China taking some intiative and China's lack of substantial response. Although Peking had been quick to celebrate the fall of the "fascist" government of Mrs. Gandhi, the maintenance of the Indo-Soviet treaty was discouraging to the Chinese leaders. Moreover, they showed no signs of being willing to negotiate the border question. In short, both New Delhi and Peking seemed to be waiting for the other to make the move. In an interview in late September, Vajpayee implicitly addressed both Moscow and Peking on this issue. When he was asked if "India's friendship with the Soviet Union will come in the way of improving relations with China," he responded that the new leaders do "not feel that the process of normalization between India and China should be at the cost of India's friendship with any other country." Having thus reassured the Soviets and warned the Chinese, he reached out to China while admonishing the Soviets: "India's existing good relations with any country need not be an obstacle to the promotion of better relations with China."[14]

While the Soviets could thus derive some reassurance from the obvious fact that it was going to take a long time and considerable understanding to remove the mutual suspicions between India and China, the obstacles to a substantial improvement in Indo-United States relations did not appear so formidable. The general climate of relations with the United States, and with the West in general, greatly improved with the Janata's assumption of office. U.S. opposition to the state of emergency was remembered in India and Carter's concern for human rights was applauded. The Carter administration hailed the Janata victory as a "reassertion of democracy" and, in July, sent Deputy Secretary of State Warren Christopher to India for talks on bilateral and international questions. In this and subsequent exchanges, the Indian response was one of warmth and cordiality. The upward trend in Indo-United States relations seemed to be on the scale of the early Kennedy years, the period of the warmest relationship. The announcement that Carter would visit India before the end of the year pointed to the likely further improvement of relations.

It was in the context of these developments that the Soviets welcomed the new prime minister, Morarji Desai, to Moscow October 21–26, 1977. It was obvious that the Soviets attached a good deal of significance to this summit, as Brezhnev again broke protocol and was on hand to greet Desai, Vajpayee, and the Indian party at the airport. Most of the top Soviet leadership was present on that occasion and at subsequent functions including the ceremony for the signing of the joint declaration. *Pravda* featured front-page stories and photographs on the visit and other Soviet media followed this lead. It was clear that New Delhi also attached particular importance to the meeting: before departure, Vajpayee said that visit had "a special significance" for a relationship that was "unique in many respects."[15] Moreover, Desai had chosen to visit the Soviet Union before going to the United States or meeting with top U.S. leaders, despite Washington's invitations to him.

The Soviet leaders thus greeted Desai with an air of cautious optimism. This was revealed by Brezhnev in his address at the banquet in Desai's honor when, after telling his guest that "the Soviet Union will continue to do everything in its power so that friendship with India will develop in all areas," he went on to say: "*If this is the line followed by the Indian leadership—and we believe it is—then Soviet-Indian relations have a good future.*"[16] Although Desai included in his response a lengthy explanation of India's "revolution through secret ballot," which had removed a leader who had taken "the people for granted," this was his only reference to internal conditions in India. (Indeed, the *Statesman* on October 26 even cited as a "highlight" of the meeting the "absence of any reference ... to developments within India.") Rather, Desai's emphasis was on the permanence of Indo-Soviet friendship, India's *gratitude* for the Soviets' "constant support on questions of vital importance to India," India's attitude of "trust and cooperation" toward the Soviet Union, and Moscow's assistance which had "helped India to advance along the path of achieving economic independence...." For all of these reasons, he said, we have a mutual desire to strengthen relations, and "we can state that the basis of our relations is not personalities or ideologies but equality, national interests and lofty common goals." Desai's reiteration that Indo-Soviet relations need not be diminished by Mrs. Gandhi's departure from office combined with Vajpayee's reference to the "unique" character of that relationship was greatly heartening to the Soviet leaders.

A close examination of the text of the Soviet-Indian joint communiqué and declaration reveals the status of the bilateral relationship.[17] It contains evidence both of continuity with and change from the Gandhi period; it even illustrates certain changes just since Gromyko's trip in April. An example of the first was the continuing absence of any mention of Moscow's Asian collective security idea, even though Brezhnev had brought this up implicitly on more than one occasion. The declaration even goes one step backward from the document signed with Gromyko in April, when, in listing principles on which peace in Asia should rest, it pointedly added "the right of every people to choose its own political and social system." Given the recent change of regime in New Delhi this sounds very much like a Soviet gesture to the Janata; indeed, Brezhnev had emphasized in other speeches the theme of "non-interference in each other's internal affairs" and the Soviets were anxious to reassure New Delhi that Moscow's previous support for Mrs. Gandhi in no way meant that they could not cooperate with the Janata regime. Broad continuity was also the case on the issue of the Indian Ocean, although statements by Desai and others indicated a growing divergence: the Janata was more explicit than Mrs. Gandhi had been in bringing the Soviet Union together with the United States as great powers that were causing tension and insecurity in the area.[18] (The reference in the joint declaration to an "exchange of opinions" on this issue may further indicate that this difference was becoming more sharply defined.)

The Desai declaration continued in several instances the trend that the Gromyko one began deviating from the previous pattern (as seen, for example, in the Gandhi declaration of mid-1976). There was, of course, an absence of reference to the internal situation in India. (Indeed, the "reactionaries" censured in 1976 were now in power!) Missing also was the exchange of abundant political compliments as seen in 1976. The tone therefore, was not nearly as warm as it had been in pre-Janata days. The atmosphere of the talks—"friendship, cordiality and mutual understanding"—was much closer to Gromyko's declaration than Gandhi's. The most revealing absence in the two 1977 declarations was reference to an atmosphere of *trust* between the two; trust had been a prominent aspect of the relationship under Mrs. Gandhi and it was no longer present. Finally, there is the continuing difference in the treatment of the 1971 treaty. Mrs. Gandhi had avoided going quite so far as the Soviet leaders in praise of the treaty. However, by the time of Brezhnev's 1973 visit and in her own 1976 trip to the Soviet Union, she had found acceptable a formulation that referred to Indo-Soviet relations being strengthened *on the basis* of the treaty, which was described as an "important factor of strengthening peace and stability in Asia and throughout the world." With Gromyko's communiqué being transitional, by the time of Desai's visit "on the basis" had been reduced to "in the spirit" and the reference to its impact on Asia, with its implications for the Asian collective security scheme, was dropped entirely. This was a very subtle yet significant diminution by India of the treaty's role.

Interestingly, the joint declaration signed with Desai seems to differ from the one signed by Gromyko only seven months earlier. For one, it is almost two times as long as the Gromyko one. Its sections on bilateral relations are longer. Perhaps most revealing, Indo-Soviet "friendship" was cited in three crucial places where it had not been in April (but had been in June 1976). This represents the improvement in Soviet-Indian relations since Gromyko's mission. The *Statesman*, in its editorial of October 21, perhaps pointed out the crux of the meeting when it said "relations between Moscow and New Delhi have so developed over the last three decades that neither can afford to expose the resultant inter-dependence to risks of impairment." Desai's visit seems certainly to have avoided any impairment to relations. While the results of the visit were mixed and relations were in several respects not as close as pre-Janata, in several other areas relations seemed to have made a significant advance since March-April.

THE UNITED STATES' AND CHINESE "CHALLENGES"

The areas that Moscow continued to scrutinize very carefully were New Delhi's relations with Washington and Peking. There was no doubt that the climate of Indo-United States relations was growing warmer. The initial step symbolizing and consolidating this improving relationship came with President Carter's arrival in India on January 1, 1978. Receiving a reception that India reserved for its most favored dignitaries—Brezhnev had been accorded it in 1973 and Vietnam's Pham van Dong was to receive it in February—Carter was greeted by large and friendly crowds at the airport and lining his route into the city and was invited to address a public rally as well as a session of Parliament. The two primary areas of focus of the talks and the public speeches were the two countries' shared belief in democratic values and human freedom and the prospects for increased bilateral cooperation. The joint declaration signed at the end of the brief visit was almost entirely devoted to an expression of the fundamental principles of equality, freedom, peace, and cooperation that should govern the conduct of relations between states—that is, the "spiritual, moral and democratic values which both President Carter and Mr. Desai so value and have stressed throughout their public and private conversations over the past three days...."[19] The Indo-United States Joint Commission met and took a number of steps to intensify cooperation in a variety of fields, and plans were laid for growth in trade between the two. (The United States was still India's principal trading partner, receiving about 13 percent of India's exports and supplying more than 25 percent of its imports.)[20]

To be sure, there were differences. Their outlooks on a number of international issues, particularly the Middle East, diverged. On the question of the Indian Ocean, Desai did urge *both* the United States and the Soviet Union to avoid a rivalry there, but he also indicated that with the denial of Somalia's Berbera base to the Soviets, India believed the major threat to peace in the region lay with the U.S. buildup of Diego Garcia as a naval base. The most important item of contention was that concerning New Delhi's nuclear intentions and escalating U.S. demands that India submit to complete safeguards in return for continued U.S. shipments of low-enriched uranium (LEU) fuel for its Tarapur plant. Desai had publicly pledged that India would not conduct another nuclear test, but he refused to sign the NPT or to agree to partial safeguards, which would represent a de facto signing of that treaty. Washington, perhaps looking ahead to a time when Desai was no longer prime minister, put little faith in such personal pledges and sought a greater commitment from India. The most difficult moment of Carter's visit came when a reporter's microphone picked up Carter briefing Vance on Desai's adamancy on the nuclear issue and then remarking: "When we get back I think we should write him another letter, just cold and very blunt." Carter's embarrassment over this may have been the reason that he departed from his original text in his address to the members of Parliament. Going beyond his original "hope that it would be possible for India and the U.S. to cooperate in the energy field," Carter announced that he had cleared another LEU shipment, of 7.6 tons, *and* that the United States would make available heavy water, which India badly needed (and which the Soviets were also offering).[21] Nevertheless, there was nothing to indicate that this issue had been resolved for the long run; indeed, by April, Vajpayee was in New York complaining that the process of Indo-United States normalization had received a setback due to the inordinate delay in the shipment of the promised fuel.

Indian reactions to Carter's visit were largely favorable. The *Statesman* editorialized on January 4 that "the mutual expressions of good will were sincerely meant" and that:

> ...the visit ranked at least with two previous historic visits since independence: those of Khrushchev and Bulganin and of Chou En-lai, the first leading to a long and cordial international relationship, the second less fortunate in its ultimate consequences. There seems no reason to suppose that the present trip will fall into other than the former category.

In terms of relations among India and the major powers, the visit was also seen as historic. "Authoritative sources" in New Delhi saw the visit as evidence that India had been "upgraded" in Washington's perception and that "China and Pakistan have ceased to influence U.S. policy towards India."[22] Significantly, Carter tended to see the visit in similar big-power terms. "Under Mrs. Gandhi," he said, "there is no doubt that the orientations of India had been away from us, perhaps towards the Soviets." But, said Carter, after two days of talks, "I felt Desai and his government have come back to a completely neutral or non-aligned position."[23]

Although Moscow could be pleased at the lack of specific agreements and the presence of important differences, the trend of improving Indo-United States relations was a disturbing one for the Soviets. Typical of the Soviet perception, *New Times* carried a major commentary that accused the United States of trying to induce India to change its foreign policy and to improve United States-Indian relations "at the expense of India's traditional friendly ties with other states, notably the Soviet Union." The article went on confidently to cite numerous examples of where Indians saw through this smokescreen of "smiling diplomacy" and recited numerous differences between New Delhi and Washington. The article's tone of confidence was belied, however, by its conclusion, which should be read as an urgent reminder, if not a warning, to the Indian leaders not to succumb to these U.S. efforts:

> If one discounts the ostentatious publicity given President Carter's visit to India, one will see that there has been no real change in the position of the United States either as regards the general situation in South Asia or the unsolved problems of American-Indian relations.... [It is not] enough to pat a giant country like India on the back to cancel all the unpaid bills of the past and make all the differences and complexities of the present disappear.... The present day realities and the complex problems facing India and other South Asian countries naturally demand an altogether different approach....[24]

Soviet insecurity in the face of the trend in Indo-United States relations, as well as Moscow's displeasure with the publicity India accorded the Carter visit, loom clearly through the Soviet rhetoric.

The Soviets also watched closely when Desai returned Carter's visit by going to Washington in June, 1978. This visit was at least as successful as Carter's, and served to consolidate further the improving United States-Indian relationship. There were more talks on economic and technical cooperation and expressions of common perceptions of developments in world politics. Desai pointed out that there was no clash on any fundamental interest between the two and relations were "much closer than they have been for some time in the past."[25] The United States even was able to obtain Indian agreement on the opposition to the presence in Africa of Soviet advisors and Cuban troops, although New Delhi did not commit itself to specific actions in respect to Cuba or the Soviet Union. As with the Carter visit, however, a great deal of attention was focussed on the continuing nuclear issue. There was no movement on either side, but the two agreed to continue their dialogue on the issue. Despite the nuclear problem, Desai said that the talks showed a "spirit of *mutual confidence* and a genuine desire to understand each other's point of view...."[26] For the Kremlin, it was precisely the degree of "mutual confidence," an ingredient seen to be small in recent Indo-Soviet relations, that was of concern.[27]

Moscow's concern with India's other major power "option," China, was also escalating during the first half of 1978. Toward the end of 1977, Peking finally gave indications of responding to New Delhi's position that the next move was up to China. Criticisms of India in the Chinese media in general were sharply curtailed; this was particularly noticeable in Foreign Minister Huang Hua's address to the U.N. General Assembly in September. The rather low-key reception for Pakistan's new President Zia ul-Haq (Bhutto had been deposed in July) in China in December seemed a further indication of China's renewed interest in normalization with India. Vice-Premier Teng Hsiao-ping's trip to Nepal in February 1978 was closely watched in New Delhi, and his behavior in Kathmandu, particularly his press conference statement that China "was eager to bring relations with India close," was cited by Indian as well as Western media as significantly conciliatory.[28] Also in February, a trade delegation, the first since the 1962 conflict, arrived for a two-week stay. This was followed by the arrival of a political delegation from the Chinese People's Association for Friendship with Foreign Countries. The meeting between its head, Wang Ping-nan, and Desai constituted the first high-level political contact between the countries since Chou En-lai's 1960 visit to India. Desai and Wang shared the view "that the border question should be solved through negotiations and by peaceful means," and Wang extended an invitation to Vajpayee to visit China, which New Delhi accepted in principle.[29]

There was also evidence of continuing problems, particularly as relations with China became a major issue in India's domestic politics on a scale rarely seen since the aftermath of the 1962 border war. Although it had been her government that had restored ambassadorial-level relations with China and had taken other early initiatives in 1976 to start the process toward normalization, Mrs. Gandhi sought to utilize the Janata's gestures toward Peking as ammunition against it in the political struggle. She argued that India was already leaning towards the United States, had diluted its relationship with the Soviet Union, and was now preparing a sellout to China. One of her followers told the Lok Sabha that a "systematic erosion of India's national interests" had been taking place since the new government took over. He then asked the rhetorical question: "Are you giving the land away for the sake of friendly neighborly relations or a smile?"[30] The opening in June of the Karakoram Highway—a 500-mile, all-weather road built by the Chinese connecting Sinkiang with a town 60 miles north of Islamabad—was seen as threatening to India's interest by sections of the Janata as well as the opposition. The road inevitably became part of the border problem, since it would also pass through or connect to roads in disputed Kashmir and would tie into a highway linking Tibet with Sinkiang, passing through the Aksai Chin area of northern Ladakh that India claimed.[31]

What was particularly significant about the Sino-Indian "search for a meaningful dialogue," was the seriousness with which the Soviet leadership seems to have viewed it. Despite the lack of substantive progress in this relationship, Moscow undertook a flurry of activity both to woo India and to denounce China. For one, the Soviets suddenly became directly and actively involved in the Indian debate over the acquisition of deep-penetration aircraft. It is striking to note that although the British, French, and Swedish had all been in the bidding for several months, the Soviet

Union had earlier dropped out. Then in March 1978, Soviet air force chief Kutahkov paid an official visit to New Delhi and forcefully offered an improved version of the Soviet MiG-23. The press reported that plans to buy Western aircraft had been put off while the government studied the Soviet offer. Kutakhov emphasized the attractiveness of the MiG-23: its cost was less (about 25 million rupees or $2.9 million versus 80 million rupees for a comparable Western aircraft), credit terms were easier, it could be repaid through Indian exports as usual (thus a foreign exchange savings for India), and the Soviets were willing to allow the plane to be made in India. The Indians remained undecided through May when Defense Minister Ram paid a visit to Moscow for a review of Indo-Soviet defense cooperation. It can be assumed that the Soviet leaders took this opportunity also to try to convince the Indians to buy the Soviet aircraft. Ram did express the hope that India would receive Soviet support "for the furtherance of its objective of speedy national self-reliance," which was an unambiguous reference to India's long-standing effort to secure a more rapid transfer of technology to India for the production of weapons under Soviet license.[32] Although there is no obvious and direct connection to the Sino-Indian dialogue, the timing of Moscow's sudden willingness to enter the bidding and the intensity with which it proceeded are intriguing and suggest at least a possible link; that is, Moscow was keen to strengthen Indo-Soviet ties at a time when it appeared that India's relations with China (and the West) were on the upswing.

Although there was not as dramatic a maneuver in the economic field, the Soviets did seek a further strengthening of relations there as well. In February the fourth session of the Indo-Soviet Joint Commission was held. Soviet Deputy Prime Minister Arkhipov traveled to India for the meeting and repeatedly emphasized that relations between India and the Soviet Union were very close and that there were yet "greater prospects for further deepening our friendship and in particular our cooperation in the field of economic activity." The session led to the signing of a long-term protocol for the expansion of economic, trade, technical, and scientific collaboration. Several subcommittees were established and some specific agreements concluded. Arkhipov left India extolling a "qualitative new phase" in relations, a phase denoted by "a search for new areas of cooperation, wider development of industrial collaboration, exchange of technologies and experience on a broader basis, and collaboration in third countries."[33]

This period also marked a substantial escalation in Moscow's polemic against China. In late March Brezhnev undertook an unprecedented 13-day tour through Siberia and the Far East, which focussed mainly on the Sino-Soviet border. Brezhnev observed maneuvers along the border and clearly conveyed the message of "the Chinese threat" and the drubbing

China would receive in any hostilities. In addition, the Soviets seemed even more concerned than India with the implications of the Karakoram Highway for India's security; the road, said the Soviets, "is clearly intended to serve above all Peking's military strategic aims" and "cannot but disquiet China's neighbors, and primarily India."[34] Finally, the Soviets seized on incidents such as the reported incursion over Indian territory of a Chinese helicopter, denied both by India and China, and sought to encourage Indian "indignation" at such an example of "another Chinese provocation against India."[35]

The most revealing aspect of the Soviet response to the Chinese "challenge" in India came with Vajpayee's visit to Moscow in Setember. The remarkable nature of this visit could not be deducted from the final communique; in fact, as the *Statesman* pointed out, in a September 20 editorial, the "joint communiqué... consisted mostly of such generalities as could have been agreed upon without a fresh round of high-level negotiations." The clear purpose of this meeting, however, was for the two sides to discuss China, and there is no reference to this sensitive issue in the communiqué. The discussion represented the culmination of an effort to discourage Vajpayee from making his planned trip to Peking, which was looming less than two months ahead. As Sino-Soviet relations had continued to deteriorate since Moscow resumed the polemic following the hiatus after Mao's death, the Soviets seemed increasingly desperate to strike a political blow at Peking. The escalating tensions between China and Vietnam, the conclusion of the long-dreaded Sino-Japanese treaty, Chairman Hua's provocative trip into Eastern Europe (Romania and Yugoslavia), and signs of sudden progress in Sino-United States relations all combined to worsen Soviet fears about the "global Chinese challenge." Peking's efforts toward India were perceived as one more example of this threat. As *Izvestia* wrote on September 29, shortly after Vajpayee's departure from Moscow:

> It is obvious that Peking, making active use of anti-Sovietism in elaborating and implementing its foreign policy actions, would like the normalization of its relations with India to automatically lead to the deterioration of Soviet-Indian relations. Realistic and far-sighted circles in India are alarmed over the fact that these designs by the present leadership are meeting with definite support from certain Indian figures who are actively coming out for "conciliation" with Peking at all costs, including the undermining of Soviet-Indian friendship and cooperation.

Thus, barring a cancellation of the China visit, for which the Soviets had been pressuring India through the CPI and even certain Janata members,[36] the Soviets hoped to receive assurances of some concrete nature from Vajpayee that any normalization between India and China would not damage Soviet-Indian ties.

Vajpayee was treated to a barrage of anti-Chinese rhetoric from the Soviet leaders, ranging from references to the USSR experience with China to warnings of Peking's designs on normalization. In his talks with Gromyko, Kosygin, and Brezhnev, whose out-of-protocol reception of the Indian minister was noted as a special gesture to India, Vajpayee was given an "outspoken, sharp and critical" appraisal of trends in China's domestic and foreign policies, which the Soviets leaders believed "pose a threat to peace."[37] In their initial meeting, Vajpayee explained to Gromyko that India wished to improve its relations with China as part of its policy of normalizing and improving ties with its neighbors. Trying to draw on the closeness of ties between Moscow and former Prime Minister Indira Gandhi, he also pointed out that the Janata was only *continuing* the process of normalization that had been initiated before it came to power. Gromyko responded by describing China's policies in reportedly sharp and bitter terms. He apparently was so emphatic in his attacks on China that he had to reassure Vajpayee that "his use of strong language was not for the love of it but the use of soft language which they might have liked in relation to China would subserve principled Soviet opposition to war."[38] It was at the luncheon that Gromyko gave for Vajpayee that the Soviet position was most clearly and publicly pronounced. Gromyko spoke at length of the need for joint efforts in Asia for peace—i.e., collective security—in view of the activity of forces that have embarked on a course of militarization and military preparations and are "seeking to aggravate the international situation." Lest his guests miss the point, Gromyko went on to castigate explicitly "the aggressive essence of the Peking leadership's great-power hegemonistic policy...." What must be done against the Chinese forces? "The schemes of the forces that are hostile to world peace and international security in Asia," Gromyko went on, "should be rebuffed, and rebuffed decisively. It is necessary to unmask and frustrate their aggressive designs and expansionist proclivities in time."[39]

Gromyko and the rest of the Kremlin leaders were seeking some form of Indian commitment to this approach. The question Gromyko asked in his speech—"Can one show any vacillation in this situation?"[40]—was in no way rhetorical. However, Vajpayee disappointed them. He did pay homage to the stability of Indian-Soviet friendship, saying it did not depend on "momentary fluctuating factors in the complicated international situation." However, he avoided identifying himself with any explicitly anti-Chinese remarks and only by his agreement with several Soviet policy perspectives—such as the possibility of avoiding war, the value of detente in Europe, and others—could he be said to have taken anti-Chinese positions. Indeed, in his evasive response to Gromyko's anti-PRC tirade at the luncheon, Vajpayee seemed to be admonishing the Soviets not to go too far in seeking to stir up anti-Chinese sentiment. He expressed the hope that the process of greater relaxation in the South Asian region *would not be affected by tensions elsewhere* and that all powers would encourage the countries of the region to "overcome old suspicions and irritations."[41]

Overall, then, the Vajpayee trip seems to have marked a direct and forceful but futile Soviet attempt to steer India away from China. The strong Soviet push for an Asian collective security system, which was part of their anti-Chinese effort, was again rebuffed. Vajpayee did stress that his visit to China would in no way affect Indo-Soviet friendship and that India had its own experience of China and New Delhi's "eyes and ears were wide open." The communique's reference to an atmosphere of "cordiality, friendship and mutual understanding" indicated that the relationship had not significantly cooled, but Vajpayee's behavior also indicated the futility of Moscow's attempt to influence Indian behavior on the Chinese question.[42]

The Soviets certainly took comfort in the early November announcement that Vajpayee's visit to China would have to be postponed due to his hospitalization for a stomach ailment. However, there seemed little room for unbridled optimism. A Janata member of Parliament, Dr. Subramaniam Swamy, had visited China in September and returned declaring that the sides were ready to solve their border issues through negotiations. Vaypayee and Huang Hua held the first foreign ministers' meeting in about 16 years at the United Nations and Vajpayee described these as "very friendly and cordial."[43] The expressions of disappointment with the cancellation, emanating from both New Delhi and Peking, were coupled with assurances that the visit would be undertaken as soon as it was convenient.

INDIA AND THE GREAT-POWER TRIANGLE

In 1979 there were complex interactions among the major powers, as well as significant developments in the regional situation and in India's domestic political scene. The nature of the interrelations among these events makes this year almost as singificant as 1969 had been for Indo-Soviet relations. Unlike 1969, however, which actually ushered in a changed relationship between Moscow and New Delhi, 1979 set the stage for a *potential* change in ties. By mid-July, foreign policy became overshadowed by the government crisis that forced Desai's resignation. Once new elections were scheduled for early 1980, foreign policy assumed a lower priority.

One development that helped set the stage for the foreign policy developments was the Janata's decision, announced in early October 1978, to purchase deep-penetration aircraft from the British. The Jaguar was selected over the Swedish Viggen (which President Carter had vetoed since it used United States-licensed engines), the French Mirage, and the Soviet MiG-23.[44] All available evidence indicates that the MiG was the least considered alternative and that the Desai govenment had determined to increase India's options in the military field. This major and long-term (ten-year) deal reportedly called for the delivery of 40 Jaguars and the subsequent building and assembling of 110 of them in India under license. Moreover, the contract also involved the purchase of Harrier vertical takeoff aircraft for the Indian navy's only aircraft carrier, the "Vikrant." While one contract with a Western supplier was hardly going to end Soviet-Indian cooperation in this area, the size and significance of this particular agreement was disturbing to the Soviet leadership. In order not to fall behind in this crucial area, the Soviets were rather suddenly more forthcoming in the negotiations on the "indigenization" of the MiG-21s being built in India. In mid-October, Indian influence seemed to be at work when Moscow stopped its procrastination and agreed to a hastened transfer of MiG-21 technology to India and an acceleration of the production of the MiG-21 bis. The Soviets also expressed a willingness to explore the possiblities of buying spare parts (in the Jaguar deal, the British had already agreed to that), accessories, and avionics produced by India.[45]

A development of perhaps greater long-term significance for Indo-Soviet relations occurred with the mid-December announcement that the United States and China would establish full diplomatic relations on New Year's Day in 1979. India saw this as the natural culmination of a process begun in 1972 and had always recognized the Peking regime as China's sole government. The External Affairs Ministry quickly pointed out, however, that it *hoped* the step would "lead to easing of international tension and more particularly promote peace and stability... in Asia." This hint of uneasiness in the Indian perception seemed related to the development's as yet unknown impact on Sino-Soviet relations and on China's behavior in Asia.[46] Teng Hsiao-ping's visit to Washington at the end of January must have increased the tension for those who saw the closer Sino-United States relationship as posing threats to Indian interests. Teng spent a good deal of his trip denouncing the Soviet Union as being the "threat to international peace, security, and stability" and calling for all states to unite against the Soviets. Moreover, he issued warnings that China might have to "teach a necessary lesson" to the Vietnamese, the "Cubans of the Orient."[47] Nevertheless, such statements did not impinge on India directly, and the Indians were quick to note Carter's openly expressed differences with Teng on relations with Moscow.[48] The old diplomatic gambit of seeking to create the image of bilateral agreement by enunciating positions unilaterally while meeting with someone was, after all, precisely what Gromyko, Kosygin, and Brezhnev had utilized during Vajpayee's Moscow visit the previous September. Since the Indians knew they had maintained their differences with Moscow then despite the Soviet rhetoric, they were not likely to be upset by Teng's unilateral declarations while on U.S. soil.

On the heels of Teng's sojourn, External Affairs Minister Vajpayee became the first Indian minister to visit Peking since 1962. Vajpayee, faced with very mixed feelings in New Delhi about the trip, called it an exploratory visit and said there was no agenda and no agreements would be signed. In many ways, the results exceeded Vajpayee's cautious optimism. The most important result was China's conversion to India's view that a border problem did in fact exist, that it was the key to any real normalization, and that it should be resolved as soon as possible. In the words of Vajpayee's subsequent report on the trip to the Lok Sabha, the issue was "at least unfrozen" and this was "not an insignificant step forward."[49] In addition, Vajpayee raised the issue of Chinese support for the Naga and Mizo revels in India's northeast and on this score, too, China seemed to be anxious to be accommodating: "I was glad to learn from Chinese leaders that such support which may have been given—the last instance was some time ago—was looked upon as a thing of the past." Moreover, there were agreements on cultural, scientific, and other exchanges as well as plans to expand trade. It was also reported that the Chinese did not seek to raise the issue of India's relations with the Soviet Union, which pleased the Indian delegation.[50] Finally, the two countries basically "agreed to disagree" on such issues as the logic of disarmament, the prospects of detente, and the inevitability of war. Vajpayee summed up the meeting in positive terms in his report:

> We have not slurred over set-backs of the past or the outstanding problems which remain. India and China have different perspectives on internal and external policies.... It is not too far-fetched to believe that neither China nor India can profit from an attitude of hostility or even detachment of a kind which characterized our relations for many years. ... Given mutual respect based on equality and dignity, India-China relations can also improve bilaterally and fit into the web of positively oriented and advantageous relationships, which is the essence of our foreign policy. Just as I would caution against euphoria, I would also urge a measure of self-confidence that any effort at improvement in relations need not mean the sacrifice of our national interests and aspirations. We have made a beginning and I come back satisfied with the decision to undertake the mission. But I also know it would be a long haul which will demand maturity and reciprocal efforts by both Governments if, in the path ahead, satisfactory results are to be obtained.

While Vajpayee struggled to keep these positive achievements of his trip in the spotlight, the focus had been dramatically shifted by China's long-feared incursion into Vietnam. The fighting was initiated while Vajpayee was still in China, and the foreign minister abruptly cut short his visit and returned home. Peking's action and its timing appeared to be a sizable blunder given all the effort the Chinese had just put into improving relations with India. India's friendly relations with Vietnam left the government little choice but to decry China's action. Desai received the news with "profound shock and distress" and called on China to withdraw its forces immediately. More than 100 members of Parliament addressed a letter to the prime minister demanding that both houses adopt resolutions "condemning" the Chinese "aggression" in Vietnam. Although the government never did go to the lengths of "condemning" or explicitly branding China as the "aggressor," a storm of indignation and opposition to China was aroused. This was certainly exploited by the pro-Soviet lobby within the Janata and elsewhere in the Indian political system. Basic anti-Chinese hostilities were genuinely aroused by the similarity of China's action in Vietnam to its attack on India in 1962 (a linkage even suggested by Teng himself).[51]

The Soviets, although they could hardly be pleased with Peking's invasion of their Vietnamese ally, were hugely relieved by the turn of events as they concerned India. In the first Soviet commentary, the author stressed the theme of "Peking's perfidious agression against India," which was still "fresh in people's minds."[52] He pointed out that China occupied about 36,000 square kilometers of Indian territory, supported India's separatists, interfered in Kashmir, and threatened India's security by strategic roads such as the Karakoram Highway. The Kremlin blatantly relished the fact that "the timing of the aggression against Vietnam to coincide with the Indian Foreign Minister's visit to China once again demonstrated to the world the duplicity of the Chinese leaders and their utter disregard for India's prestige." With a mixed sense of glee as well as continued hope that this would be the reality, the author concluded by asserting that "even those Indian politicians who until recently had illusions with regard to Peking are beginning to realize that its policy is motivated by agressive hegemonism."

Soviet Premier Kosygin could hardly have asked for a better prelude to his March visit to India. Although the meeting had been talked about during 1978, the dates were not set until early in February— that is, just before Vajpayee's trip to Peking—and the timing undoubtedly reflected a Soviet desire to counter immediately and strongly any progress in Sino-Indian relations. Kosygin arrived in New Delhi less than three weeks after Vajpayee's return. He left no doubt that China was to be the central focus of his visit when, in his meetings with Desai and Vajpayee on the day of his arrival, he sought a "detailed assessment" of Vajpayee's visit to China.[53] After listening to Vajpayee's report, Kosygin further illustrated his "preoccupation" with China in his address to Parliament and at the dinner in his honor that evening. Thus began a six-day visit, with six to seven hours of private talks with Desai, in which Kosygin lambasted China in every public statement he made. In his parliamentary address, he referred to the Chinese action as "criminal" and sought to align India with the Soviet position. No peaceful country and no honest person, he said, should remain indifferent when the aggressor, "showing brazen contempt for human life, for world public opinion, is trampling underfoot international law, the lofty principles of peace and independence, sovereignty and equality, everything that has become the people's banner in the struggle against domination and oppression...."[54] Lest the members of Parliament miss Kosygin's implication that India *must* stand with the Soviet position, he asserted that forces had emerged in the world that would not allow such an outrage: "These forces include India; they include the Soviet Union."[55] The Soviets stood ready to lend their most active support, he said, to any initiative by the Parliament of India for cooperation in the struggle against aggression and the "policy of blackmail and diktat." At the civic reception for Kosygin at the Red Fort in Delhi, the Soviet premier continued his onslaught against China for this "crime" and promised that the aggressor would have to pay. Later in his visit, Kosygin used all the bluntness he could muster when he warned the Indians that "China might want to teach India a lesson at some point in the future, just as it had sought to do with Vietnam in the present."[56]

Clearly, Kosygin was seeking to create an impression of identity of views between India and the Soviet Union on the Chinese issue. Throughout his visit, in fact, he contended that the two states had "no differences, none at all." At the end of his stay, Kosygin remarked that "the talks have ended very successfully indeed and we have agreed on all subjects."[57] That this was hardly the case is intimated by Desai's statement on the same occasion that "we have agreed even where we differ." Desai also said there were "no misunderstandings" and even that is a far different situation from one of "identity of views." (In the joint communiqué, the phrase was "wide-ranging coincidence of their views.")[58] On the Chinese issue, Desai was adroit in not identifying India with Kosygin's strident assault. While deploring the turn of events in Indochina and calling for the withdrawal of troops, he rarely even mentioned China by name and apparently made clear to the Soviets that normalization with China would still be pursued when circumstances permitted. In the final communiqué, the two sides went only so far as to cite the "massive and armed attack," not "aggression" as Kosygin preferred, by China on Vietnam and to demand "an immediate, unconditional and total withdrawal of Chinese troops from the territory of Vietnam." This was no gain for the Soviets as this had been India's principled yet restrained position from the beginning. Moreover, the Indians were also somewhat embarrassed by what the *Statesman* referred to as Kosygin's "violently abusive language."[59]

On the issue of the new Vietnam-installed regime in Cambodia, Kosygin also failed to get the Indians to follow the Soviet line. India's position had been that it was willing to recognize the new regime in Phnom Penh once that government requested it and was in effective control of the country. Although the regime had officially asked for recognition, India still had not given it when Kosygin arrived. Indeed, Desai had broken India's silence on Vietnam's invasion of Cambodia by criticizing Hanoi on Indian television shortly before Kosygin's arrival. Despite Kosygin's reportedly strenuous efforts, he was unable to obtain Indian agreement on recognition of the Heng Samrin regime. The disagreement was substantial enough that there was no mention whatsoever of this issue in the final communique.

Kosygin had not come empty-handed. He had economic agreements and benefits to offer India: indeed, in the *Statesman's* opinion, "The Russians had never been as forthcoming as during this visit." Kosygin also offered sophisticated military weaponry and this was followed up on in September.[60] The meeting was, in many respects, a very positive one. Numerous areas of agreement were still present, and economic ties were strengthened, all "in the *spirit*"—rather than "on the *basis*" as the Soviets would have liked—of the 1971 Indo-Soviet treaty. Desai, even while remaining adamant that he would "not reject overtures for normalization of relations in keeping with our policy of friendship with all," assured the Soviets that "the normalization of relations with any country will not in any way impinge upon the strength and the quality of our relations, particularly with good friends such as the Soviet Union." Indeed, Desai seemed to say this so often that, when he once stated that "we have *repeatedly* assured you...," he seemed to be implying he was tired of having to reassure the insecure Soviets so frequently.[61] Nevertheless, despite all the USSR rhetoric, their glossing over differences afterwards,[62] and Kosygin's efforts, the Soviets did not get all they wanted from the meeting, particularly on the primary issue of China.

Economic Ties

Kosygin's visit also illustrated the relative stability of Soviet-Indian economic relations, in spite of certain problems, as well as Moscow's willingness to utilize economic ties as a tool in its influence seeking. Although the Soviets could take a very business-like approach in certain economic dealings, at other points they seemed mainly motivated by political, rather than economic, considerations. An example of the former was the final conclusion of an agreement on the ratio between the ruble and the rupee. This agreement, which took four years of often acrimonious negotiation, was reached near the end of 1978 and although it removed a significant irritant from their relationship and represented a compromise, most analysts saw it as a victory for the Soviets at India's expense.[63] On the other hand, Kosygin made the politically significant and economically costly gesture of offering an additional 600,000 tons (over the 1.5 million already promised) of crude oil to India for 1979. India had been seeking additional supplies from the Soviets, particularly to compensate partially for the decline in Iranian supplies, and had been turned down just three months earlier. A long-term agreement on economic, trade, scientific, and technical cooperation was also signed with India. Intended to cover a 10–15 year period, it was to provide "specific and prospective directions, projects and the form of mutually beneficial cooperation." Specific agreements were reached that accelerated the transfer of technology in various fields from the Soviet Union to India. This was particularly significant since the West was now providing more competition in this area than previously. Western terms had softened from 6–7 percent interest and short repayment periods, to 0–2 percent with some grants and 40–50 years to repay, compared with the Soviets' 2.5 percent repayable over 12 years. In addition, the Janata regime was more interested in Western technology, more tolerant of multinational corporations, and more sympathetic to India's private sector.[64]

In the area of trade, the value was projected to grow by another 50–100 percent during 1981–85. In 1978 there was a total turnover of Rs 1,000 Crore, and the protocol for 1979 had projected growth to Rs 1,200 Crore. By the end of 1979, there was evidence that trade had exceeded this goal, reaching Rs 1,600 Crore. Moscow's deputy minister of commerce and trade, I.T. Grishin, arrived in New Delhi in December and signed a protocol that envisaged a further jump to Rs 1,900 Crore in 1980. In all the agreements, continued emphasis was placed in joint ventures in third countries and provisions for a Soviet "buy-back" of production.[65]

Overall, then, Kosygin's visit, in addition to illustrating the Indo-Soviet differences, provided a further indication that both sides were anxious to strengthen and expand mutually beneficial economic and technological cooperation. The Soviet "investment" in the Indian economy was indeed substantial. By this point, Soviet aid had financed 30 percent of India's steel capacity, 70 percent of its oil extraction facilities, 30 percent of its oil-refining capacity, 20 percent of its power-generating capacity, and 80 percent of its metallurgical equipment production. Of the more than 70 industrial and other projects in operation or being set up, a large percentage were in these areas. The Soviets never missed an opportunity to emphasize the USSR contribution to India's "economic independence." Among the mass of publications turned out by the Information Department of the Soviet Embassy in New Delhi was a "Soviet-Indian Cooperation Series." Often included here and in the Embassy's weekly *Soviet Review* was the list of Soviet projects in addition, of course, to glowing articles about these "projects for prosperity."

Nuclear Issues in Politics

The Soviet Union had gotten involved in the nuclear issue through its 1976 agreement with Mrs. Gandhi's government to supply 200 tons of heavy water. Although 50 tons were shipped immediately without any formal safeguard accord, it became apparent early in 1977 that Moscow was insisting on comprehensive safeguards. After difficult and unsuccessful negotiations, the Soviets asked India to conclude an agreement with the International Atomic Energy Agency (IAEA). Four rounds of talks and almost a year later, an agreement was reached that included what one analyst has called "creeping, partial safeguards."[66] Thus, the Soviets had avoided repeating the U.S. posture of "full-scope" safeguards, which was totally unacceptable to India. Moreover, after Vajpayee's September 1978 meeting in Moscow, it was reported that the Soviets were also offering low-enriched uranium (LEU) to New Delhi, again under IAEA rather than "full-scope" safeguards. In the context of Indo-United States friction over U.S. shipments of LEU, the Soviet offer was significant (and realistic since it was already shipping LEU to France, West Germany, and communist states). Early in 1979, India and the Soviet Union also signed an agreement for USSR assistance in developing fast breeder-reactor technology.

The evidence of Soviet behavior on the nuclear issues suggests a somewhat tentative and qualified effort to come to India's aid in a situation of conflict with the West. In this sense, the heavy-water and LEU offers are similar to Soviet offers on Bhilai, Bokaro, and other projects in India's economic development. However, in the nuclear field Moscow demanded safeguards, even if not as complete as the ones the United States sought. As Paul Power depicted:

> With the U.S. acting a heavy role and the Soviets playing Mr. Accommodator in the same nonproliferation performance of "safeguards are good for you," India had no choice other than to accept the Soviet terms, which are less onerous than American terms.[67]

Early in 1979, however, it became known that India had decided not to make use of the Soviet heavy-water offer. Thus, the Soviets ran into the same extremely sensitive nationalism that had proved an insurmountable obstacle to the United States on the issue. Moscow was, like the United States, unable to influence New Delhi on the issue, nor were the Indians able to influence the Soviets.

By this time, the nuclear issue in South Asia had become more complicated by reports that Pakistan had developed a new plant that could produce weapons-grade enriched uranium. The United States indicated that it "shared India's concern" and took the step of cutting military and eonomic, but not food, aid to Islamabad. Nevertheless, the issue became a recurrent one in India's Parliament and reports that the government was "having second thoughts" on Desai's vow not to produce nuclear bombs and that the country needed to "keep its options open" were countered with statements from Desai, in particular, that a "Pak bomb will not provoke India" nor change its policy.[68] With the change of government in July, however, there was a new rash of statements from government officials to the effect that India would have to evaluate several factors in making a decision on whether to build nuclear weapons. The new defense minister, C. Subramaniam, stated that "he would not be naive enough to declare on behalf of all future generations and Governments that India would not make nuclear weapons."[69]

DESAI'S LAST VISIT TO MOSCOW

The visit of 83-year-old Morarji Desai, barely one month before his government fell from power, generally confirmed the status of relations. He received a warm welcome (unusually so, according to some sources), had cordial talks with the top Soviet leadership, and signed a communiqué full of glowing references to Indo-Soviet friendship and cooperation. He presided over the signing of the agreement for the Visakhapatnam steel mill and for a third Indian earth satellite. The Soviets also offered him further crude oil supplies.

Among all these indications of close ties between the two countries, there were still issues on which they differed. Desai's visit had originally been intended to be no more than a transit stopover on a European trip; its conversion into an official visit was probably urged by the Soviets in hopes of obtaining more Indian support for Soviet policy positions or at least creating the impression of closer viewpoints. It is apparent, judging from Brezhnev's speech at the dinner for Desai on June 11, that Moscow's primary concern continued to be China and Sino-Indian relations.[70] Desai was once again treated to a reminder of the concern that "both of our countries" share regarding "China's recent aggression against Vietnam, the continuing threats to take up arms again to 'teach someone a lesson.'"

China's behavior "makes the situation extremely complicated and creates considerable danger for Asian countries," Brezhnev reiterated. Despite these Soviet efforts, which also included a book review of Morarji Desai's memoirs in which the reviewer focussed almost exclusively on Desai's perception of "China's hegemonistic ambitions" in addition to his warm regard the Soviet Union,[71] Desai managed to keep India at a respectful distance. On China, he defended dialogue with them on the basis of the peaceful settlement of disputes and the lessening of tension, just as the Soviets were pursuing at this time with the Chinese. China was not even mentioned in the joint statement released at the end of the meeting.[72] On Afghanistan, there was a call for peace and noninterference in the joint statement but it is vague and in no way focusses on Pakistani "subversion," as Moscow argued. Indeed, Desai's response to Kosygin's laying of blame on Islamabad for the growing problems in Afghanistan was only to assert that "India was solely interested in seeing that there was no trouble in Afghanistan...." In any case, the increasing tensions in South Asia led to the omission from the final communiqué of any reference to the Soviet Union's usual "appreciation" of India's efforts to lower tensions in the region (a reference that always left out India's efforts toward China, of course).

On two other issues, there were also significant differences. One was Kampuchea (Cambodia) and Desai gave Brezhnev a lengthy explication of India's stand of refusing to recognize the new regime. Second, Desai also resisted what were probably more subtle attempts at influence on India's role in the nonaligned movement. Moscow's supporters in the movement for some time had been urging members to see the Soviet Union and the socialist camp as the "natural ally" of the nonaligned. These efforts by Cuba, Ethiopia, Vietnam, and others had been resisted particularly by India and Yugoslavia at the Coordination Bureau meeting in Colombo in early June and Desai continued this resistance.

There were even certain signs of the exercise of influence by India at the meeting. For one, the paragraph in the joint statement on the Indian Ocean left out the usual Soviet disclaimer on international law and, while seemingly focussing on the question of military bases went on to "condemn any attempts to build up foreign military presence in the Indian Ocean under any pretext whatsoever." Such a sweeping condemnation was not characteristic of Moscow's earlier statements and was regarded in Delhi as "Soviet support for the Indian stand."[73] On the other hand, the Soviets avoided any reference to great-power rivalry in the area and could interpret the phraseology to refer to the U.S. consideration of creating a Fifth Fleet, permanently stationed in the Indian Ocean, as a response to tension emanating from Iran and Afghanistan. In any case, this compromise hardly indicated that Moscow and New Delhi had a common stand on the issue as the *Soviet Review* (no. 31) trumpeted to its Indian readers. This was clearly confirmed in the fall when Moscow once again abstained on the Indian Ocean resolution at the thirty-fourth General Assembly session. Moscow went to substantial lengths to justify its vote in the face of its "invariable" support for the concept of peace and security for the area and its willingness to take constructive measures to bring this about. The key was "the failure of the resolution to put the blame for the rising tension in the Indian Ocean where it truly belongs [imperialists' military bases] and the indirect attempt to put some of the blame for the continued arms race in this region on the Soviet Union...."[74] Thus, a narrow, but significant, Indo-Soviet difference remained on this issue.

Desai was undoubtedly being sincere when he assured Brezhnev that "the Soviet Union has a reliable friend in India, one whose policy is founded... on a solid basis of feelings of warmth, goodwill and recognition of mutual interests...." Desai's reference later to "very frank" talks, that is, disagreement, was passed off by the *Overseas Hindustan Times* (June 28), for example, in these terms:

> It is in fact this emerging ability to agree to disagree on certain regional or international political issues, whilst maintaining without diminution the fraternal ties, that constitute the secure bedrock of Indo-Soviet relations.

Indeed, while these important differences kept relations from being as "close and cordial" as Moscow liked to contend,[75] the "coincidence or similarity of views" (in the words of the joint statement) on world political issues was indeed substantial. An examination of the voting on key issues in the 1979 General Assembly reveals a continuation of a far greater coincidence of Indian views with the Soviet Union than with the United States.

CHANGING GOVERNMENTS

By the middle of July, the Janata regime had become so divided that Desai's government fell. With support from Mrs. Gandhi's Congress (I), Charan Singh was able to oust Desai and become prime minister. When Mrs. Gandhi withdrew her support less than a month later, this new government had to resign. The Lok Sabha was dissolved and, after more frantic maneuvering, Charan Singh and his coalition ministry were asked to carry on as a caretaker cabinet. The country then began to prepare for its seventh general election. Moscow's undeniable interest in these developments in India was tempered by too many unknowns, particularly who would succeed as prime minister and at what political cost to alliance building. Perhaps learning from their mistakes in 1977, the Soviets proceeded cautiously since they did not know with whom they would be dealing. Soviet news reports of the political crisis in India were factual and offered criticisms only in quoting Indian assessments. The Soviets concentrated on four themes. One was that Singh and External Affairs Minister S.N. Mishra had stressed that there would be no foreign policy change, that is, no shift from nonalignment. Second, Moscow underlined that Indian assessments all noted that foreign policy issues were not a concern in the campaign debates. Third, the Soviets stressed that "all the leading political parties have confirmed their support of such an important aspect of this policy as the maintenance of friendly relations with the U.S.S.R." Finally, the Soviets put emphasis on the steadfast nature of Soviet-Indian ties and the USSR support for India.

Indicative of Moscow's concern with developments in India and its eagerness to remind India of the importance of Indo-Soviet relations, Premier Kosygin made a special stopover in Bombay in September on his way home from a visit to Ethiopia. He was met by Mishra, who described the stop as a great gesture to India and the talks as "very fruitful and cordial." Although virtually nothing is known of the details of the meeting besides the fact that they exchanged impressions about the Havana nonaligned meeting, it is likely that Kosygin sought to assess the current political situation in India and reinforce relations. In messages of greetings to President Reddy and Prime Minister Singh, he stressed the Indo-Soviet treaty, the importance of bilateral ties for each country, peace in Asia, and world security, and expressed his "confidence" that relations between India and the Soviet Union "will develop successfully" and grow stronger.[76]

The Sixth Nonaligned Summit, held in Havana in early September 1979, represents one of the forums through which Soviet-Indian relations in this period can be analyzed. In recent years, the Soviets had put an increasing amount of emphasis on the nonaligned movement.[77] Since the 1973 Algiers summit, Fidel Castro had led a small group of "radical" states in pushing the thesis that the Soviet Union was the "natural ally" of the nonaligned and that the movement's thrust had to be exclusively anti-Western. As the Havana session approached, the Soviet Union stepped up its efforts to underline the common interests between the nonaligned states and the Soviet camp and to denounce U.S. diplomacy for its efforts to divide the movement and drive a wedge between it and its "natural allies." The Soviets also devoted substantial efforts, although not pressure, on India as a key member of the movement and a recognized "moderate." For example, in an article praising the role of Nehru—a "safe" topic even in New Delhi's turbulent politics in late 1979—the Soviets referred to him as "at the source of the policy of nonalignment." In a clear reference to the current situation, they argued that he "tirelessly defended its progressive, anti-imperialist aspects, and rejected the idea of non-alignment being interpreted as a sort of neutrality in the struggle for peace and national rights."[78] Moreover, a major article upholding this same theme of "natural allies" and denouncing "equidistance" between the capitalist and socialist camps, written by a former correspondent in India and published in *New Times*, was republished in *Soviet Review* in New Delhi just prior to the meeting.[79]

Moscow's efforts had mixed results. In a meeting where the movement seemed to move somewhat further to the left but in which neither the radicals nor the moderates could claim a clear victory, even Cuba backed off from trying to promote the "natural allies" thesis. India was one of the opponents of this thesis and New Delhi's continued opposition helped to moderate Castro's position. The Soviet Union did better, however, when India supported the Cuban compromise solution on Kampuchea's representation. The best the more radical states could get in this situation, since there was insufficient support for the Heng Samrin regime, was to keep the seat vacant rather than let it be occupied by Pol Pot. India's support of this position, obviously favored by the Soviets, seemed basically consistent with its denunciation of Pol Pot but non-recognition of Heng Samrin. Thus, the actual exercise of Soviet influence here seems doubtful. Nevertheless, Moscow's distinct pleasure with New Delhi's position was enhanced when India took an active role two weeks later at the United Nations in seeking to keep Kampuchea's seat vacant there too. The vote on a resolution to seat representatives of the former Pol Pot regime was 71 in favor, 35 against, and 34 abstentions, with India joining the Soviet Union, Cuba, and other nonaligned "radicals" in voting against. Although New Delhi was still not recognizing nor voting to seat the Heng Samrin regime, its unusual willingness to be out of step with broader world opinion on the issue must have been satisfying to Moscow, whether it had influenced this stance or not.

The visit later in September of a high-level team to confer on the purchase of arms gives further evidence of the nature of Soviet-Indian relations. The mission was led by the civil-service head of the Indian Ministry of Defense and included representatives of all three services. They reportedly went to look at modern missile systems for the air force: MiG-23s, missile-carrying cruisers and corvettes, and tanks. The Soviets appeared eager to be forthcoming. A Soviet spokesman said at the conclusion of the meetings that "the U.S.S.R. would allow no obstacles, including prices, to impair its assistance to India's defense needs."[80] The visit was also significant in that the Jaguar deal had become a major domestic issue in India and there was considerable talk of a review and possible cancellation of that deal. No agreement was reached immediately on the MiG-23s, although India's defense minister later referred to "satisfactory progress" in the talks and hoped that new equipment, including the MiG-23, would "soon be with the Indian Air Force."[81] The two sides did agree to a sale of AN-32 transport aircraft and Mi-8 helicopters. Moreover, it was known that India was seriously evaluating a large-scale purchase of the T-72 battle tank. The significance of this visit lies mainly in its illustration of the fact that Indo-Soviet military ties were hardly dead after the Jaguar deal. The Soviets were certainly anxious to maintain cooperation, particularly in the MiG program, and may have offered attractive items and terms on this basis. Even so, the two did not conclude a large-scale deal, as the Soviets obviously did not present an offer "too good to refuse." Their wariness, as well as India's, probably also reflected the extent to which the whole arms situation was also related to India's political confusion.

OBSERVATIONS ON THE ELECTION

As India prepared to go to the polls January 3 to 6, 1980, Soviet interest naturally heightened. Although the Soviets recognized as well as Indian observers that the election was being fought over personalities and not issues or policies, there were some foreign policy differences that had been emerging. One of these was the issue of recognition of the Vietnam-backed government in Phnom Penh. Mrs. Gandhi and the Congress (I) came out stridently for immediate recognition of this "new revolutionary Government" while the other groups, led by Charan Singh and Jagjivan Ram, favored a continuation of the "watching and waiting" approach. The Congress (I) also sounded stronger on strengthening defense, asserting India's "sovereign right to use nuclear technology," and not bowing to external pressures, particularly from the United States. Moreover, the Congress (I) criticized the general thrust of the Janata's foreign policy and implicitly promised a closer relationship with the Soviet Union: India, read the party's election manifesto, "was relegated to the humiliating position of a non-entity," one that had alienated "the sympathy and support of friends who had stood by us in need."[82]

It is not difficult to imagine that, in this context, the Soviets had a growing interest in Mrs. Gandhi's return to power. Nevertheless, they remained officially neutral and any preference was kept implicit. Moscow had apparently learned a lesson from its partisanship in a losing cause in the 1977 election and had no desire to repeat that mistake. Even more importantly, however, Moscow had seen substantial continuity in Indo-Soviet relations even under such a "right-wing" administration as the Janata. To be sure, there were greater differences between the two countries than before and the exercise of Soviet influence was more difficult. In sum, while the Soviet leaders would prefer Mrs. Gandhi, by the end of 1979 they were aware that relations with her had not been as close as they would have liked nor those with the Janata as distant as they had feared. In any case, like the rest of the world, Moscow could only await the outcome of the electoral exercise of the world's largest democracy.

NOTES

1. See *Los Angeles Times*, March 25, 1977; and S.D. Muni, "Major Developments in India's Foreign Policy and Relations, January-June 1977," *International Studies* (New Delhi), January-March 1978, pp. 84–90.
2. *Indian Express*, March 25, 1977.
3. Muni, "India's Foreign Policy," pp. 90–91.
4. A seminar in New Delhi in September 1971 gave vent to these suspicions and produced a book provocatively entitled *Shadow of the Bear: The Indo-Soviet Treaty;* see S.C. Gangal, "Major Developments in India's Foreign Policy and Relations, July-December 1977," *International Affairs*, January-March 1971, p. 51.
5. See V. Sofyin, "Foreign Policy Contours," *New Times*, no. 16, April 1977, p. 12.
6. *Statesman*, April 26, 1977. Other coverage in that paper is found on April 27 and 28. See also *Far Eastern Economic Review* (hereafter cited as *FEER*), May 20, 1977, p. 34; *New York Times*, April 25–28, 1977; and *The Times*, April 7, 27, 1977.
7. *Statesman*, April 27, 1977. Emphasis added.
8. *Pravda*, April 28, 1977.
9. For example, compare V. Tretyakov, "Faithful to the Principles of Friendship," *New Times*, no. 19, May 1977, p. 4; and "India is Neutral Again," *The Economist* (London), April 30, 1977, pp. 12–13.
10. *Statesman*, April 27, 1977.
11. *Statesman*, April 28, 1977. See also the analysis in R. V. R. Chandrasekhara Rao, "The Janata Government and the Soviet Connexion," *The World Today*, February 1978, pp. 70–76.
12. *The Times*, April 7, 1977.
13. *The Military Balance, 1978-1979* (London: International Institute for Strategic Studies, 1978), p. 106.
14. *FEER*, October 7, 1977, p. 32. See also Golam W. Choudhury, "New International Patterns in Asia," *Problems of Communism*, March-April 1979, pp. 14–28.
15. See *Statesman*, October 21, 1977. See also the editorial, "Mission to Moscow," in the same issue.
16. *Pravda*, October 22, 1977. Emphasis added.
17. *Pravda*, October 27, 1977.
18. See Donaldson, *Soviet-Indian Alignment*, p. 36; and Gangal, "India's Foreign Policy," p. 51.
19. *Statesman*, January 4, 1978. Lengthy excerpts from the joint declaration are also contained in this issue. See also Nancy Jetly, "Major Develpments in India's Foreign Policy and Relations, January-June, 1978," *International Studies*, July-September 1979, pp. 369–72; and *FEER*, January 20, 1978, pp. 16–20.
20. These figures and an excellent analysis of the course of Indo-United States relations into 1979 are found in Norman D. Palmer, "Indo-American Relations: The Politics of Encounter," *ORBIS*, Summer 1979, pp. 403–20.

21. See A. Hariharan, "Accord Survives Carter's Aside," *FEER*, January 13, 1978, pp. 28–29.
22. *Statesman*, January 1, 1978.
23. Stephen Barber, "Carter's New Directions," *FEER*, January 20, 1978, p. 16.
24. Natalia Beglova, "Behind the American 'Smiling Diplomacy,'" *New Times*, no. 4, January 1978, pp. 24–25.
25. *Hindustan Times*, June 14, 1978. See also *Christian Science Monitor*, June 12, 1978.
26. From Desai's statement to Parliament on his trip; *Overseas Hindustan Times*, August 3, 1978. Emphasis added.
27. The fact that the Kremlin replaced its ambassador, as announced by *Pravda* on December 24, 1977, with one who was a specialist in U.S. affairs may be a further indication of the seriousness with which Moscow viewed India's budding "U.S. connection": see the excellent discussion in Nisha Sahai, "Soviet Specialists in South Asia," *International Studies*, January-March 1979, pp. 103–6.
28. *Statesman*, February 5, 1979; *Times of India*, February 5, 1979; and *Christian Science Monitor*, March 1, 1978.
29. See *Times of India*, March 12, 1978; and *FEER*, March 24, 1978, p. 5.
30. *FEER*, August 11, 1978, p. 19.
31. For discussion of the complex geography of these highways, see *FEER*, September 1, 1978, pp. 18–19; and *Christian Science Monitor*, August 22, 1978.
32. See *Hindustan Times*, May 24, 1978. See also *Christian Science Monitor*, May 26, 1978.
33. From Jetly, "India's Foreign Policy," pp. 367-77.
34. A. Turanov, "Road for Chinese Expansion," *New Times*, no. 31, July 1978, p. 23.
35. For the Chinese reaction to such alleged provocations, see *Peking Review*, no. 40, October 6, 1978, p. 39.
36. Kuldip Nayar from New Delhi in *New Times*, September 21, 1978.
37. *Statesman*, September 13, 1978.
38. Ibid.
39. *Pravda*, September 13, 1978.
40. Ibid.
41. *Statesman*, September 13, 1978.
42. *Pravda*, September 19, 1978.
43. *Overseas Hindustan Times*, October 26, 1978.
44. For an analysis of the various considerations involved in the Indian decision, see Raju G. C. Thomas, "Aircraft for the Indian Air Force: The Context and Implications of the Jaguar Decision," *ORBIS*, Spring 1980, pp. 85–101.
45. See Mohan Ram in the *Christain Science Monitor*, November 8, 1978. See also A. Hariharan, "Aircraft Deal Airborne at Last," *FEER*, October 20, 1978, p. 37; and *Overseas Hindustan Times*, November 2, 1978.
46. *Times of India*, December 17, 1978. See also *Overseas Hindustan Times*, December 28, 1978.
47. For example, see *Christian Science Monitor*, January 21, 1979; and *Los Angeles Times*, February 1, 1979.
48. See *Statesman*, January 31, and the editorial, February 6, 1979.
49. *Indian and Foreign Review*, March 1, 1979, pp. 5–7. See also A. Hariharan, "Success with a Sting in the Tail," *FEER*, March 2, 1979, p. 25.
50. *Times of India*, February 18, 1979.
51. See *Overseas Hindustan Times*, March 1, 1979; and *Indian and Foreign Review*, March 1, 1979.
52. V. Tretyakov, "Visit Wrecked," *New Times*, no. 10, March 1979, p. 24.
53. See *Statesman*, March 10–16, 1979; *Indian and Foreign Review*, March 15 and April 1, 1979; and *Overseas Hindustan Times*, March 22, 1979, which also contained the text of the joint communiqué. See also *FEER*, March 23, 1979, pp. 9–10, and March 30, 1979, pp. 29–30.

54. *Statesman*, March 10, 1979.
55. *Statesman*, March 11, 1979.
56. Cited in Robert Rand, "Kosygin Ends His Visit to India," *Radio Liberty Research*, RL 89/79, March 15, 1979, p. 2.
57. *Overseas Hindustan Times*, March 22, 1979.
58. Ibid.
59. The *Statesman*, in its editorial of March 16, 1979, asserted that Deng's (formerly Teng Hsiao-ping) behavior in the U.S. had been questionable, but that "compared to the Soviet leader's performance on Indian soil, Mr. Deng's was almost a model of rectitude."
60. See Walter K. Andersen, "India in Asia: Walking on a Tightrope," *Asian Survey*, December 1979, p. 1247.
61. *Pravda*, March 11, 1979. Emphasis added.
62. For example, see Vasily Tretyakov, "Bonds of Sincere Friendship," *New Times*, no. 13, March 1979, pp. 4–5.
63. See Jayanta Sarkar, "India Unties the Soviet Knot," *FEER*, January 19, 1979, pp. 74–76.
64. See Mohan Ram, "India Plays Off East and West," *FEER*, April 20, 1979, p. 56.
65. *Overseas Hindustan Times*, January 10, 1980.
66. Paul F. Power, "The Indo-American Nuclear Controversy," *Asian Survey*, June 1979, p. 585.
67. Ibid., p. 586.
68. Respectively, see *Christian Science Monitor*, April 10, 1979; the editorial in *Overseas Hindustan Times*, May 24, 1979; and *Overseas Hindustan times*, May 17 and July 5, 1979.
69. *Overseas Hindustan Times*, November 8, 1979. See also Mohan Ram, "The South Asian Arms Race," *FEER*, November 16, 1979, pp. 38–39.
70. *Pravda*, June 12, 1979. Indian coverage of the visit is in the *Statesman*, June 3 and 11–15, 1979. The text of the joint statement is found in *Overseas Hindustan Times*, June 28, 1979.
71. See G. Bondarevsky, "Memoirs of Morarji Desai," *New Times*, no. 25, June 1979, pp. 26–27.
72. *Statesman*, June 15, 1979.
73. See the editorial in *Overseas Hindustan Times*, June 28, 1979.
74. A. Alexeyev and A. Fialkovsky, "Peace and Security for the Indian Ocean," *International Affairs*, no. 9, September 1979, p. 53. This article constitutes perhaps the most explicit defense of the USSR voting record on the issue.
75. See the assessment of Desai's visit by A. Usvatov, "Close and Cordial," *New Times*, no. 26, June 1979, p. 7.
76. See *Indian and Foreign Review*, October 1, 1979, p. 6: and *Soviet Review*, no. 44, 1979.
77. For an excellent discussion of the movement and particularly the Havana meeting, see William M. LeGrande, "Evolution of the Nonaligned Movement," *Problems of Communism*, January-February 1980, pp. 35–52.
78. Erik Komarov, "Nehru, Builder of the New India," *New Times*, no. 46, November 1979, pp. 21–22.
79. See Victor Sidenko, "Non-Aligned Perspectives and the Blind Alley of 'Equidistance,' " *New Times*, no. 29, July 1979, pp. 4–6: and *Soviet Review*, no. 38, 1979, pp. 17–22. A lengthier Soviet analysis is found in A. Klimov, "On the Havana Conference," *International Affairs*, no. 9, September 1979, pp. 43–50.
80. Cited in Andersen, "India in Asia," p. 1248.
81. *Overseas Hindustan Times*, November 15, 1979. See also *Daily Telegraph*, August 11, 1979; and *FEER*, December 14, 1979, p. 24.
82. The various parties' election manifestoes are excerpted in the *Overseas Hindustan Times*, December 13, 20, and 27, 1979.

7

RETURN TO "NORMALCY"?: INDIRA BACK IN OFFICE

In the January 1980 election, Mrs. Gandhi made a surprisingly overwhelming return to power. Her Congress party not only jumped from 34.5 percent of the popular vote to 42.6 percent, but the Congress (I), despite predictions that no party would obtain a majority in the Lok Sabha, benefitted as it had in every year except 1977 from the fragmentation of its opposition and also captured two-thirds of the seats.[1] Mrs. Gandhi's frequently split party was now reestablished in almost as strong a position as in 1971.[2] With Mrs. Gandhi the prime minister once again, the situation in India and in Soviet-Indian relations seemed ready to return to normal.

The Soviets were quick to applaud Mrs. Gandhi's victory and her commitment to build a socialist society, to "investigate the role played by the multinationals," and to "return to economic planning, which was abandoned when the Janata Party was in power."[3] While thus arguing for change in domestic policies, the Soviets made only implicit criticisms of Janata foreign policies: Moscow praised the Congress campaign promise to recognize the Heng Samrin regime in Kampuchea and urged India to resist efforts by Washington and Peking to cause a rift between New Delhi and Moscow. It was clear that the Soviets were pleased that Mrs. Gandhi was back in power. In their message of congratulations to her, Brezhnev and Kosygin hailed her as "a prominent political figure and statesman of India, as a consistent adherent of the course of Jawaharlal Nehru who stood at the source of the Soviet-Indian friendship." Most significantly, they praised her *personal contribution* to the "expansion and deepening of Soviet Indian relations...."[4]

Even before the elections, however, the context within which any party would be operating was drastically altered by Moscow's invasion of Afghanistan in late December. New Delhi was faced with a dilemma. On the one hand, the Soviet Union was India's most important ally and the relationship had seemed likely to get closer with a more sympathetic prime minister in power. To the extent that Moscow's action had crushed the possibility of a fanatic Islamic state in Afghanistan, as in Iran, and had reduced U.S. and Chinese meddling in Afghanistan's internal situation, India could be well pleased. Moreover, who would become India's major-power supporter if it denounced the Soviet Union? On the other hand, most of the nonaligned world, not to mention the United States and China, expressed strong opposition to the Soviet move. The introduction of actual USSR army units into another country, one which had been nonaligned and not part of the Soviet bloc, was a situation that was repugnant to India's historic foreign policy principles. How could India maintain its stature in world politics and not oppose Moscow's action? What was India to do as the regional context seemed to be reverting to the very tense 1969–71 period, when local states squared off against each other and external powers lined up behind their respective "clients"?

INDIA AND THE AFGHAN INVASION

The details of the Soviet Union's action cannot be our concern here.[5] For us, it is important to note that New Delhi had been watching the deterioration of the situation in Afghanistan with increasing unease. India's rapid recognition of the new Marxist regime (it was the second country, after the Soviet Union, to do so) after the April 1978 coup was indicative of its keen hopes for the return of stability there. The Indian government was all too ready to agree with the Soviets, as Vajpayee did during his visit in September 1978, that the situation was an internal matter of Afghanistan's and all powers should avoid interfering. In the aftermath of the events in Kabul in late December, the Indian reaction focussed on two themes and these, with shifting degrees of relative emphasis, have dominated the Indian stance ever since. First, New Delhi reiterated that it had "always opposed outside interference in the internal affairs of one country by another." While still prime minister, Charan Singh expressed India's deep concern at the Soviet action and summoned the Soviet ambassador to make it clear that, in India's view, the sending of troops would have "far-reaching and adverse consequences" for the entire region. The Soviets should withdraw their troops and return the situation to "normal." In virtually the next breath, Indian leaders underlined the second thread of New Delhi's official perception: a major danger of the situation in Afghanistan and the invasion was that the arms race in the region was likely to be restored and accelerated. One New Delhi newspaper said that "Washington's decision to lift its earlier embargo on the arms sales to Pakistan" was "still worse" news than the Soviet move. Despite attempts by President Carter and U.S. Ambassador Goheen to persuade the Indians that new arms for Pakistan would only be to contain the Soviet intervention along Pakistan's borders, New Delhi was adamant in professing to see the move as a threat. The Foreign Office stated that it was "the Government of India's earnest hope that no country or external power would take the steps which might aggravate the situation...."[6]

The initial posture adopted by the new Gandhi government shifted the balance in favor of the second theme. At the United Nations, Indian Ambassador B.C. Mishra remained silent when the issue came before the Security Council at the request of the United States and 51 other states, including many of the nonaligned group. After the issue was transferred to the General Assembly under the "Uniting for Peace" process, Mishra became the first non-Soviet bloc envoy to speak essentially for the USSR position. Addressing a resolution sponsored by 17 nonaligned nations which appealed to all states to refrain from interfering in Afghanistan and, without identifying the troops involved, called for an "immediate, unconditional and total withdrawal of the foreign troops from Afghanistan," Mishra said in part:

> India cannot look with equanimity on the attempts by some outside powers to interfere in the internal affairs of Afghanistan by training, arming and encouraging subversive elements to create disturbances inside Afghanistan.

Mishra added that "we are against the presence of foreign troops and bases in any country" but then immediately went on to say:

> However, the Soviet Government has assured our government that its troops went to Afghanistan at the request of the Afghan Government first made by President Amin on December 26, 1979, and repeated by his successor on December 28, 1979. And we have been further assured that Soviet troops will be withdrawn when requested to do so by the Afghan Government.

Although he later mentioned that India "hopes" that "Soviet forces will not remain there a day longer than necessary," his fundamental conclusion was that "we have no reason to doubt assurances, *particularly from a friendly country like the Soviet Union with whom we have many close ties.*"[7]

India's stand in the General Assembly's debate caused a good deal of shock and surprise particularly among Western observers who had hoped for New Delhi's support against the Soviet action. The fact that India was not completely supporting Moscow, however, became apparent first of all in the vote on the resolution. India joined 17 other countries in abstaining (and 12 others who were "absent or not participating") while the resolution passed overwhelmingly, 104 to 18. Shortly thereafter, Mrs. Gandhi made her first statement on Afghanistan since assuming office. After a meeting with Britain's foreign secretary, Lord Carrington, Mrs. Gandhi stated bluntly that "no country is justified in entering another country," thus further qualifying India's official position.[8] Moreover, in an interview with the U.S. news magazine, *Time*, Mrs. Gandhi went so far as to say that she "disapproved" of the Soviet presence in Afghanistan.[9] Mrs. Gandhi summarized her position in a by-election speech by first reminding her audience that Soviet troops were sent into Afghanistan "only after Pakistan started training the Afghan rebels and sending them in to topple the Government there," and then adding that, nevertheless, India was opposed to the USSR presence and "it had told that country so."[10]

India's low-key and compromise position raises immediately the question of influence. What is the evidence that Moscow was able to influence New Delhi to support it or at least not to oppose it on the Afghan issue? Indications of potential Soviet influence are plentiful yet circumstantial. For one, it is apparent that the Soviets attempted to persuade India to support Moscow's position. Moreover, it is undeniable that New Delhi's stance in opposition to almost all noncommunist Asian states and more than two-thirds of the nonaligned states in the United Nations hurt India's stature in the nonaligned movement and, in that vaguest of all forums, world public opinion. On the other side of the coin, India's relative consistency of position on the issue raises doubts about the existence of Soviet influence. Even prior to the election, Mrs. Gandhi had stated she was opposed to interference by any country in the affairs of another but added that the USSR "interference" in Afghanistan was not a "one-sided affair."[11] India's concern with foreign interference in regional affairs was one of long-standing, and there was indeed evidence of at least Chinese and Pakistani support for Afghan rebels prior to the Soviet incursion. Finally, India's position on the USSR invasion of Czechoslovakia in 1968 bears a striking resemblance to its response to the Afghan situation in 1980. In 1968, too, Mrs. Gandhi's government had avoided any condemnation of the Soviet Union but had expressed disapproval of the Soviet action and "anguish at events." India had also abstained on a U.N. resolution (in the Security Council) mainly due to one of its operative clauses that "condemned" the Soviet Union. Perhaps the greatest similarity stands out in Mrs. Gandhi's reference in 1968 to dealing with "political realities" and her 1980 statement that "I do not excuse the Russians but you have to take a realistic look at the situation."[12] This "realistic look" included external subversion in Afghanistan, Soviet interests there, Amin's request for assistance, and the Soviet Union's present substantial commitment.

What all of this evidence seems to point to is that, once again, India and the Soviet Union had a coincidence of interests. That is, their respective views of the Afghan situation were similar in more respects than they differed. These similarities were relatively more pronounced under Indira Gandhi than under Charan Singh due to differences in their own personal percepetions. New Delhi therefore worked out a two-pronged approach to the situation: it adopted a very low-key and mostly behind-the-scenes effort to bring about a Soviet disengagement, while it adopted a much more visible program of seeking to limit the global and regional response that might threaten Indian interests. New Delhi's argument was that only if a major military buildup in South Asia was avoided would it be possible to get the Soviets to leave Afghanistan.

India reacted strongly to the Western response to the invasion. When U.S. Defense Secretary Brown's visit to China in early January resulted in the specific agreement that both countries should move quickly to increase military aid to Pakistan, Mrs. Gandhi responded by criticizing this United States-China "combination" whose action would pose a danger to India and the rest of the Third World.[13] India reiterated its concern in a message to the Chinese leadership and personally to Washington via Clark Clifford, the president's special envoy who arrived in Delhi at the end of January. Clifford argued that the U.S. aim was only to prepare Pakistan as a bulwark against the Soviets. The Indians rejected this, pointing out that this would hardly be adequate to contain the Soviets *should* they decide to launch a southward thrust; this buildup would, however, "help escalate an already bad situation and upset the military balance in the region."[14] Mrs. Gandhi also turned down Clifford's proposal for a regional security arrangement, which Carter had raised in his State of the Union address, arguing that such lineups were bound to further heighten tensions. (This was consistent with India's policy, which had also rejected participation in Moscow's Asian collective security system for a long time.)

On the whole, despite major points of disagreement, Clifford's visit seemed to quiet Indian fears somewhat. Under the terms of a 1959 agreement, the United States had promised to help Pakistan if it was attacked by the Soviet Union. Therefore, Carter's pledge to aid Pakistan was defensive in nature and not threatening to Indian security. Meanwhile, Zia had rejected a $400 million U.S. military and economic aid offer as "peanuts" and was anxious not to appear too anti-Soviet. India could take some comfort in the prevailing perception in Pakistan that it "could not ignore *the fact that the U.S. sensitivity to Indian reaction* appeared to be determining the size and nature of the aid package, denuding it of relevance to our defensive capacity."[15] China's behavior was also helpful in keeping a lid on the escalation of tensions in the region and preventing a complete polarization of forces as had occurred in 1971. Chinese Foreign Minister Huang Hua's visit to Pakistan did not emerge as overly threatening to India; what unease New Delhi may have felt was at least partially dispelled by Huang Hua. When appearing at a dinner in Peking celebrating the thirtieth anniversary of the Republic of India, he called for the improvement of Sino-Indian relations and the promotion of "mutual understanding and cooperation."[16] The strong denunciation of the Soviet invasion by the foreign ministers of the 35 members of the Islamic Conference may have been a further factor conditioning oil-poor India's stance. In any case, New Delhi undoubtedly enjoyed being the center of diplomatic attention. Before Soviet Foreign Minister Gromyko could get to India, Mrs. Gandhi had already met with Britain's Lord Carrington, Bangladesh's President Ziaur Rahman, U.N. Secretary-General Kurt Waldheim, French President Valery Giscard d'Estaing, Austrian Chancellor Bruno Kreisky, and the United States' Clark Clifford.

MOSCOW'S MULTIFACETED STRATEGY

There can be no doubt that India's position on the Afghanistan question was of major importance to the Soviets. Given the tremendous negative reaction to the Soviet move—from the United States and China, from Asian states, the nonaligned, and the Islamic Conference states—the Soviets needed support from any quarter. The lopsided lineup in the General Assembly vote on the Afghan resolution indicated the desperate situation in which Moscow found itself. Moreover, India's prestige in the nonaligned movement and within the Third World in general made India that much more significant. Finally, all of the Kremlin's efforts to keep India divided from Washington and Peking would be lost if the two latter powers should somehow persuade India to cooperate with them in taking action against the Soviet Union. Indeed, the Soviet media was quick to point out to the new Indian government the direct threat the United States and China represented to India. According to a January *New Times* article;

> Washington is again providing Pakistan with sophisticated weapons which can be turned against India at any moment, building up its fleet in the Indian Ocean, and expanding its base on Diego Garcia. The United States' Chinese friends continue to train and arm saboteurs recruited from among separatists in the northeastern states of India, seeking to use them to destabilize the political situation in the country and eventually gain control of some Indian regions. Peking has not yet returned the 36,000 square kilometers of territory it seized from India.[17]

Pravda argued that India's fears of U.S. and Chinese attempts to "encircle India" were justified: the plans for global domination, hatched by Washington and Peking, who had "identical interests" in South Asia, included building up Pakistan militarily as a counterpoise against India and a bastion against the Soviet Union.[18]

Moscow moved quickly to assess the new Indian government's policy preferences and to underline the significance of continued close relations between India and the Soviet Union. Its initial step was the same one taken immediately after the Janata election victory in March 1977: the dispatch of Foreign Minister Andrei Gromyko to New Delhi. Gromyko arrived in mid-February, which was barely a month after the elections, and there are indications he would have been there sooner had India's busy diplomatic schedule permitted.[19] Gromyko's major goal undoubtedly was to obtain Indian support for Moscow's military intervention in Afghanistan. To this end, he tried very hard to reexplain the causes and necessity of the Soviet Union having to send "limited military contingents" into Afghanistan. The major justification for this, of course, was the interference from Washington, Islamabad, and Peking. This reflected Gromyko's ancillary goal for visiting New Delhi: to reinforce India's perception of the United States' dual role of first causing the crisis and then prolonging it through its military response.

Gromyko seems to have been largely successful on this second goal. His speech at a dinner hosted in his honor by new External Affairs Minister P.V. Narasimha Rao contained some of the toughest anti-United States language uttered by a Kremlin leader since the invasion six weeks earlier. The United States was accused of subverting detente, escalating the arms race in South Asia, and seeking further aggression against Afghanistan. It was this U.S. action, particularly the extension of military aid to Pakistan, that prevented the situation from stabilizing. Although Rao was not nearly so explicit nor vehement in his own address, the External Affairs Ministry issued its own statement at the end of Gromyko's visit, which stated that the United States was hampering efforts to get the Soviet Union to withdraw its troops. Moscow's armed intervention could not be looked at out of context, said J. N. Dixit, the Ministry's spokesman, as "many things are happening in the world which impinge on the situation in Afghanistan": U.S. use of Indian Ocean-Persian Gulf military facilities, strengthening of Diego Garcia, "massive buildup" of U.S. naval force in the region, and reports that "certain countries are openly saying" they are training Afghan rebel fighters.[20] Although New Delhi had expressed these opinions before, Gromyko had to be pleased with at least this indication that India held the United States as much to blame as the Soviet Union for the tensions gripping the region.

Even on this theme, however, Gromyko may have gone a bit too far and not only differed from his hosts but irritated them as well. He devoted a good deal of his attacks on U.S. policy to rather harsh warnings to Pakistan. In one particularly ominous statement, Gromyko remarked that if Pakistan went "along the path followed by the USA and China," it would "derive nothing good out of it and will actually undermine its position as an independent state."[21] Gromyko's assault on Pakistan came at a delicate moment for India when one aspect of its diplomacy to lessen regional tensions was aimed directly at negotiations and building rapport with Pakistan. New Delhi's discomfit with Gromyko's approach—one spokesman, when asked about India's reaction, said rather frankly, "You do not tell your guest what to say"—was clearly seen in its avoidance of any mention of Pakistan by name. Dixit did not refer to Pakistan directly when enumerating grievances against the United States and even Rao, at the dinner where Gromyko launched his attacks, was most circumspect in urging "all countries concerned"—this would refer to the Soviet Union as much as to Pakistan—to "refrain from any action contributing to a further escalation of tension in the region and to accept that problems between countries can and must be resolved through peaceful negotiations."[22]

On his major goal of obtaining Indian support, Gromyko clearly failed. At the same time, however, New Delhi failed in its objectives of persuading the Soviets to withdraw or, falling short of that, of obtaining some positive Soviet measures to defuse the situation such as a timetable for even a partial withdrawal. Mrs. Gandhi described her exchange with Gromyko as "frank"; Gromyko was said to have "explained the Soviet point of view" while the Indian leaders "conveyed ... India's assessment...."[23]

The most Gromyko did in the face of India's different perception was to take note and appreciate "New Delhi's point of view." Even Gromyko's agreement to "consider measures by which tension in the region could be defused" seemed hollow when it was followed by his vehement attack on Washington and Islamabad. In the end, as Dixit reported, there was no change in the Soviet position: "Mr. Gromyko reiterated the stand previously expressed by the Soviets on this issue."[24] Despite the fact tht the controversy over Afghanistan had dominated, if not monopolized, the several hours of talks as well as public speeches and statements, the joint statement contained no reference whatsoever to the issue, which is a certain sign of substantial disagreement.[25]

Further evidence of continuing differences in Soviet and Indian perceptions and of their ongoing attempts to influence one another, was seen in the brief visit to India by Nikolai Firyubin, the USSR deputy foreign minister, in early April. Firyubin, who had accompanied Gromyko on his trip in February, arrived in New Delhi after a swing through Southeast Asia and Nepal. His arrival coincided with the visits of representatives of two close Soviet allies, the Cuban foreign minister and the Vietnamese prime minister. These visits hardly seemed to be coincidental, as India claimed, but rather were likely part of a concerted Soviet effort to gain wider support for its Afghan intervention. Although neither New Delhi nor Moscow revealed anything about Firyubin's talks, it is known that his main theme on the rest of his itinerary was Afghanistan and that he had worked especially hard, to no avail, to get Kathmandu to change its position of calling for the immediate withdrawal of Soviet troops from Afghanistan.[26] The Cuban envoy's visit was explicitly about Afghanistan while he had recently been shuttling back and forth between Kabul, Islamabad, and Moscow. Pham van Dong's six-day state visit was a much broader and more ceremonial affair, but it too involved the Afghan issue. Had either the Soviets or Indians been successful in influencing the other, there would have been no need for such a group of proselytizers converging on New Delhi. Despite the overall success of Dong's visit, even the Vietnamese leader conceded frankly that there were differences with India on the Afghanistan issue. Since Hanoi's and Moscow's perceptions on the issue were identical, it is evident that New Delhi had not become more agreeable. Once again, as the Chinese gleefully observed, differences on Afghanistan were so substantial that no mention of it was made in the final communiqué after Dong's visit.[27]

Despite these differences, or perhaps because of them, both the Soviet Union and India were anxious to emphasize the basic stability and mutual benefits of their relationship. Feburary 1980, which marked the twenty-fifth anniversary of the beginning of Soviet-Indian economic cooperation, represented an ideal opportunity. Deputy Chairman Arkhipov again led a delegation to India to celebrate the "Silver Jubilee." There were meetings and speeches as well as celebrations in Bhilai where the first project had been initiated. There were further talks about collaboration in establishing a steel plant in Nigeria and a nuclear power plant in Libya. The Soviets also agreed to do business with the Indian private as well as public sector. Moscow missed no opportunity to publicize the celebrations, reiterating frequently the importance to India of Soviet friendship, the benefits of cooperation, and the constancy of relations.[28] Moscow was obviously anxious to underline these attractions of Indo-Soviet ties at a time when relations were somewhat strained by the Afghanistan issue. As one commentary pointed out, "International cooperation is an active dynamic process. *It is in constant need of attention, development and improvement.*"[29]

Moscow's eagerness to solidify the Soviet-Indian relationship was revealed more clearly by the visit to Moscow of an Indian Defense Ministry team in May. This delegation, consisting of top officials, armaments experts, and financial advisers, journeyed to the Soviet Union to resume negotiations, which were last held in September 1979. The results of this mission were very substantial. The Soviets agreed to a $1.63 billion credit for India to purchase weapons and equipment over a 10–15 year period. The terms were beneficial: the credit was repayable over 15 years after a 2-year grace period at a 2.5 percent rate of interest. At least as important for India were the items the Soviets agreed to sell at this time. These included 5 highly sophisticated MiG-25 "Foxbat" aircraft, an unannounced number of fast attack boats equipped with missiles, and 100 T-72 tanks with another 600 to be produced in India under license.

The significance of this arms deal was substantial for a variety of reasons. It seems obvious, for one, that Moscow was anxious to arrive at an agreement. The meeting was the culmination of 18 or 19 months of negotiations, according to Indian reports, and suddenly the logjam was broken. Since Indira Gandhi was more inclined than Morarji Desai to conclude a large-scale deal with the Soviet Union and since the delivery of new U.S. arms to Pakistan was almost a foregone conclusion, some of the movement that finally led to the agreement most likely came from India; nevertheless, it was the Soviet Union that was now providing an attractive offer to India—in quantity, repayment terms, kinds of weapons, and license producing. India was anxious to play down the significance of the deal, so it would not damage further its position among the nonaligned. In this vein, India also continued to make veiled references to its ongoing differences with the Soviets over Afghanistan. A spokesman for the External Affairs Ministry, for example, argued strenuously that "India's bilateral defense supplies arrangements and India's assessment and approach to international issues are unconnected. These are separate matters."[30] Still, the Soviets had to have been pleased with this new manifestation of the closeness of Indo-Soviet ties. Military relations had always been perceived in world politics as a particularly sensitive indicator of friendship and agreement, and if the Jaguar deal had been a blow to the Soviets, the May 1980 agreement now put things back on track. Moscow could take specific pleasure in the rather common sentiment in India expressed in one press editorial:

> While accepting aid from outside until there can be a greater degree of self-reliance, the guiding factor will be whether the supplier will remain a

friend in need or in the event of an emergency desert the recipient and ground all his weapons. *Moscow has time and again proved it can be depended upon, while the contrary has been this country's experience with some other suppliers of essential equipment.*[31]

While this did not represent influence—in fact, it was the antithesis of influence since it implied Moscow's obligation to aid India when the latter faced a need or an emergency—it at least provided the Soviets with an important influence-seeking tool in their relations with India.

RESURGENCE OF THE CHINESE FACTOR

The Soviet invasion of Afghanistan had further worsened relations between Peking and Moscow, as China emerged as one of the most vociferous of all states in denouncing the Soviet action. Sino-Indian relations, however, after an initial downturn, began to rebound almost immediately. The early signals for better relations came from the Chinese side and included such gestures as sending a new ambassador almost immediately after Mrs. Gandhi's election victory without waiting for India's replacement in Peking to arrive and having the Chinese foreign minister attend India's Republic Day celebration in Peking for the first time in 20 years. This trend continued through May and in June it was announced that PRC Foreign Minister Huang Hua would be visiting India before the end of the year.

India's and China's mutual concern with the Afghan crisis and its possible repercussions seemed to contribute significantly to the desire of the two states to move toward improved relations, albeit extremely cautiously. China's response to the Afghan situation emerged as more measured than India first believed and the two began to see the value in responding to each other's position. As Huang Hua said at the Republic Day reception, "The present turbulent and tense international situation places a greater obligation on both China and India to promote mutual understanding and cooperation."[32] The visit in early May of Pakistani President Zia to China provided further evidence to India of Peking's positive intentions. For the first time, the Chinese leadership failed to take up the Kashmir theme after Pakistan's leader introduced it.[33] When over 30 heads of state and prime ministers converged on Belgrade shortly thereafter for Yugoslav President Tito's funeral, Mrs. Gandhi held a number of summit meetings, including one with Chinese leader Hua Kuo-feng. This represented the first talks between the two countries at that level since the Nehru-Chou parley 20 years earlier. Chairman Hua apparently spared little in seeking to persuade Mrs. Gandhi that China was anxious for better relations and was eager to take action toward that end. He clearly implied Peking's support for Indian leadership of the non-aligned movement as opposed to Cuba's. The two leaders agreed that better Sino-Indian relations were essential to promote peace and stability in Asia and that bilateral problems could be solved only if the two countries avoided confrontations and resorted to mutual consultations. Hua finished off the talks by suggesting that "both countries should concentrate on the present and the future and put aside past differences."[34]

Moscow's concern with these developments was once again blatantly obvious. The Soviet warning to India of the threat to it and others of a Washington-Peking-Islamabad axis was emphasized with new intensity. The Soviets went to great lengths to picture to the Indians the Zia summit in Peking as "cooperation on a militarist basis." Moscow said, the "Chinese-Pakistani alliance in the making" was putting "the squeeze on India" in Kashmir and in nuclear cooperation to mention just two examples.[35] An authoritative article entitled "Peking's Policy of Heightening Tension," appeared in the May 26 edition of *Pravda* under the name "I. Alexandrov," long-thought to be a pseudonym whose articles represent the consensus of the top Kremlin leadership. *Soviet Review* circulated that piece in India as it did other articles on the strategic dangers to India of the Karakoram Highway, China's threat to Asian security, and Peking's expanding contacts with imperialist powers.

In early August, just prior to the planned visit to India of Huang Hua, *Pravda* again featured a major article on the Chinese threat to India, this time written by V. Shurygin, who was the paper's correspondent in New Delhi.[36] The article was a particularly bitter rehash of the various anti-Indian actions taken by China over the years. China's "anti-Sovietism" was denounced and Shurygin pointed out that:

> China has officially branded the Soviet Union as its enemy No. 1, whereas India correctly regards it as a dependable and selfless friend, which has always given a helping hand to the country at times of trial.

This seeming tone of confidence is belied, however, in Shurygin's conclusion. Referring to the great attention focussed in recent months on Indian-Chinese relations, he warned the government in New Delhi "to be very cautious and avoid hasty steps that could be detrimental to the country's national interests." Shurygin went on to underline that "India's friendly contact and all-round cooperation with the Soviet Union are a main trend in the country's foreign policy" and—here was presented Moscow's recurrent nightmare—this relationship "*cannot be a subject of bargaining in the matter of normalization of Indian-Chinese relations."* In the face of this steady barrage of Soviet warnings, there was a recognition in New Delhi of Sino-Indian problems. Mrs. Gandhi and the Indian leaders, for example, noted differences in China's and India's approach to the Afghan issue and cautioned China against taking an attitude toward Asian countries, particularly India, in the context of superpower politics, for example, India's relations with the Soviet Union. Peking was also urged not to utilize relations with India's neighbors "to sour India's relations as it tended to do in the past." However, New Delhi noted with appreciation Peking's refusal "to play the Pakistani card against India," and, in general, maintained a guardedly optimistic tone.[37]

The Peking visit of Eric Gonsalves, secretary in the Ministry of External Affairs, justified and somewhat accelerated this optimism. At the banquet in Gonsalves' honor on June 20, the Chinese vice-minister for foreign affairs stated that Peking was "willing to further improve its relations with India on the basis of the Five Principles of Peaceful Coexistence." He pointedly added that "China and India are the two big nations of Asia"—thus reiterating Peking's long-held perception of geography in which the Soviet Union was not considered an Asian state—and therefore "they have a responsibility to safeguard peace in Asia and the world." Gonsalves replied that his mission sought to remove as far as possible "the abnormal state of affairs between India and China and develop their relations."[38]

The most significant step in relations occurred the next day when, in an interview with the editor of the New Delhi defense journal *Vikrant*, Vice-Premier Teng Hsiao-ping (Deng Xiaoping) called for improved relations and took two fresh initiatives toward that end.[39] First, he confirmed China's implicit dropping of support for Pakistan's call for "self-determination" in Kashmir, declaring it to be a bilateral problem between India and Pakistan that "should be settled amicably." Second, he offered to settle the long-standing border dispute with the specific proposal that each side agree to the present line of control. Teng was thus suggesting that China would give up its claim to about 115,000 square kilometers in the east, if India would reconcile itself to the situation in the Aksai Chin area. Since India rejected all of the Chinese claim and wanted to retain the territory in the east as well as regain land in the west, India did not find this proposal acceptable. Nevertheless, the offer was significant in that it was the first time it had been made publicly since Chou En-lai had proposed it prior to the 1962 border war. The Indian Government, moreover, welcomed it as a starting point for negotiations and as evidence that Peking wanted the process of normalization resumed.[40]

Despite the productive nature of Gonsalves' visit, little more than a month later, "reliable diplomatic sources" reported that Huang Hua would not be coming during 1980. The Chinese explained this move as being due to Hua's extremely busy schedule for the remainder of the year, but certainly no one in New Delhi was in any doubt as to the real cause: India's recognition in early July of the Heng Samrin regime in Kampuchea.[41] The timing and effect of this significant decision by India once again raises the question of the possibility of Soviet influence. After all, this move was one that the Soviets strongly favored for its effect on their own campaign of support for Vietnam and its "client" regime in Phnom Penh. Moscow could and did revel in this "big gain for Kampuchea," which would undermine China's "hegemonistic schemes" in Indochina and would also lead to an increase in recognition for Heng Samrin among the nonaligned now that it was "clear which way the wind was blowing."[42] In addition, the Soviets had been working strenuously to prevent any India-China normalization from going too far, and they knew that the Indian decision to recognize the Heng Samrin regime would at least temporarily disrupt such a process. For what was, then, a move clearly in the interests of the Soviet Union, there is still no evidence of Soviet pressure on India. In Rao's visit to Moscow in early June, which was the closest contact between the two countries prior to New Delhi's announcement, there is no indication in the available and fairly extensive record of that meeting that Kampuchea was a major issue and certainly no hint of any unusual Soviet pressure or Indian policy change. We know quite a bit less about Firyubin's visit in April, but there is nothing to indicate that any policy change was made then, either.

Since recognition of the Heng Samrin regime had been part of the Congress (I) election manifesto, and India's close ties with Vietnam were a matter of public record, the real question may be why did India wait for some six months to carry out this plank of its foreign policy platform. Although a wide variety of explanations have been offered, a scenario that emphasizes Indian domestic politics and relations with China as well as ties with the Soviet Union may well be closest to the truth. One consideration was that suspicions of China still were high within India. This was apparent in: (1) the reaction to Gonsalves' Peking visit when there were calls in the Lok Sabha not to even talk to China until "Indian territory" had been returned; (2) criticism of Chinese offers as inadequate; and (3) reminders of Peking's insult to India when in invaded Vietnam during Vajpayee's 1979 visit. Thus, the step of recognizing Heng Samrin would serve several purposes. It would give China a taste of its own medicine of February 1979, could serve to tell China its border proposals were not acceptable, and would, most of all, substantiate India's frequently stated position that improvement in Sino-Indian relations would not be at the expense of India's other ties, specifically, friendship with the Soviet Union. With India's independence thus asserted, the "Soviet lobby" in New Delhi would be mollified, and the country would be free to pursue normalization with China when the situation improved. India could then see itself affirming its principles, teaching China a small lesson, and showing its friendship for the Soviet Union—all of which would undermine domestic resistance to improved relations with China. Any movement toward normalization with Peking had thus been balanced ahead of time.

This explanation presents us with an interesting example of influence. To the extent that the explanation is accurate, it would indicate that the Soviets exercised influence, but in a very indirect manner. That is, Moscow had influence because India—specifically, an important segment of the elite—saw USSR ties as so important that differences with the Soviets on China and Afghanistan had to be compensated for by some gesture that Moscow would appreciate. The gesture chosen was important to the Soviets and in keeping with Mrs. Gandhi's stated policy and thus not costly. However, it did create some problems for New Delhi. For one, Peking postponed Huang Hua's visit and waited to assess the degree of what it perceived as Soviet influence on India's policy making. Second, there was no rush by the nonaligned to recognize the Heng Samrin government. In the second of what was becoming the annual debate on Kampuchea's representation in the United Nations in October, the General Assembly rejected the move to oust the Pol Pot regime. Despite India's recognition and intense Soviet lobbying efforts, the vote was slightly worse for Heng Samrin, 74 to 35 against him with 32 abstentions, than it had been in 1979 (71-35-34). Thus, India's policy once again raised questions about its nonaligned status and led to renewed charges of the country's isolation in world affairs.

THE CONTINUING AFGHAN ISSUE
AND THE EXCHANGE OF VISITS

In early June Indian Foreign Minister Rao journeyed to Moscow for an "official friendly visit." An informed Indian government source revealed Rao went to seek "the unconditional withdrawal of Soviet troops from Afghanistan without waiting for an international guarantee of the security and integrity of that country."[43] Soviet Foreign Minister Gromyko seemed to substantiate this report when he preempted Rao's message at a luncheon on the day of the Indian's arrival by bluntly telling his guest: "It must be clear to all that the attempts to change the realities existing in Afghanistan are futile. *Any discussions concerning this*, any attempts to interfere in the internal affairs of Afghanistan *are pointless.*"[44] In addition, the Soviets tried again to bring India around to the USSR position on Afghanistan. It was apparently to this end that the Soviets talked Rao into extending his stay from three to more than four days.

It is clear that neither side was successful in influencing the other on the Afghan issue. Once again, there was no mention of Afghanistan in the final statement at all. The Soviet media thoroughly covered all aspects of Rao's visit without ever mentioning Afghanistan except to give the Soviet viewpoint. Bilateral relations seemed healthy judging from the statement and from Rao's address to Parliament upon his return. The issue of Afghanistan, he said, "has not allowed even the slightest clouding of our bilateral relations; these have indeed grown from strength to strength during the last five months."[45] In the words of the joint statement, talks and discussions were held "in a warm and friendly atmosphere," relations were developing "in the spirit of" the treaty, and both sides saw the visit as "as positive contribution to the development of mutual understanding and friendship between the Soviet Union and India."[46]

Nevertheless, Rao returned home admitting that he had failed to change the Soviet position on Afghanistan and expressed discouragement that it no longer looked like the Soviet "assistance" to Kabul would "remain limited in time as originally intended...." As he said in his statement to Parliament:

> It is time for us to ask ourselves the question whether the Soviet troops meant for assisting Afghanistan have not become, or are not likely to become, a pretext for those who wish to create further instability in that country. Our fear is that beyond a reasonable time frame this could well come to pass....[47]

Rao's various references to his talks with Brezhnev and Gromyko being "candid," "frank," and "concrete, businesslike" indicated clearly that in the "exchange of opinions" Rao had been unable to persuade the Soviets of this fear. All he could say in this regard was that the Soviet Union *seemed* "to have fully understood and respected the views held by India," and that is very different from agreeing with them.

The two sides again failed to influence each other during Indian President Reddy's largely ceremonial visit to the Soviet Union in late September and it was clear that any substantial changes would have to await Leonid Brezhnev's forthcoming visit to India. The excitement with which the Soviets surrounded Brezhnev's December 1980 trip was every bit as extreme as that accompanying his last state visit in November 1973. His departure was preceded by a massive buildup in the Soviet media of the "tremendous significance" of the visit. The USSR multilanguage publication, *Soviet Review*, filled two issues with virtually nothing beside Soviet and Indian paeans of praise for the "forthcoming visit of L. I. Brezhnev," and another issue comprised the texts of all speeches delivered and the joint declaration. An entourage of nearly 300 accompanied Brezhnev; a large press contingent was included, and live television coverage in color was beamed back to the Soviet Union and Eastern Europe via a temporary satellite.

It seems clear that, for Moscow, this excitement was intended to be a major part of the visit. Brezhnev held only three hours of official talks with Mrs. Gandhi, and the agreements he signed on economic and technical cooperation and trade for 1981–85 had all been worked out in advance, represented no innovations in the relationship, and could easily have been signed by lesser officials just as they had been in the past. For the Soviets, however, the hearty welcome Brezhnev received in India, which produced evidence of the closeness of Soviet-Indian ties, was significant in itself. This really was a symbolic and demonstrative meeting directed at the Indian domestic audience and the states of the nonaligned movement primarily. Soviet propaganda was full of praise for the Soviet-Indian relationship, which was described as a "striking reflection of the principles of peaceful coexistence," according with India's "esteemed" policy of nonalignment, and through which India's economic development and independence had been furthered. Moscow spared little effort to remind India of the value of its ties with the Soviet Union. At the same time, the Soviets sought to convince Indians and others in the nonaligned movement of the "positive part Moscow plays in world politics."[48]

Clearly, the issue that motivated Moscow's desire for such a visit was Afghanistan. Despite the Kremlin's strenuous year-long lobbying efforts, the Soviet Union did not fare much better than it had in January on the vote in the General Assembly supporting troop withdrawal. The Soviets could be pleased that the resolution had been watered down but the numbers were still discouraging: 111 states supported the resolution, only 22 opposed it, 12 abstained, and 9 were absent or not voting compared to 104-18-18-12 in January.[49] Although India once again abstained, Moscow's failure to gain ground—particularly in key groups such as the Islamic Conference, where support for the resolution grew from 28 to 31 of the 40 member states with only 2 states supporting the Soviets—was of real concern. Undoubtedly, Moscow hoped that Brezhnev's visit and the benefits he might offer would be enough to induce India to change from abstention to support for the Soviet position. Long before Brezhnev's arrival, Western diplomats were quoted as saying that his goal would be to "enlist India's aid in softening or staying off ... sharp third world criticism" of the USSR intervention in Afghanistan: "The Soviets need a few more statements of support in their kind of words. They would love to have the Indians say the 'right things' on Afghanistan."[50] That there was going to be no change in the Indian position seemed clear from President Reddy's banquet speech on the evening of Brezhnev's arrival. Without softening his position on the Soviet Union by warning of Western, Chinese, or Pakistani subversion or provocation in South Asia, he stated flatly that "We in India remain opposed to any form of intervention, covert or overt, by outside forces in the internal affairs of the region." However, Brezhnev reiterated his previous position. He launched vehement attacks against those who were seeking to subvert Afghanistan and who were maintaining tension and preventing the withdrawal of Soviet troops and normalization of the situation. The meetings with Mrs. Gandhi were referred to even by the Soviets as "frank" and it appears that both Brezhnev and the Indian prime minister simply reaffirmed their positions on the issue of Afghanistan. Mrs. Gandhi told him that India could not condone military intervention and Brezhnev told her that only when threats to the country were ended would the reason for USSR military presence vanish. Until then, he said, the Soviet Union would discharge "to the end its duty of rendering assistance to Afghanistan."[51] It was to be expected, given this continuing disagreement, that Afghanistan would not be mentioned in the final statement, just as it had not in all meetings since the invasion, and this proved to be the case.

Brezhnev and his delegation—which included Gromyko, Firyubin, and Arkhipov—were concerned, secondly, with at least maintaining and supporting India's position on Afghanistan. That is, if the Soviets were unable to influence India to change its position, they would certainly strive to reinforce New Delhi's stance, that is, to keep it from moving further from Moscow. The Kremlin's concern on this score was somewhat urgent by this time, since the meeting of the nonaligned foreign ministers was scheduled for New Delhi in February. The nonaligned movement had been struggling all year to adopt a "common line" on Afghanistan and to deal with what Yugoslavia and others, including India,[52] saw as the threat to the movement's principles from the pro-Soviet radical minority. The barrage of Soviet rhetoric supporting the movement and India's high prestige within it was intended to allay Indian fears of drifting from the mainstream of the movement. The basis of Moscow's defense of India's stance in the movement, particularly its compromise position on Afghanistan, was the warning to India of U.S. "imperialist" and Chinese "hegemonist" forces' hopes of splitting India and the Soviet Union apart. One Soviet commentary prior to Brezhnev's visit said:

> The social systems of the U.S.S.R. and India differ from each other. It is not surprising, then, that at times differences of nuance are to be observed in their assessments of some international problems. But in vain do the opponents of rapprochement between the two countries count on capitalizing on this. The important thing is the identity of their basic positions of principle, their awareness of the sameness of their fundamental historical interests.[53]

The loss of Indian support in the nonaligned movement would have been devastating to the Soviets, and this emphasis on "the sameness" of the two countries' "fundamental historical interests" was a major theme during the visit and following it.

On the issue of Afghanistan, then, neither had changed its position nor influenced that of the other. On a couple of other issues, there also were indications of continuing, if fairly narrow, Indo-Soviet differences. Although the Sino-Indian rapprochement had been in an almost suspended state since New Delhi's recognition of the Heng Samrin regime in Kampuchea, Brezhnev apparently utilized his visit, evidently more tactfully than Kosygin had in 1979, to try to slow down or stop any normalizaton and to encourage the Indians to take a firmer stand against Peking's foreign policy. In one of their meetings, Mrs. Gandhi had felt compelled to explain the progress made in the normalization of relations with China and had then gone on to assure the Soviet leader that this would in no way affect India's ties with the Soviet Union.[54]

A second area of some difference had to do with the Indian Ocean. The United States had reversed President Carter's March 1977 pledge of demilitarization of the area and, in December 1979, the U.S. flotilla in the Indian Ocean was larger than it had ever been, and Washington was moving rapidly ahead with development of Diego Garcia. The Afghan invasion became the justification for a further buildup, and the number of U.S. ships in the ocean grew from about 24 at the beginning of 1980 to close to 30 by April and more than 40 by September. Although Soviet naval strength in the region increased from 24 to 32 over the same period, the Soviets ignored this in unleashing a steady stream of invectives denouncing Washington for "building up [its] military muscle" and for increasing "the imperialist threat in the Indian Ocean."[55] At the initial banquet, however, President Reddy had expressed to Brezhnev India's strong disapproval of the *competitive naval race* going on in the Indian Ocean and "the efforts being made to change the non-aligned character of the littoral states...."[56] At an official press briefing, Indian spokesman Dixit was apparently not satisfied with USSR spokesman Zamyatin's reply to a question from a Soviet newsman about the U.S. military buildup in the area; Dixit amended his response to include Mrs. Gandhi's reaction of broad concern over the increased naval presence of several countries.[57] The joint declaration left both with room for their own interpretation and thus probably satisfied both: Diego Garcia was cited specifically as an example of a base that should be removed, and also condemned were "any attempts to build up foreign military presence in the Indian Ocean under any pretext whatsoever."[58] The different perceptions the two had on this issue—Moscow of a U.S. buildup and New Delhi of an "upward spiral of competitive naval presence"—indicated a widening divergence between the Soviet Union and India. India's very restrained response to Brezhnev's five-point proposal for peace and security in the Persian Gulf was further indication of this divergence. As Mrs. Gandhi tactfully said, "it appeared to be a constructive suggestion and was worthy of careful consideration."[59] In short, while India found itself in far closer agreement on the issues of the overall Indian Ocean-Persian Gulf area with Moscow than with Washington, its views were only similar to Moscow's, not identical.

A significant aspect of Brezhnev's visit were the inducements he apparently brought along with him. One was the agreement for Soviet assistance in the implementation of a broad range of projects totaling over Rs 40 billion in India's next five-year plan. Steel and alumina expansion and oil prospecting were particularly emphasized. Moreover, their previously stagnant mutual trade had grown substantially—the Soviet Union was, by this time, India's third largest trading partner and second-best customer for Indian exports—and a new five-year protocol was signed that pledged the two sides to double the total value of trade again by 1985. There were also reports that Brezhnev's delegation had furthered the negotiations on the supply to India of the MiG-25, and the Indian Air Force would be getting the first lot shortly. Brezhnev's most significant contribution to India, however, was his agreement to raise the USSR's crude oil supplies by one million tons per year. This was an agreement of tremendous importance for New Delhi, which had been scrambling for new sources of oil since the conflict had erupted between Iran and Iraq, which together supplied about 70 percent of India's oil imports. When Mrs. Gandhi reported the Soviet deal to Parliament, saying that these additional imports would be paid for not with hard currency but with more exports to the Soviet Union and that "we appreciate this friendly gesture," her announcement was greeted with rousing cheers from the members of Parliament. That this was a significant step for Moscow to take was clear when it became apparent that the Soviet Union was having to cut its exports to Western Europe, at the cost of precious hard currency, in order to increase supplies to India and certain other developing states.[60]

Since New Delhi had sought and failed to obtain this increased supply of crude oil before, notably during Reddy's visit earlier in the fall, and since there had been speculations about Moscow's holding it out as a "bargaining chip" for Brezhnev's visit,[61] it needs to be asked whether it had any effect on Indian behavior. Since India's position on Afghanistan did not change, the new supply of crude oil obviously had no impact there. It is possible that the oil supply was an instrument that *reinforced* or sustained India's position on Afghanistan and kept it from turning further against the Soviet position. There is no indication, however, that Mrs. Gandhi's government was considering such a policy shift.

The oil offer, therefore, may best be seen as a very significant gesture of Soviet support for India and for Soviet-Indian relations. It should be noted that, for the first time since Mrs. Gandhi's visit to Moscow in June

1976, the atmosphere of relations between the two countries was described as one of "friendship and *trust*" in the final statement. The term "trust" had never been employed by the Soviets during the Janata period, and it seemed to signal the restoration of a closer Indo-Soviet relationship now that Indira Gandhi was back in power. Brezhnev had said in one of his speeches that "I make no secret of the fact that we have always had a particular liking for Mrs. Indira Gandhi, that outstanding political and state figure of contemporary Asia."[62] Thus, despite anti-Soviet demonstrations in New Delhi over Afghanistan—which necessitated very tight security around Brezhnev's visit—and such untoward events as former Premier Desai's charge that Brezhnev had urged him in 1979 not to talk to China and to "teach Pakistan a lesson"[63] and the flap created by Brezhnev's meeting with the CPI leadership, Indo-Soviet relations seemed to have been stabilized. Although there would be differences with Mrs. Gandhi, the Kremlin could indeed have confidence in her and her policies—the kind of confidence it could never have with Desai or Charan Singh.

While Brezhnev's visit did not indeed offer "any substantive evidence concerning India's improved capacity to bargain for a better stature than before,"[64] neither was there any evidence that Moscow was influencing Indian behavior beyond the extent to which India sought to act in a restrained and cautious manner in order to retain its ties with the Soviet Union. The "profound satisfaction" with which the joint statement said the two leaders viewed their bilateral relations and the "new content" of those ties referred particularly to the restoration of "trust" and to the crude oil and economic agreements. The continuing strong nature of bilateral ties, however, did not necessarily mean influence on international issues. While Brezhnev's mission may not have been intended to change India's position but only "to bolster Moscow's image before the non-aligned countries,"[65] even so, as the Chinese recognized, "Brezhnev did not get everything he wanted."[66]

1981: THE STATE OF RELATIONS

Despite the confirmation of degrees of difference on such issues as Afghanistan, the Indian Ocean, and India's possible normalization with China, it was obvious that neither New Delhi nor Moscow saw Brezhnev's visit in December as a failure. Indeed, both placed great emphasis on its contribution to the strengthening of bilateral ties, which were of value to both parties. As Mrs. Gandhi told the Lok Sabha shortly after Brezhnev's departure:

Though India's perceptions of global problems did not always tally with the Soviet Union's, *the two countries were careful to see that these differences did not come in the way of their bilateral relations* or affect their common commitment to strive for world peace. Nor has the divergence in the socio-economic systems of the two countries posed any problem to the development of the multifaceted friendship between them which has benefited the people of India and the Soviet Union, contributing to world peace and stability too. Since *Indo-Soviet relations were not directed against any third country*, the pursuit of good neighborly ties by both had not adversely affected this friendship in any way.[67]

The Twenty-sixth Congress of the Communist Party of the Soviet Union held in late February provided an opportunity for the Soviets to give public expression to *their* view of Indo-Soviet relations. In his Central Committee Report to the Congress, Brezhnev said:

> Comrades, a big place in the Soviet Union's relations with the newly-free countries is, of course, accorded to our cooperation with India. We welcome the increasing role played by that large country in international affairs. Our ties with it are continuing to expand. In both our countries, Soviet-Indian friendship has become a deep-rooted popular tradition.
>
> As a result of the recent negotiations in Delhi with Prime Minister Indira Gandhi and other Indian leaders, the entire range of Soviet-Indian relations has been taken substantially further.
>
> Joint action with peaceful and independent India will continue to be one of the most important areas of Soviet foreign relations.[68]

Two aspects of Brezhnev's comments deserve special mention. One is that, compared to his description of India and Soviet-Indian relations in his report to the Twenty-fifth CPSU Congress in 1976, his 1981 description is briefer, milder, and far less enthusiastic. There is no reference to the impact of their relations on South Asia or Asia in general nor any reference to the solidarity Soviet people were said in 1976 to feel with India's foreign and domestic policies. In other words, relations in early 1981 had not regained the lofty status they had occupied in early 1976. On the other hand, however, India is the *only* country singled out for more than a passing mention in the section of Brezhnev's speech devoted to the development of relations with newly independent countries. This represents a significant gesture on Moscow's part and indicates that relations were of particular importance, even if they were not back to the level of earlier years.

Continuing cooperation in the economic and military fields gave substantive evidence to the solidity of the bilateral ties between Moscow and New Delhi. In January First Vice-Chairman of the USSR Council of

Ministers Ivan Arkhipov made another trip to India to cochair with External Affairs Minister Rao the session of the Inter-Governmental Soviet-Indian Commission. The Soviets agreed to build a thermal power station in northern India and the two governments established joint commission in several areas, including evergy and coal. A month later, a trade potocol for 1981 was signed. This provided for a further increase in turnover, from an expected Rs 19 billion in 1980 to Rs 22 billion. In the military sphere, negotiations were continuing on the items to be purchased by India under the large credit extended by the Soviets the previous May. Discussions had been initiated for the multirole, swing-wing MiG-23 "Flogger" aircraft. Moreover, there was growing controversy over the Jaguar deal, particularly concerning the local manufacture aspect, and negotiations had been held both with the French and with the Soviets concerning filling that potential void.

India's relations with the other major powers, China and the United States, had also undergone no abrupt changes that might have threatened Moscow's relationship with New Delhi. There were some signs of improvement in Sino-Indian relations, however. India stated that it "greatly appreciated" the "amicable manner" in which the Chinese resolved a border incident in August,[69] and the Chinese government went out of its way to make a gesture of goodwill after serious floods in India in mid-August. By December, it seemed clear that Peking indeed sought to resume negotiations toward better relations. The major news agencies of the two countries signed an agreement to exchange correspondents, and the Chinese deputy foreign minister gave an immediate interview to the Press Trust of India's correspondent sent to Peking in which he called for the resolution of the border question on the basis of "mutual respect." A flurry of other feelers on the border issue soon followed.

Significantly, this upsurge in hints that China was anxious to get the normalization process going again came just prior to Brezhnev's visit to India. Although Peking treated Brezhnev's stay in Delhi in a very low-key manner,[70] the Chinese clearly were seeking to undermine the Soviet leader's talks with Mrs. Gandhi. The timing of these gestures was not missed by the Soviets. Nor were they unconcerned about the possibility of a Sino-Indian border settlement setting a very troublesome precedent for the settlement of Sino-Soviet territorial differences. Once again, there was upswing in the quantity and vehemence of Soviet denunciations of China's "hegemonistic" policies in South Asia. Moscow contended that China's buildup of Pakistan, its subversion in India, its anti-Indian position on the Afghan issue, and other Chinese actions directly contradicted "Peking's assurances about its desire to normalize relations with India."[71]

India's relations with the United States were at once better than those with China, yet plagued with chronic problems that appeared likely to prevent them from becoming any closer in the foreseeable future. Nuclear fuel problems dominated the agenda through 1980 and the first several months of 1981. In May 1980 the U.S. Nuclear Regulatory Commission voted against granting a license to ship the next load of fuel on the grounds that India had not accepted the safeguards required in the 1978 Nuclear Non-proliferation Act. President Carter overturned the ban in June and then the fight switched to Captitol Hill. Committees in both houses voted against the sale as did the full House of Representatives. Amid renewed concerns in India of possible U.S. "violation" of the contract the two countries had signed, the Senate finally approved the sale by the narrowest of margins, 48 votes to 46. Before that vote even took place however, India had submitted a request for another shipment of fuel, thus assuring that this issue would continue to irritate relations, even though the issue was more one of principle than of substance, since experts increasingly believed that India was verging on total independence in nuclear energy development.[72] Other issues presented ongoing problems as well: (1) U.S. protectionist policies that hampered Indian exports and hurt trade relations; (2) Mrs. Gandhi's March 1980 statement that dropped Desai's categorical pledge that India would conduct no further nuclear tests and asserted that whether or not India would move in that direction would be determined by national interests;[73] (3) renewed reports that Washington's ally, Pakistan, was moving toward producing a bomb; and (4) continuing differences with the United States on the Indian Ocean.

The Soviets kept open their offer of heavy water for India but continued to demand safeguards and to refuse any supplies of other fuels, such as low enriched uranium. Thus, Moscow had little opportunity to benefit directly from this problem in United States-Indian relations. Nor did the Soviets have anything to say about the possibility of India conducting further nuclear tests and the implied possibility of developing nuclear weapons; Moscow opposed this but refused to allow this opposition to affect Soviet-Indian relations. The Soviets did direct their attention to two irritants in Washington-New Delhi relations: the Indian Ocean and Pakistan. On the former, the Soviets kept up a steady stream of denunciations of U.S. military expansion in the region and stressed the similarity[74] (not identity) of Soviet and Indian positions on the problems of the Indian Ocean. On the latter, the Soviets denounced the possibility of Pakistan developing a bomb and lambasted the West and China for their alleged aid in Islamabad's effort.[75]

Despite Mrs. Gandhi's call for a "new beginning" in Indo-United States relations as the Reagan administration took office and continuing negotiations on arms sales (especially for TOW antitank missiles), it was apparent that problems would remain. For one, the Reagan administration was seen in India as being more hawkish and inclined toward confrontation with the Soviet Union. This outlook, combined with the long-held U.S. perception that India and the Soviet Union had a comfortable relationship, was likely to exacerbate problems in relations. As one Indian newspaper editorialized shortly after Reagan's inauguration:

> As far as Asia is concerned, the basic strategy of outright support for Japan, selective approval of China and a tilt in favor of Pakistan is to be expected. The Indian Ocean will certainly become a focal point of American military, naval and air activity. For India this will pose many unpleasant challenges.[76]

Initial moves by the new U.S. president served to confirm new Delhi's fears. He reversed Carter's naval policy and pledged an approach aimed at countering the Soviet Union in all key oceans, particularly the Indian Ocean.[77] Reagan also indicated that he would consider any request for weapons from Afghan "freedom fighters," thus seeming to escalate the tension there. In March the new government carried on extensive discussions with Pakistan on the resumption of large-scale military aid. After two days of talks in Washington between the new secretary of state, Alexander Haig, and Pakistani Foreign Minister Agha Shahi, it was announced that the United States had agreed to offer Islamabad a $2.5 billion five-year military and economic aid package on easy credit terms.[78] Predictably, India reacted by warning the United States that this step would only create new tensions in the region. Mrs. Gandhi told Parliament that India could afford to ignore these developments "only at grave peril to its security interests." Never in the last two decades, she concluded, had the "international outlook been as grim as it was today."[79] One of India's greatest fears in the wake of the USSR Afghan invasion was coming to pass: Pakistan was being further armed. Moscow sympathized with the threat that Islamabad, Washington, and, of course, Peking presented to India.[80]

Given this situation of real and significant differences in India's relations with both China and the United States, we might well ask again just how close was the Indo-Soviet relationship. The five-day meeting of the foreign ministers of the 96-nation nonaligned movement held in New Delhi in February provided an opportunity to make such an assessment. Although neither Moscow's attitude toward this meeting nor India's behavior in it reveal the details of the relationship, they do provide a certain insight on it and suggest some of the issues and parameters of the Soviet-Indian influence relationship as of early 1981. It had seemed clear that Moscow had attached a special role to the nonaligned movement and to India's role in it, especially since the invasion of Afghanistan. This had certainly been apparent in Brezhnev's visit in December. Leading up to the New Delhi foreign ministers meeting, the Soviet press was full of articles praising the movement and stressing the thesis that the Soviet Union was the "natural ally" of the nonaligned movement, which was also "naturally" anti-imperialist, a thesis Cuba had expounded upon with some success at the Havana summit in September 1979. Given their isolation within the Third World in the aftermath of Afghanistan, the Soviets desperately needed a meeting that would at least be soft in its criticism of the USSR action, if not supportive. Most of the movement's members, however, had taken a stance in opposition to the invasion in the United Nations and elsewhere. The New Delhi meeting would be a crucial test of acceptance of the Soviet action and close Soviet allies, such as Cuba and Vietnam, were busy lobbying other states on Moscow's behalf.

The Soviets did a great deal of their own lobbying and with no state more than with India. The most revealing indication of Moscow's concern with the meeting and with the role that India might play appeared within what was in all other respects a typical Soviet article celebrating India's Republic Day in late January.[81] The emphasis was on Soviet-Indian bilateral ties and the normal aspects were stressed: Indo-Soviet friendship, the value of consultations and exchange of visits, Brezhnev's visit specifically, economic and technical cooperation, and "the identity of fundamental goals" and the similarity of positions on such issues as the Indian Ocean. Although the nonaligned foreign ministers' gathering, only two weeks away, was not mentioned, there were two key paragraphs devoted to the nonaligned movement. These implicitly gave support to the "natural ally" thesis by: (1) reiterating Nehru's opposition to an interpretation of nonalignment as "disinterested observer" or "indifferent pacifist"; (2) referred to his definition as being "an uncompromising anti-imperialist and anti-colonial attitude, struggle against all manifestations of aggression, international diktat and violence"; and (3) asserted the identical or similar views between nonaligned and socialist countries. What made this article unique, however, was that Moscow chose to go beyond this reasonably subtle call on India for support to a somewhat less subtle one and one that indicated the depth of Moscow's current concern. The author, discussing the Soviet Union's support for newly independent countries such as India, first cited Soviet support in the Goa incident of 1961: when "the imperialist states attempted to push through a Security Council resolution censuring India's legitimate action," the Soviets vetoed this "anti-Indian demarche of the West." Then the author moved on to the Bangladesh conflict where, once again, "the Soviet Union helped to repulse the massive attack unleashed against India in the United Nations by Western states and China...." Having thus established the precedent of Soviet support for India in its time of need, the author pointed out that Mrs. Gandhi recognized, as she had told Brezhnev at a mass rally during his 1973 visit, that "true friendship is that which is extended in an hour of trial." He continued his effort to remind Mrs. Gandhi of all the Soviets had done and her own appreciation of it. She was said to have noted that "when one is in trouble or danger, it is especially important to hear a voice of support and assistance, to hear words of sympathy and feel a helping hand." Finally, she was said to have remarked that the Soviet Union had demonstrated this help and support "on repeated occasions." All indications are that the Soviets were here asking for a direct return, in similar goods, of past Soviet support for India. The Afghanistan crisis and the reaction to it, including among the nonaligned, had produced the Soviet Union's own "hour of trial." The Soviet Union needed "a voice of support and assistance," "words of sympathy," and "a helping hand." Moreover, New Delhi owed this to Moscow given Moscow's repeated sacrifices for India.

Moscow's effort to influence India's behavior at the meeting seems to have worked, at least partially. As the host state, India was given the responsibility of preparing the draft declaration. The "blandly worded" result was described as a "draft with no teeth" and perceived by many states to be "blatantly anti-United States and pro-Soviet."[82] This was true particularly on three issues central to Soviet-Indian relations: Afghanistan, Kampuchea, and the Indian Ocean. On the first, India's declaration went beyond the previous Indian position and moved closer to Moscow. It did not even mention the Soviet intervention and merely expressed the need to deescalate tensions and seek a political settlement of the fighting there. Although India had recognized the Heng Samrin regime and had close relations with Vietnam, New Delhi had always reiterated its opposition to the presence of foreign troops anywhere; in the draft, however, Kampuchea was not even mentioned. Finally, on the Indian Ocean New Delhi appeared to backtrack from the position Reddy had expressed to Brezhnev as recently as two months earlier, by specifically citing the U.S. Diego Garcia base while deemphasizing the idea of "superpower rivalry" (and, of course, not mentioning Soviet bases and other military facilities in places such as South Yemen and Ethiopia).

India's positions on these issues were not dramatic reversals of its earlier stances, but the shifts in emphasis and nuance were definitely there and definitely in Moscow's favor. If Moscow had thus influenced New Delhi on these issues, the Indians were forced to backtrack once the conference began. On the Indian Ocean, dissenters demanded that the declaration name all bases, i.e., also the Soviet Union's, or none. The latter option was chosen and India agreed to go along with the majority formulation that voiced disapproval of the existence of foreign bases and supply facilities and regretted big-power presence in all forms and manifestations in the Indian Ocean. Despite Hanoi's warnings before the meeting that any mention of Kampuchea would exacerbate the regional situation, India was forced to back down on this issue as well. The issue was enlarged to take note of "tensions in and around Kampuchea," but the final declaration did call for the withdrawal of "all foreign forces," mentioning only Kampuchea by name. Finally, on the issue of greatest importance to the Soviets, Afghanistan, the Indians also had to step down, but they salvaged somewhat more of a compromise. The final formulation called for a settlement on the basis of withdrawal of foreign troops—which was close to Pakistan's call for a Soviet withdrawal—and the strict observance of nonintervention and noninterference in the country's affairs—which was closer to what India and, certainly, the Soviet Union wanted.

The final declaration was thus a compromise, if only in the sense that it did not specifically name the Soviet Union or Vietnam as the "culprits" in Afghanistan and Vietnam. The general impression, in India and in the West, was that "the pro-Soviet tilt" that had come to dominate the movement in recent years had been ended.[83] Peking also saw it as a victory for the "real nature" of the movement and a "heavy blow" to the Soviets.[84] Two of Moscow's closest allies and those most directly affected by the planks in the final resolution, Afghanistan and Vietnam, expressed "reservations." The Soviets' reaction was one, implicitly, of disappointment. They published only very general assessments that barely mentioned differences within the meeting and gave no indication that certain pro-Soviet positions had been altered.[85] In terms of Soviet-Indian relations, moreover, Moscow was apparently not too impressed with India's efforts, which was indicated by the fact that it was hardly mentioned, much less praised, in Soviet commentary. Indeed, another Soviet assessment clearly categorized India's contribution below the states of Vietnam, Laos, Angola, Ethiopia, Nicaragua, Afghanistan and "a number of other countries"; the latter were all making a "valuable contribution" to the movement, while India was "again" (since the return of Mrs. Gandhi?) described only as playing an "active part."[86] Moscow's lack of enthusiasm may be due to the fact that India appeared to give in too easily to the reaction to its pro-Soviet positions in the draft declaration. After a vain "diplomatic offensive" of unknown intensity by India to muster support for its draft, Indian leaders seemed to have sat back and been more than willing to accept compromise solutions to the serious differences besetting the conference. There is no evidence of Indian lobbying, such as was done by the Havana, Hanoi, and Kabul representatives. Indeed, India emerged as one of the chief spokesmen for the unity of the movement. Thus, it is apparent that India shifted its stance, which suggested Soviet influence, only until substantial resistance was met and then quickly returned to its original position. It is too early to tell if India would suffer a setback to its nonaligned leadership status in the wake of its temporary defense of Soviet positions.

INFLUENCE AND CONTINUING ISSUES

In the months after the February 1981 nonaligned foreign ministers' meeting in New Delhi, it was obvious that India still maintained a compromise position on Afghanistan despite Moscow's influence attempts. While this was of concern to Moscow in certain respects, it certainly was pleasing to the Soviets in its anti-Western aspects. The major differences between India and the West were displayed clearly during British Prime Minister Margaret Thatcher's visit in April 1981. Moreover, the U.S. decision to provide Pakistan with arms was creating the necessary spillover effect in India that Moscow hoped for: New Delhi saw this arms deal as another Pakistani attempt to achieve military parity and, moreover, a reflection of a change in U.S. foreign policy toward South Asia.

Just as this continuing and indeed growing United States-Indian friction was of no little comfort to Moscow, signs of progress in Sino-Indian relations were, of course, alarming. In April, Chinese Vice-Premier Teng Hsiao-ping told the visiting Janata Party leader, Dr. Subramaniam Swamy, that China was ready to resolve the border question or, "if conditions are not ripe now for the settlement," China was willing to move to "other aspects of normalization . . . ." Teng also contended that bilateral relations had been "soured" by a superpower "which always tried to fish in troubled waters" (the 1962 border conflict was due to the "manipulations" of then Soviet leader Krushchev, for example). He told Swamy that the first item on China's agenda was the normalization of relations with India.[87] The Soviet position continued to be one of denouncing "Peking's anti-Indian schemes" and of reminding India of all the issues that lay between India and China. One article cited Chinese aggression against "sacred Indian land," reminded New Delhi of the 1962 Parliamentary resolution not to negotiate with China until the territory had been returned, and pointed out that the border problem was "only a part of the complex problems" dividing the two countries: "The deadlock in their relations is also a direct result of Peking's political orientation, its rapprochement with the imperialist circles and the simultaneous intensification of its expansionist tendencies in South Asia."[88] China's military support for Pakistan and its "rabid anti-Sovietism" were further issues. India's approach of willingness to settle disputes was "*on the whole*"—that is, not entirely—"realistic, logical and constructive." In a clear warning to New Delhi, this rather typical, if somewhat more blunt, article concluded:

But India does not want to win the favor of its quarrelsome neighbor *at the price of* concessions detrimental to its sovereignty, interests, prestige and *good relations with other countries, mainly the Soviet Union*, its tried and tested friend who has come to its aid on more than one occasion.

The bluntness of such warnings will probably increase if, as announced in early May, the five-day visit to India by the Chinese foreign minister, Huang Hua, takes place as scheduled. Yet Moscow is not likely to have much more success influencing Indian behavior on this issue than in the past. Indian and Soviet interests and perceptions of international issues remained close, but the exercise of influence by either was hugely difficult.

NOTES

1. The Party has never had more than 44.7 percent of the popular vote, yet its share of the seats in the Lok Sabha before 1977 had ranged from 54 percent to close to 75 percent.
2. For election data, see Norman D. Palmer, *The Indian Political System*, 2nd ed. (Boston: Houghton Mifflin, 1971), ch. 10; Ram Joshi and Kirtidev Desai, "Towards a More Competitive Party System in India,'" *Asian Survey*, November 1978, pp. 1091–1316: *Overseas Hindustan Times*, January 17, 1980; and *Indian and Foreign Review*, March 1, 1980.
3. Boris Chekhonin, "Looking into the Future," *New Times*, no. 4, January 1980, pp. 10–11. See also A. Usvatov, "The Return of Indira Gandhi," *New Times*, no. 2, January 1980, p. 11.
4. *Soviet Review*, January 17, 1980. Emphasis added.
5. Among many sources, see Robert Rand, "A Chronology of Soviet-Afghan Relations: April 1978-January 1980," *Radio Liberty Research*, RL 17/80, January 2, 1980; Louis Dupree, "Afghanistan under the Khalq," *Problems of Communism*, July-August 1979, pp. 34–50; and Jiri Valenta, "The Soviet Invasion of Afghanistan: The Difficulty of Knowing Where to Stop," *Orbis*, Summer 1980, pp. 201–18.
6. *Overseas Hindustan Times*, January 10, 1980.
7. *Times of India*, January 13, 1980. Emphasis added. See also *Los Angeles Times*, January 12, 1980; and *Overseas Hindustan Times*, January 24, 1980.
8. *Los Angeles Times*, January 17, 1980.
9. *Time*, January 21, 1980, p. 42.
10. *Overseas Hindustan Times*, March 6, 1980.
11. *Overseas Hindustan Times*, January 24, 1980.
12. *Overseas Hindustan Times*, May 29, 1980.
13. *Los Angeles Times*, January 12, 1980.
14. *Overseas Hindustan Times*, February 14, 1980. See also *Los Angeles Times*, January 30, February 1–2, 1980.
15. *Los Angeles Times*, April 1, 1980.
16. *Beijing (Peking) Review*, no. 5, February 4, 1980, p. 4.
17. Chekhonin, "Looking into the Future." The same issue also featured an article on China's subversive efforts in Afghanistan.
18. *Pravda*, January 19, 1980. The article was reported in the *Times of India* on the next day.
19. See *Radio Liberty Research*, RL 35/80, January 21, 1980. Extensive coverage in the

Indian press is found in the *Statesman,* February 12–15, 1980. The joint statement was carried in full by *TASS* on February 14.
20. *Los Angeles Times,* February 15, 1980.
21. *Statesman,* February 13, 1980. See also *FEER,* February 29, 1980, p. 20.
22. *Statesman,* February 13, 1980.
23. *UPI,* February 12, 1980.
24. *Los Angeles Times,* February 14, 1980. See also *Overseas Hindustan Times,* February 28, 1980.
25. *TASS,* February 14, 1980.
26. *Statesman,* April 7, 1980; and *UPI,* April 6, 1980.
27. "Soviet, Vietnamese and Cuban Lobbying Missions in Asia," *Beijing Review,* no. 17, April 28, 1980, pp. 11–12.
28. For example, *Soviet Review,* produced in India, carried many more articles on Indo-Soviet economic cooperation than usual; also, S. Almazov and Y. Karpov, "Silver Jubilee," *New Times,* no. 9, March 1980, pp. 18–19.
29. A. Nizamov, "India at the Start of the 1980s," *International Affairs,* no. 3, March 1980, p. 19. Emphasis added.
30. *Overseas Hindustan Times,* June 12, 1980. See also *Los Angeles Times,* May 29; *Far Eastern Economic Review* (hereafter cited as *FEER*), June 6, pp. 9–10; and *The Military Balance, 1980-1981* (London: The International Institute for Strategic Studies, 1980), p. 106.
31. *Overseas Hindustan Times,* June 12, 1980.
32. *Beijing Review,* no. 5, February 4, 1980, p. 4. See also *The Times* (London), June 24, 1980.
33. *Beijing Review,* no. 19, May 12, 1980, p. 4; and *FEER,* May 16, 1980, pp. 23–24.
34. *Indian and Foreign Review,* May 15, 1980. See also *Overseas Hindustan Times,* May 22, 1980; and *Statesman,* May 6 and 9, 1980.
35. *New Times,* no. 21, May 1980 p. 24.
36. "Cold Winds from the Himalayas," *Pravda,* August 7, 1980. Emphasis added.
37. *Overseas Hindustan Times,* June 5, 1980.
38. See *Beijing Review,* no. 26, June 30, 1980, p. 7; and *Indian and Foreign Review,* July 1, 1980.
39. See *Times of India,* June 22, 1980; and Arul B. Louis, "A Thaw in the Himalayas," *FEER,* July 4, 1980, pp. 26–27.
40. See *Statesman,* July 3, 1980.
41. *Statesman,* August 6, 1980. See also *FEER,* August 15, 1980. pp. 14–15.
42. *New Times,* no. 29, July 1980, p. 11. The author did admit that "all of the non-aligned countries that have not yet established diplomatic relations with Phnom Penh may not of course follow India's example at once . . . ."
43. *New York Times,* June 3, 1980; and *Overseas Hindustan Times,* June 19, 1980.
44. *TASS,* June 3, 1980. Emphasis added.
45. *Indian and Foreign Review,* July 1, 1980, p. 6. See also *TASS,* June 15, 1980, p. 5.
46. *Soviet Review,* no. 28, June 16, 1980.
47. *Indian and Foreign Review,* July 1, 1980.
48. In addition to the November 17, December 4, and December 15, 1980 issues of *Soviet Review,* see issues no. 49, 50, and 51 of *New Times.* The titles of the *New Times* articles indicate their theme: "The Fruits of Friendship," "Mission of Peace and Friendship," and "Dynamic and Stable Relationship." See also F. Yurlov, "Soviet-Indian Friendship: Factor of Peace and Progress," *International Affairs,* no. 3, March 1981, pp. 59–64.
49. See Ted Morello, ' Moscow Puts the Pressure On." *FEER,* November 7, 1980, pp. 11–12; and "Case for the Prosecution (No. 2)," *FEER,* November 21, 1980, pp. 11–12.
50. *Christian Science Monitor,* October 17, 1980.

51. *TASS*, December 9, 1980. See also *Christian Science Monitor*, December 10, 1980.
52. See Mohan Ram, "Sticking to the Guidelines," *FEER*, May 30, 1980, p. 36.
53. "The Soviet Union and India," *New Times*, no. 47, November 1980, p. 1.
54. *Overseas Hindustan Times*, December 18, 1980.
55. For example, see *New Times*, no. 15, April 1980, pp. 24–25; and *International Affairs*, no. 6, June 1980, pp. 101–05.
56. *Overseas Hindustan Times*, December 18, 1980.
57. *Christian Science Monitor*, December 10, 1980.
58. *Soviet Review*, no. 58, December 15, 1980.
59. *Overseas Hindustan Times*, December 25, 1980. See also *Los Angeles Times*, December 11, 1980; and, for an analysis of the proposals, Bruce Porter, "Brezhnev's Proposals on Persian Gulf Security," *Radio Liberty Research*, RL 475/80, December 11, 1980; and Mohan Ram, "An Offer that Can be Refused," *FEER*, December 26, 1980, pp. 16–17.
60. *AP*, February 2, 1980.
61. *Soviet Review*, no. 58, December 15, 1980.
62. *Christian Science Monitor*, October 17, 1980.
63. *Overseas Hindustan Times*, December 18, 1980. A Soviet refutation—Mrs. Gandhi's government also refuted it—is in *New Times*, no. 51, December 1980, p. 6.
64. Jyotirindra Das Gupta, "India in 1980: Strong Center, Weak Authority," *Asian Survey*, February 1981, p. 160.
65. *Overseas Hindustan Times*, December 25, 1980.
66. *Beijing Review*, no. 51, December 22, 1980, p. 8. Also see Mohan Ram, "The Not-so-Warm Welcome," *FEER*, December 12, 1980, p. 10; and *FEER*, December 19, 1980, pp. 15–16.
67. *Overseas Hindustan Times*, December 25, 1980. Emphasis added.
68. The text is published as a supplement to *New Times*, no. 9, February 1981. The Soviet Embassy distributed it in India as issue no. 11 of *Soviet Review*, March 5, 1981. A lengthy and glowing article on "India and CPSU Congresses" was also carried in *Soviet Review*, no. 9, February 19, 1981, pp. 12–27.
69. *Overseas Hindustan Times*, September 4, 1980. See *Beijing Review*, no. 35, September 1, 1980, p. 8.
70. See *Beijing Review*, no. 51, December 22, 1980, pp. 8–10.
71. *Izvestia*, December 23, 1980. See also V. Borisov, "Peking: Hegemonism in Action," *International Affairs*, no. 1, January 1981, pp. 34–42; and Mohan Ram, "China Opens the Indian Door," *FEER*, December 5, 1980, pp. 38–39.
72. See *Los Angeles Times*, September 20, 1980, and February 18, 1981.
73. See *Christian Science Monitor*, March 19, 1980, and *Overseas Hindustan Times*, March 27, 1980. An editorial in the latter applauded Mrs. Gandhi's decision as providing "nuclear clarity."
74. *New Times*, no. 4, January 1981, p. 9.
75. See Vyacheslav Boikov, "A-Bomb for Pakistan," *New Times*, no. 13, March 1981, pp. 28–30.
76. *Overseas Hindustan Times*, February 5, 1981.
77. *Los Angeles Times*, March 4, 1981.
78. *Los Angeles Times*, April 22, 1981.
79. *Overseas Hindustan Times*, April 23, 1981. See also *Overseas Hindustan Times*, April 2, 9, 16, and 30, 1981.
80. For example, see A. Usvatov, "Furthering Alien Interests," *New Times*, no. 14, April 1981, pp. 14–15.
81. Andrei Fialkovsky, "'We Rejoice at Your Achievements,'" *New Times*, no. 4, January 1981, pp. 8–9.

82. See Mohan Ram, "The Draft with no Teeth," *FEER*, February 13, 1981, p. 10; *Los Angeles Times*, February 14, 1981; *Overseas Hindustan Times*. February 19, 1981; and Ram, "Moscow in the Firing Line," *FEER*, February 20, 1981, pp. 8–9.
83. For example, see *Overseas Hindustan Times*, February 26, 1981; and *Los Angeles Times*, February 14, 1981.
84. *Beijing Review*, no. 8, February 23, 1981, pp. 11–12.
85. For example, see V. Gordeyev and S. Irodov, "The Delhi Conference," *New Times*, no. 8, Feburary 1981, pp. 8–9. See also A. Pavlov, "The Non-Aligned Movement and the Struggle Against Imperialism," *International Affairs*, no. 4, April 1981, pp. 77–81.
86. Victor Sidenko, "Twenty Years," *New Times*, no. 6, February 1981, p. 6.
87. *Overseas Hindustan Times*, April 23, 1981.
88. Yuri Lugovskoy, "Peking's Anti-Indian Schemes," *New Times*, no. 11, March 1981, pp. 16–17. Emphasis added.

8
THE PARAMETERS OF
AN INFLUENCE RELATIONSHIP

Many of the hypotheses with which we began this study seem borne out after analyzing the nature of influence in Soviet-Indian relations from 1969 into the 1980s. Certainly, this influence relationship was determined by the interactions between domestic developments in India (we know far less on this score regarding the Soviet side) as well as regional events and great-power relationships. Changes on any one of these three levels impinged on the other two and forced the Soviet-Indian relationship into a new context. Any one of these threads is ignored only at the risk of substantial misperceptions of the situation. Moreover, the hypothesis that presence does not equate with influence also seems to have been supported. We witnessed the evolution of a substantial Soviet presence in India—in economic and military aid programs, as well as personnel, diplomatic support, and the like—yet it was clear that influence did not automatically follow (or precede). Soviet "inputs" in terms of this presence did not equal "outputs," that is, influence over Indian behavior.

One of the central issues in assessing influence in the Soviet-Indian relationship is distinguishing it from coincidence of interests. If two states, such as the Soviet Union and India, have the same perception of certain issues or of their interests, there would be no influence operating between them. Agreement or coincidence would not be influence. For example, does the failure of India to condemn the Soviet Union for its intervention in Hungary in 1956, Czechoslovakia in 1968, or Afghanistan in 1980 signify Soviet influence at work? Or does it rather indicate that India appreciated at least some of Moscow's motivations and that India also realized the practical futility of "condemnations" and the value of playing a mediatory role in East-West tensions? If it is the former, it means that Moscow's leverage was operational as early as 1956 and, given the newness of the relationship then, this seems doubtful. If it is the latter, it illustrates a rather consistent perception of world politics over the years in New Delhi, a perception that places India much closer to the Soviet Union than to the United States.

The West seems always to have assumed that if a state looked at the world in terms different from its own, and similar to Moscow's, that the Soviets had influenced those perceptions. However, there are many factors that help to explain the undeniable truth that Indian perceptions of world politics have tended to be closer to those of the Soviet Union than to those of the United States; these include India's colonial experiences and foreign policy principles, the Soviets' economic development and challenge to the West in world affairs, as well as the West's specific policies, such as the repeated arming of Pakistan. As Robert Wesson has argued in a different context, it is likely that these mutual perceptions, "the background of relations and attitudes,"[1] between Moscow and New Delhi have been more important to the relationship than any concrete measures by either to exert influence. In any case, there is no evidence in Soviet-Indian relations of a crude application of pressure. Yet, they have agreed far more often than they have disagreed. For Washington, the basis for the strain in Indo-United States relations over the years examined here has not been Soviet influence in India but rather, as an Indian analyst wrote early in 1981, that "the real difference between India and the U.S. is that their international perceptions are widely varying."[2]

Perhaps coincidence of interests can at times be viewed as joint influence. In the process of moving toward a treaty in 1969 and finally signing it officially in 1971, the perceptions and interests of the two sides came closer together, almost to the point of identity. In these common perceptions, each side was able to influence the other: the Soviets influenced India to qualify its nonalignment by leaning toward the Soviet Union, and New Delhi influenced the Soviets to forego their policy of balance between Pakistan and India. The treaty and Soviet support during the war over Bangladesh did indeed enhance Soviet-Indian relations[3] yet differences, even over the significance of the treaty itself, have remained; Soviet references to the treaty representing a "new stage" in relations or providing the "basis" for those relations have rarely been reiterated by the Indians.[4]

The general conclusion evident from this study is that the instances of the successful exercise of influence by either side have been rare. Mrs. Gandhi, not surprisingly, has always contended this. During Brezhnev's 1973 visit, for example, she stated that the Soviet leaders had never tried to influence an Indian decision[5] and, during his 1980 trip, she emphasized that "neither country" had "ever sought to impose its perceptions on the other."[6] As she proceeded to say on the latter occasion, "our agreement on vital issues outweighs divergence," and the degree of agreement has been the crucial ingredient in most cases where some influence may have been successfully exercised. For instance, while Moscow may be said to have influenced New Delhi not to go to war earlier in 1971, by October the Soviets had come to agree with India—that is, they were influenced by New Delhi—on the necessity of a short-term conflict. More recently, the Soviets have been relieved that India has not condemned them for the Afghan invasion, and they may have influenced New Delhi in this by reinforcing their past attitudes. Yet, this would appear to be another case of joint influence, or coincidence of interests, in that Moscow has paid for New Delhi's behavior via a huge new arms deal and further economic aid, especially crude oil sales. Moscow may have contributed to the Indian decision to recognize the Heng Samrin regime in Cambodia in 1980 (but perhaps only at the cost of New Delhi going further with its normalization with China). The Soviets did seem to influence New Delhi's role in the nonaligned foreign ministers' meeting in early 1981 but only up to the point where India met resistance from its nonaligned brethren. Then Indian positions reverted to past ones with little evidence of struggle, and Soviet influence vanished. Direct Soviet influence thus appears to have been limited, short-lived, and often expensive.

Aside from these cases of possible Soviet influence or joint influence, there are some instances that appear to be examples of the exercise of Indian influence over Soviet behavior, of the weaker state influencing the superpower. Although New Delhi did not have enough clout to prevent Moscow from offering arms aid to Pakistan in 1968, for example, the Indians were able to influence the Soviets to stop the program shortly thereafter. India's playing of the "China card" in fall 1972 and again in mid-1976 influenced the Soviets into a variety of concessions toward India: recognizing some of the Indian positions regarding the Sino-Indian border, further aid, rhetorical support, and an offer of crude oil. The symbolic significance of this Soviet offer of crude oil to India probably cannot be overstated. India had tried since at least 1972 to obtain Soviet oil but had failed. The Soviets' own needs, those of its Eastern European comrades, and the hard-currency earnings generated by sales of it to the West, held a higher priority for Moscow. Then, in December 1976, at a time when prospects for a Sino-Indian normalization seemed particularly good, the Soviets were suddenly forthcoming. This Soviet use of its own oil as a "weapon" shows up again only in 1979 and 1980: while in New Delhi in March 1979, Kosygin offered to increase the quantity sold and Brezhnev did the same in December 1980; the first offer followed Vajpayee's mission to China and the latter also was extended when Indian interest in more normalized ties with Peking was again growing. A final example of likely Indian influence came with Soviet uncertainty about the new Janata regime. This was evidenced by Gromyko's offer in April 1977 of a new aid package on the most reasonable terms Moscow had ever offered New Delhi and when previous Soviet credits had barely been touched. These instances, combined with Soviet military aid offers and certain Soviet policy concessions, such as on the Indian Ocean, suggest weaker states can indeed influence stronger ones despite the disparities in capabilities.

It is almost as difficult to know when an attempt at influence has failed as to realize that one has succeeded. Often we may not even know an attempt has been made. We do know, however, that the Soviets tried strenuously on several occasions to obtain Indian endorsement of their Asian collective security idea. Although India seemed to come close to supporting it on a couple of occasions, Moscow clearly failed here. The Soviets also were unable to persuade India to allow them to mediate between India and Pakistan after the 1971 war as they had at Tashkent after the 1965 conflict. The Soviets got nowhere in their efforts to have India sign the NPT or avoid developing a nuclear device. (Fairly stringent Soviet safeguards on nuclear fuels may, however, have had an impact on India's nuclear program.) Each side has been able to influence the other's similar but not identical views on the Indian Ocean issue only slightly. Finally, it does not appear that Moscow has been very successful in influencing New Delhi to forego normalization with Peking; normalization has not taken place and progress in this area has been painstakingly slow, but this seems due more to the inherent problems in Sino-Indian relations than to Soviet attempts at influence.

The overall nature of Soviet-Indian relations has been marked more by failure than success in attempts at influence; yet the relations have been characterized by far greater agreement than difference in perceptions of issues in world politics. How can this be explained? Certainly one key part of the answer is to be found in a comparison of Soviet and Indian foreign policy goals. The point has been made throughout this study that there has been a great similarity in these goals. However, at a fundamental level there would appear to be a major and all-pervasive difference: for India the primary concern in foreign policy has always been Pakistan—as Bhabani Sen Gupta has noted, Pakistan "casts its shadow on India's domestic politics and affects the Indian "psyche" far more than any other external factor"[7]—while for the Soviet Union, the highest priority has been China. Relations between New Delhi and Moscow, then, have been closest when both have perceived a close link between Pakistani and Chinese "threats." This was the case in 1969 to 1971, in 1975, and again in 1980 following the Afghan invasion. However, when Indo-Pakistani and Sino-Soviet tension has eased somewhat, such as in the 1972–74 period, both New Delhi and Moscow have probed for an improvement in relations with the other's adversary. When this has failed, both have reverted to trying to persuade the other of the "danger" of dealing with that same adversary. It is at these times that relations have become closer.

If there is a single theme that may be said to have dominated the whole history of Soviet-Indian relations and to characterize the nature of that relationship, it is the Soviet attitude toward China. Moscow has made unremitting efforts to convince India of the danger which China has represented to it—directly along the border and through the various insurrectionist groups Peking is said to be supporting, as well as indirectly, by means of support for Pakistan economically, militarily, and politically (e.g., on Kashmir). At times when New Delhi has been more actively pursuing the course of normalization, Moscow's warnings have escalated in number and in stridency. After citing a lengthy list of Chinese provocations, the Soviets would implicitly demand to know how the Indians could even consider the possibility of any truly "normal" relationship with the Peking regime. The centrality of China in Soviet foreign policy should not be understated nor should the significance of South Asia, in general, and India, in particular, in Moscow's anti-Chinese crusade.

At the same time, Moscow has also regarded India as politically significant in its own right, certainly to a greater degree than has Washington.[8] The Soviet Union has also been more successful than the United States in persuading the Indians that Moscow was basing its policy on Indian interests as such rather than only viewing those interests as a function of broader strategic concerns.[9] Indeed, it has been the general rule that the Soviet leaders have backed off from the Chinese issue when it became clear the Indians were becoming uncomfortable with Moscow's diatribes. If for no other reason than geopolitics, the Soviet Union is going to perceive its interests engaged over the long term in South Asia. Even the Pakistanis, who have been at odds with the Soviets far more than the Indians, have realized the significant impact of the Soviet Union's geographical proximity and high degree of interest in the region's affairs. Early in 1980 President Zia admitted that:

> ... you can't live in the sea and create enmity with whales. You have to be friendly with them. The Soviet Union is on our doorstep. The United States of America is 10,000 miles away.[10]

In seeking explanations for the nature of the Soviet-Indian relationship, in addition to goals we need also to consider capabilities. The Soviets have indeed brought substantial capabilities to bear in their pursuit of influence in India. This is especially true in the areas of economic and military assistance, where Moscow has been clearly willing to allocate its resources toward the establishment of influence. This has had mixed results. There have been certain problems but, in general, Moscow has not been unskillful in applying its resources. The Soviet effort in molding Indian public opinion has been particularly revealing. According to recent statistics,[11] the Soviets direct 50 percent more radio broadcasts to India per week than does the United States, their monthly magazine has eight times the circulation and one-third the price of the United States', they translate far more books, and they distribute far more journals. Although these attempts to influence attitudes have not been completely successful, and there remains a large segment of the Indian elite that is not sympathetic to the Soviet Union, a vast majority of Indians see the Soviet Union as the most trustworthy of the great powers.[12] Moreover, the Soviets have been aided by a "pro-Soviet lobby" in India; at times this lobby has included close advisers of Mrs. Gandhi's, usually the CPI, and, most recently, a newly revived organization called the "Friends of the Soviet Union."[13]

Overall, then, there have been a number of factors that were conducive to, and other factors that obstructed, the establishment and exercise of influence by either state. Among the former, similarity of views has been the most significant. As one Indian journalist commented, this "natural" friendship was simply based on a "convergence of interests."[14] Personality has been not an unimportant factor in the relationship as seen in the different perceptions of the Soviet Union held by Indira Gandhi and Morarji Desai. Yet this has been circumscribed by the degree of common interests; that is, relations under Desai, for example, did not become as strained as the West expected and the Kremlin feared, and relations under Mrs. Gandhi's state of emergency showed almost the opposite tendency. Among the obstacles, in addition to the difference in goals, India's sensitivity to its independence has made it highly suspicious of any action that even resembled an attempt to influence it. The internal disarray in India, particularly since 1975, has also been a limitation, both on India's attractiveness as a "target" and on the likelihood of the Soviets having any meaningful success. On Moscow's side, its virtual obsession with China as opposed to India's own interest (long-term) in better relations with that country, has been a limitation on Soviet policy. The Soviet Union's other interests, such as detente, stability in South Asia, naval expansion in the Indian Ocean, and Afghanistan, have also conflicted with Soviet goals vis-à-vis India.

What we are left with, then, as the basic explanation for the nature of the Soviet-Indian influence relationship, and this gets back to the issue of goals, is the question of *need*. Who has needed whom more? The Soviet-Indian relationship through the 1970s and into the 1980s has indeed been, as Robert Donaldson asserted, a "shifting balance" of "mutual dependency."[15] India has needed the Soviet Union for support in times of crisis vis-à-vis Pakistan or in times of uncertainty as the Sino-United States rapprochement has developed. India has also needed the economic, technical, and military assistance that the Soviets have been able to provide. Moscow, on the other hand, has needed India against China, and to a lesser extent against the United States, as well as to serve as an entree for the Soviet Union to the nonaligned movement, the Third World, and Asia. The degree of need that each has felt has depended on the importance of the particular issue and the options available. In the 1969–71 period, each state needed the other's support vis-à-vis the main adversary, Pakistan for India and China for the Soviet Union. After the actual crisis in Sino-Soviet relations passed in 1969, New Delhi's need for support was greater due to the significance of the coming struggle with Islamabad over Bangladesh and India's isolation from the United States and China. Even then, however, India's influence predominated in that Moscow ultimately agreed to India taking military action against Pakistan. (It should be noted that one of the "code" words we have spotted, "trust," did not appear in their joint description of the relationship until Firyubin's visit in October.) After the war, India's stronger regional position greatly reduced its dependence on the Soviet Union. Although the relationship stayed close, both sides explored relations with other regional and external powers. When those cautious efforts collapsed, which was symbolized particularly by Washington's lifting of the arms embargo to Pakistan, their mutual need was fairly even and the close relationship was restored. During India's state of emergency, Moscow apparently became convinced that New Delhi's need was less, which was signified by the April 1976 policy change toward China, and the Soviets responded with a wide variety of inducements to India to prevent this "normalization." The Janata perceived even less Indian need and sought to improve ties with Washington and Peking. Even this regime, however, realized the fundamental importance to India of the Soviet relationship, and the policy changes were carefully calibrated not to jeopardize the "essentials" of this relationship. Since the end of 1979, the sense of need has seemed to heighten in both countries, but perhaps more so in the Soviet Union. Mrs. Gandhi's suspicions of the United States and its arming of Pakistan have been counterbalanced by Moscow's need for support in the wake of the Afghan invasion. The Soviet appeal to India, prior to the nonaligned foreign ministers' meeting in New Delhi in February 1981, to help the Soviet Union in its "time of trial," as it had helped India in 1971, could not have been a clearer expression of this Soviet need. The Afghan issue has been of critical importance to Moscow, and its options among the "moderates" of the nonaligned movement are limited. Thus, the Soviets have been willing to offer economic and, especially, military assistance to obtain Indian support, or at least prevent Indian opposition. This is a clear example of the exercise of influence by India. To the extent that the Soviets have kept India from changing its policy, it would also be an example of at least some degree of Soviet influence as well. It is natural to expect that a weaker state will be dependent upon, or have needs from, a superpower. It goes against "conventional wisdom" to assert that the opposite may also be true. The record of the Soviet-Indian influence relationship between 1969 and 1981 should confirm, however, that both have been true in different periods and sometimes even simultaneously; indeed, it may be argued that, on the whole, it has been the Soviet Union's need for India that has been greater and, therefore, India has exercised a relatively greater amount of influence.

Nevertheless, this record indicates the existence of only very limited actual influence or leverage of a substantial nature by either side. Influence has taken the other's views and interests into consideration when making a policy decision. This form of influence is not insignificant and, by all indications, has occurred regularly in the Soviet-Indian relationship. This also may represent implicit rather than manifest influence, reinforcing rather than modifying influence, and indirect and long-term influence rather than direct and immediate influence. These areas of influence are exceedingly difficult to analyze with any precision but are no less significant for an influence relationship. These kinds of influence, however, have not produced the major policy changes we have been looking for; they have tended to mean influence only on the margin or periphery of relations. Looking at the overall picture of Soviet-Indian relations, one is inclined to agree with a former U.S. ambassador to India, who wrote in 1971 that "by now" each superpower, the Soviet Union and the United States, "should have discovered that its own capacity to influence India and Asia is strictly limited." He then went on to prophesy, in this writer's opinion accurately, that "we have learned this lesson the hard way and the generally cautious leaders of the USSR are unlikely to repeat our folly."[16]

Soviet-Indian relations have been very close and remarkably stable despite this apparent difficulty of exercising influence. Relations have certainly never been as distant nor probably as close as Western media have reported. The West has tended to overstate shifts in relations. There have indeed been alterations in the relationship but between 1969 and 1981 these changes took place within surprisingly narrow parameters.

There is little in the current relationship to indicate that there will be any abrupt change in Soviet-Indian relations in the foreseeable future. Indeed, over the course of the period analyzed many themes and patterns in the relationship had recurred. A last-minute perusal of the Indian press reveals more of the same: the Chinese foreign minister was to visit India at the end of June;[17] a dispute with Dacca had erupted over an island in the Bay of Bengal; the Bangladesh leader, Ziaur Rahman, had been assassinated and this generated new concerns for regional stability and great-power involvement; there were continuing discussions about the number of Pakistani divisions on the border; and, finally, looking particularly at nuclear questions, there were renewed worries in India about "how peaceful are Pak intentions?"[18] In addition, the early 1981 visit to India of Marshal N.V. Ogarkov, head of the General Staff of the USSR Armed Forces and first deputy defense minister, made it obvious that old patterns were not dead.

This is not to suggest that there will be no change within India, in New Delhi's foreign policy, or in Moscow's external conduct. There have been significant changes in all these areas and others since 1969. What is striking, however, has been the stability of the Indo-Soviet relationship. When Mrs. Gandhi remarked to Leonid Brezhnev at a civic reception in New Delhi in December 1980 that "Indo-Soviet friendship ... is of equal importance to both India and the Soviet Union,"[19] she was not only tactfully reminding her guest of his country's need for India. The Indian prime minister was also drawing attention to the essence of the bilateral relationship: this relationship has been important and has paid dividends to both partners. Much of this has been due to the skill with which New Delhi has utilized its more limited capabilities and also to the sensitivity with which Moscow has conducted its influence-seeking policies. Indians have long contended what one U.S. official in New Delhi recently confirmed: the Soviet Union has "a good relationship with this country because the Soviets have never asked the Indians for anything the Indians couldn't gracefully give."[20] At the same time, such close relations, but not Soviet influence, have not always meant Indian influence either; it has been a "simplistic view" in the West, said one Indian official, that "since India had good relations with the Soviet Union, New Delhi can automatically solve all problems involving Moscow...."[21]

For the future, India and the Soviet-Indian relationship are faced with the same dynamics as in 1969 and ever since: for India, how can its independence from big powers be further developed, and its ties with China and the United States expanded, while still maintaining its strong relationship with the Soviet Union? For the Soviet Union, how can it limit such diversification while expanding its own role in the South Asian region and maintaining its strong relationship with India? While the future will not duplicate the past, the themes, patterns, dynamics, and tradeoffs are likely to be the same for New Delhi and for Moscow as they have been. Each will successfully influence the other on occasion, but, generally, such influence will likely remain limited. The Soviet-Indian relationship, nevertheless, will continue to be highly significant for the two countries involved, the region, China and the United States, and for the overall world political scene.

NOTES

1. Robert Wesson, *The United States and Brazil: Limits of Influence* (New York: Praeger, 1981), p.166.
2. *Overseas Hindustan Times*, February 5, 1981.
3. See Richard B. Remnek, *Soviet Scholars and Soviet Foreign Policy: A Case Study in Soviet Policy Towards India* (Durham, N.C.: Carolina Academic Press, 1975), p.79.
4. For example, compare Brezhnev's message on the first anniversary of the treaty to Mrs. Gandhi's comments a few days earlier; *Hindustan Times*, August 11, 1972, and *Indian Express*, August 5, 1972, respectively. See also the discussion in Robert H. Donaldson, *The Soviet-Indian Alignment: Quest for Influence* (Denver: University of Denver Monograph Series in World Affairs, 1979), pp.46–47.
5. *Pravda*, November 28, 1973.
6. *Soviet Review*, no. 58, December 15, 1980.
7. Bhabani Sen Gupta, "South Asia and the Great Powers," in William E. Griffith, ed., *The World and the Great Power Triangles* (Cambridge, Mass.: M.I.T. Press, 1975), p. 186n.
8. See the discussion in Chester Bowles, "America and Russia in India," *Foreign Affairs*, July 1971, pp.637–38.
9. See Leo E. Rose, "The Superpowers in South Asia: A Geostrategic Analysis," *Orbis*, Summer 1978, pp.395–413.
10. *Los Angeles Times*, January 16, 1980.
11. See *Los Angeles Times*, November 9, 1980; and *Time*, March 9, 1981, pp.15–17.
12. See Stephen Clarkson, "The Low Impact of Soviet Writing and Aid on Indian Thinking and Policy," *Survey*, Winter 1974, pp.1–23; and Bhabani Sen Gupta, *Soviet-Asian Relations in the 1980s and Beyond: An Interperceptional Study* (New York: Praeger, 1976), passim.
13. See *Overseas Hindustan Times*, March 12, 1981; and Mohan Ram, "Brezhnev's New Fulcrum." *Far Eastern Economic Review*, March 20, 1981, pp. 27–28.
14. Girish Mathur in *Indian and Foreign Review*, December 1, 1980, pp.8–9.
15. Donaldson, *Soviet-Indian Alignment*, p.63.
16. Bowles, "America and Russia in India," p.649.
17. See the editorial on "Ties with China" in *Overseas Hindustan Times*, June 11, 1981.
18. *Overseas Hindustan Times*, May 28, 1981.
19. *Soviet Review*, no. 58, December 15, 1980.
20. *Christian Science Monitor*, December 8, 1980. For earlier Indian assertions, see Sen Gupta, *Soviet-Asian Relations*, p.154.
21. *Overseas Hindustan Times*, November 13, 1980. See also the editorials on the island and "Pakistan's bomb," in *Overseas Hindustan Times*, June 4, 1981.

BIBLIOGRAPHY

Andersen, Walter K. "India in Asia: Walking on a Tightrope," *Asian Survey* 19 (December 1979), pp.1241–53.

Bakshi, Jyotsna. "Soviet Attitude Toward Bangladesh Liberation Movement," *Indian Journal of Political Science* 38 (April-June 1977), pp.179–99.

Banerjee, Jyotirmoy. *India in Soviet Global Strategy*. Calcutta: South Asia Books, 1977.

Barnds, William J. *India, Pakistan, and the Great Powers*. New York: Praeger, 1972.

_____. "Soviet Influence in India: A Search for the Spoils that Go with Victory," in Alvin Z. Rubinstein, ed., *Soviet and Chinese Influence in the Third World*. New York: Praeger, 1975.

_____. "Moscow and South Asia," *Problems of Communism* 21 (May-June 1972), pp.12–31.

_____. "The USSR, China, and South Asia," *Problems of Communism* 26 (November-December 1977), pp.44–59.

Bowles, Chester. "America and Russia in India," *Foreign Affairs* 49 (July 1971), pp.636–51.

Chari, P. R. "Indo-Soviet Military Cooperation: A Review," *Asian Survey* 19 (March 1979), pp.230–44.

Chawla, Sudershan. *The Foreign Relations of India*. Encino, Calif.: Dickenson, 1976.

Chawla, Sudershan, and D. R. Sardesai, eds. *Changing Patterns of Security and Stability in Asia*. New York: Praeger, 1980.

Chopra, Pran. *India's Second Liberation*. Cambridge, Mass.: M.I.T. Press, 1974.

Choudhury, G. W. *India, Pakistan, Bangladesh and the Major Powers: Politics of a Divided Subcontinent*. New York: Free Press, 1975.

_____. "New International Patterns in Asia," *Problems of Communism* 28 (March-April 1979), pp.14–28.

Clarkson, Stephen. *The Soviet Theory of Development: India and the Third World in Marxist-Leninist Scholarship*. Toronto: University of Toronto Press, 1978.

_____. "The Low Impact of Soviet Writing and Aid on Indian Thinking and Policy," *Survey* 20 (Winter 1974), pp.1–23.

Datar, Asha L. *India's Economic Relations with the USSR and Eastern Europe, 1953 to 1969*. Cambridge: Cambridge University Press, 1972.

Donaldson, Robert H. *Soviet Policy Towards India: Ideology and Strategy*. Cambridge, Mass.: Harvard University Press, 1974.

_____. *The Soviet-Indian Alignment: Quest for Influence*. Denver: University of Denver Monograph Series in World Affairs, 1979.

_____. "Soviet Policy in South Asia: Aspirations and Limitations," in Roger E. Kanet and Donna Bahry, eds., *Soviet Economic and Political Relations with the Developing World*. New York: Praeger, 1975.

_____. "India: The Soviet Stake in Stability," *Asian Survey* 12 (June 1972), pp.475–92.

Drieberg, Trevor, Harji Malik, and D. K. Joshi. *Towards Closer Indo-Soviet Cooperation*. New Delhi: Vikas Publications, 1974.

Galbraith, John Kenneth. *Ambassador's Journal*. New York: New American Library, 1970.

Gandhi, Indira. "India and the World," *Foreign Affairs* 50 (October 1972), pp. 65–77.

Ghebhardt, Alexander O. "The Soviet System of Collective Security in Asia," *Asian Survey* 13 (December 1973), pp.1075–91.

_____. "Soviet and U.S. Interests in the Indian Ocean," *Asian Survey* 15 (August 1975), pp.672–83.

Hensel, Howard M. "Asian Collective Security: The Soviet View," *Orbis* 19 (Winter 1976), pp.1564–80.

Horn, Robert C. "Indian-Soviet Relations in 1969: A Watershed Year?," *Orbis* 19 (Winter 1976), pp.1539–63.

_____. "Sino-Soviet Relations in an Era of Detente," *Asian Affairs* 3 (May-June 1976), pp.287–304.

Imam, Zafar. *Soviet View of India, 1957–1975.* New Delhi: Kalyani Publishers, 1977.

Jackson, Robert. *South Asian Crisis: India, Pakistan, and Bangladesh. A Political and Historical Analysis of the 1971 War.* New York: Praeger, 1975.

Jain, J. P. *Soviet Policy Towards Pakistan and Bangladesh.* New Delhi: Radiant Publishers, 1974.

Jain, R. K., ed. *Soviet-South Asian Relations, 1947–1978.* 2 vols. New Delhi: Radiant Publishers, 1978.

Jetly, Nancy. *India-China Relations, 1947–1977: A Study of Parliament's Role in the Making of Foreign Policy.* Atlantic Highlands, N.J.: Humanities Press, 1979.

Jukes, Geoffrey. *The Soviet Union in Asia.* Berkeley: University of California Press, 1973.

Kapur, Ashok. "Indo-Soviet Treaty and the Emerging Asian Balance," *Asian Survey* 12 (June 1972), pp.463–74.

Kapur, Harish. *The Soviet Union and the Emerging Nations—A Case Study of Soviet Policy Towards India.* Geneva: Michael Joseph, 1972.

_____. *The Embattled Triangle: Moscow, Peking, New Delhi.* New York: Humanities Press, 1973.

Kaushik, Devendra. *Soviet Relations with India and Pakistan.* New Delhi: Vikas Publications, 1971.

Khalizad, Zalmay. "India's Bomb and the Stability of South Asia," *Asian Affairs* 5 (November-December 1977), pp.97–108.

McLane, Charles B. *Soviet-Asian Relations.* New York: Columbia University Press, 1973.

Menon, Rajan. "India and the Soviet Union: A New Stage of Relations," *Asian Survey* 18 (July 1978), pp.731–50.

Naik, J. A. *Soviet Policy Towards India: From Stalin to Brezhnev.* New Delhi: Vikas Publications, 1970.

_____. *India, Russia, China and Bangladesh.* New Delhi: S. Chand, 1972.

Nayar, Kuldip. *Between the Lines*. Bombay: Allied Publishers, 1969.

───. *Distant Neighbors: A Tale of the Subcontinent*. New Delhi: Vikas Publications, 1972.

Nayyar, Deepak, ed. *Economic Relations Between Socialist Countries and the Third World*. Montclair, N.J.: Allanheld, Osmun, 1977.

Palmer, Norman D. "Indo-American Relations: The Politics of Encounter," *Orbis* 23 (Summer 1979), pp.403–20.

Patil, V. T. "Soviet Policy Towards Pakistan," *Indian Journal of Political Science* 38 (October-December 1977), pp.451–61.

Rao, R. V. R. Chandrasekhara. "Indo-Soviet Economic Relations," *Asian Survey* 13 (August 1973), pp.793–800.

Remnek, Richard B. *Soviet Scholars and Soviet Foreign Policy: A Case Study in Soviet Policy Towards India*. Durham, N.C.: Carolina Academic Press, 1975.

Rose, Leo B. "The Superpowers in South Asia: A Geostrategic Analysis," *Orbis* 22 (Summer 1978), pp.395–413.

Sahai, Nisha. "Soviet Specialists in South Asia," *International Studies* (New Delhi) 19 (January-March 1980), pp.87–109.

Sen Budhraj, Vijay. *Soviet Russia and the Hindustan Subcontinent*. Bombay: Somaiya Publications, 1973.

───. "Moscow and the Birth of Bangladesh," *Asian Survey* 12 (May 1972) pp.482–95.

───. "India and the Soviet Union." *International Studies* 17 (July-December 1978), pp. 739–57.

Sen Gupta, Bhabani. *The Fulcrum of Asia: Relations Among China, India, Pakistan, and the USSR*. New York: Pegasus, 1970.

───. *Soviet-Asian Relations in the 1970s and Beyond: An Interperceptional Study*. New York: Praeger, 1976.

───. "The Soviet Union and South Asia," in Roger E. Kanet, ed. *The Soviet Union and the Developing Nations*. Baltimore: Johns Hopkins Press, 1974.

───. "South Asia and the Great Powers," in William E. Griffith, ed. *The World and the Great Power Triangles*. Cambridge, Mass.: M.I.T. Press, 1975.

Seth, S. P. "Russia's Role in Indo-Pak Relations," *Asian Survey* 9 (August 1969), pp.614–24.

Sharma, R. K., ed. *The Economics of Indo-Soviet Trade*. Bombay: Allied Publishers, 1979.

Simon, Sheldon W. "China, the Soviet Union, and the Subcontinental Balance," *Asian Survey* 13 (July 1973), pp.647–58.

Singh, K. R. *The Indian Ocean: Big Power Presence and Local Response*. Columbia, Mo.: South Asia Books, 1978.

Singh, V. B., ed. *Indo-Soviet Relations, 1947–77*. New Delhi: Sterling Publishers, 1978.

Stanislaus, M. Sebastian. *Soviet Economic Aid to India*. New Delhi: N.V. Publications, 1975.

Stein, Arthur. *India and the Soviet Union*. Chicago: University of Chicago Press, 1969.

Tahir-Kheli, Shirin. "Chinese Objectives in South Asia: 'Anti-Hegemony' vs. 'Collective Security,'" *Asian Survey* 18 (October 1978), pp.996–1012.

Tanzer, Michael. *The Political Economy of International Oil and the Underdeveloped Countries*. Boston: Beacon Press, 1969.

Thakur, Ramesh. "India's Vietnam Policy, 1946–1979," *Asian Survey* 19 (October 1979), pp.957–76.

Thomas, Raju G. C. "Aircraft for the Indian Air Force: The Context and Implications of the Jaguar Decision," *Orbis* 24 (Spring 1980). pp.85–101.

INDEX

Afghanistan, 141–42; 1973 coup, 89; 1979 invasion of, 181–85, 195, 197–98, 207, 213
Aksai Chin, 32–33, 56
Algeria, 1971 Kosygin visit to, 69
Arkhipov, Ivan, 160, 188, 197, 202

Baghdad Pact, 10, 12
Bangladesh (and East Pakistan), 59–60, 66–73, 77–79, 119–20, 124, 140
Bhutto, Z. A., 59, 71, 78, 141, 158; 1972 visit to PRC, 80; 1972 visit to USSR, 81–82; 1974 visit to PRC, 98–99; 1974 visit to USSR, 100–3; 1974 visit to U.S., 105–6; 1976 visit to PRC, 129–31
Binh, Madame, 50, 54
Brezhnev, L. I., 24, 29, 37–38, 59, 67, 112, 121, 124–26, 134, 153–54, 162, 173, 180, 214; 1973 visit to India, 89–93; 1980 visit to India, 195–201, 221

Cambodia (Kampuchea), 50, 172, 175, 193–94, 206–7
Carter, Jimmy, 156–58
Chavan, Y. B., 103ff, 121, 123–24
collective security system, 29–30, 32, 51, 54, 77, 90, 92–93, 121–22, 133, 140, 216
Communist Party of India (CPI), 3, 9, 23, 47, 58, 118, 125, 142, 200
Communist Party of the Soviet Union (CPSU): slogans, 4, 13; Twentieth Congress (1956), 4–6; Twenty-fourth Congress (1971), 59; Twenty-fifth Congress (1976), 124–25; Twenty-sixth Congress (1981), 201–2

CPI—Marxist, 118
cultural center (Trivandrum), 47, 54
cultural relations, 3–4, 218
Czechoslovakia, invasion of (1968), 21–22

Desai, Morarji, 21, 25, 147ff, 158–59, 168, 218; 1977 visit to USSR, 153–56; 1979 visit to USSR, 171–73
Dhar, D. P., 38, 49, 55, 63, 70, 72, 81, 85–86, 100–1, 117
Diego Garcia, 121, 134–35, 198

economic relations, 3, 5–9, 23–24, 48, 85–86, 91–92, 100–1, 108–9, 121, 127–129, 133–34, 137–39, 150, 161, 169–70, 172, 188–89, 199–200, 202
emergency, India's state of, 78, 116–18, 142–43, 148, 153

Farakka Barrage, 53, 57, 124
Firyubin, N. P., 38, 49, 55, 81, 85, 140, 197; 1968 visit to India, 22–23, 26–27; 1970 visit, 53–54; 1971 visit, 70; 1976 visit, 126–27; 1980 visit, 188
Ford, Gerald, 103, 105–6, 141

Gandhi, Indira, 21–22, 25–26, 30–31, 34–36, 46–47, 53, 69–70, 78, 80, 87, 112, 116ff, 126–27, 141–43, 159, 173ff, 176–77, 181, 187, 190–91, 199, 214, 218, 221; 1953 visit to USSR, 4; 1970 visit, 55–56; 1971 visit, 67–68; 1976 visit, 129, 131–35, 147, 154–55
Gandhi, Sanjay, 142
Giri, V. V., 54–56, 70
Goa (and Daman and Diu), 10

229

Gonsalves, Eric, 192
Great Britain, 2, 208
Grechko, Marshal, 28, 67, 110–11
Grishin, I. T., 108–9, 138
Gromyko, Andrei, 38, 49, 55, 121, 154–55, 162–63, 194, 197; 1971 visit to India, 63–66; 1977 visit, 149–51; 1980 visit, 186

Huang, Hua, 163, 194
Hungary, Soviet invasion of (1956), 21–22

Indian National Congress (INC), 2, 23–24, 34–36, 46–47, 58, 78, 142, 180, 193
Indian Ocean, 14, 77, 90–91, 94–96, 104, 121, 134, 173, 198–99, 203–4
Indo-Pakistan conflicts: 1965, 12–13; 1971, 72–73
Indo-Soviet treaty (1971). *See* Treaty of Peace, Friendship and Cooperation
Iran, 88–89, 141–42

Jan(a) Sangh, 25, 147–48
Janata, 142–43, 147ff, 180ff

Kampuchea. *See* Cambodia
Kapitsa, Mikhail, 52
Karakoram Highway, 159, 191
Kashmir, 9–12, 53, 57, 59–60, 79, 81, 99–100, 130–131
Kaul, T. N., 49–52, 55–56, 70, 83–84, 141
Khrushchev, Nikita S., 4–6,
Kissinger, Henry, 62–63, 71, 86; 1974 visit to India and Pakistan, 104–6
Kosygin, Alexei, 12–13, 24, 37–38, 49, 55, 61, 67, 82, 85, 88, 121, 162, 180; 1968 visit to India, 20, 23; 1969 stopovers, 36–37; May 1969 visit to, 28–29; 1979 stopover, 174–75; 1979 visit, 167–70
Kuo-feng, Hua, 129–30, 190
Kutakhov, Pavel, 70–71, 160
Kuznetsov, V. V., 55, 72

Lenin, V. I., 1–2, 5
Lok Sabha, 21–22, 25, 58, 142, 180, 200–1

Malenkov, G. M., 3
maps (Soviet), 23, 56, 85
Marx, Karl, 1
Menon, K. P. S., 3–4
military assistance and relations, 8, 67, 72, 87–88, 110–12, 127, 151–53, 159–61, 164–65, 168, 175–76, 189–90, 201–2
Mishra, B. C., 182
Mishra, S. N., 174
Moynihan, Daniel Patrick, 87, 103
Mujib, Sheik (Mujibur Rahman), 59ff, 69, 83, 119

Nagas, 19
Naxalites, 19
Nehru, J., 3, 9–10, 13; 1927 visit to USSR, 2, 10; 1955 visit, 4, 8–9
Nixon, Richard M., 18, 33, 55, 62, 71, 80, 103
nonalignment and nonaligned movement, 6–7, 9, 55, 126, 172, 183; Colombo summit (1976), 135–36; Havana summit (1979), 174–75; New Delhi foreign ministers' meeting (1981), 204–7
Nuclear Non-Proliferation Treaty (NPT), 20
nuclear weapons, 77, 99, 102, 104; fuel, 139–40, 156–57 169–72, 203; test, 96–98

oil, 109, 138–39, 171, 199, 215

Pakistan, 2, 10–14, 16, 18–20, 27–28, 30–34, 39–43, 51–57, 62–63, 66ff, 77, 87, 98–99, 105–8, 112, 126, 129–31, 171, 181–82, 184–87, 203–4, 208–9, 216–17; Soviet arms to, 13, 24–27
peaceful coexistence, 5
People's Republic of China, 3–4, 10–14, 17–19, 28–34, 39–42, 50–51, 54–

57, 60, 62–63, 71, 77, 80–85, 90, 98–99, 106–8, 112, 120, 122–24, 126, 129–33, 152–53, 158–68, 171–72, 184–85, 190–94, 198, 202–3, 208–9, 215–16, 218–19
Podgorny, N., 53, 61, 67–68

Radhakrishnan, S., 3
Ram, Jagjivan, 56, 87–89, 151, 160, 176
Rao, P. V. Narasimha, 186, 194
Reagan, Ronald, 203–4
Reddy, N. S., 195
Roy, M. N., 1

Sikkim, 106ff
Simla summit (1972), 78
Singh, Charan, 173–74, 176
Singh, Dinesh, 31, 37–40, 54
Singh, Kewal, 37, 48, 103, 126, 141; 1970 visit to USSR, 49–52; 1975 visit, 121–22
Singh, Swaran, 31, 53–55, 64, 69–70, 103, 120; 1969 visit to USSR, 40; 1971 visit, 62; 1972 visit, 83; 1974 visit, 100
Sino-Indian border clashes: 1959, 10–11; 1962, 10–12; 1975, 120–21
Skachkov, S. A., 23–24, 26n, 48, 55, 85
Southeast Asia Treaty Organization (SEATO), 10
Stalin, J. V., 1–3
Swatantra, 25

Tashkent, 12–13, 19, 79, 83, 216; "spirit", 19, 53
Teng Hsiao-ping, 159, 164–65, 192
trade, 3–4, 8, 58, 85–86, 128–29, 137–39, 169–70
Treaty of Peace, Friendship and Cooperation (1971), 16, 30n, 42, 64–66, 69–70, 149

Ulianovski, R. A., 117
United Nations, 10, 12, 21, 66–67, 72, 84, 94–96, 120, 137, 173, 182–83
United States, 3, 10–12, 17–20, 31, 33, 55, 60, 71, 77, 79–80, 86–88, 92, 103–6, 112, 121, 141, 153, 156–58, 164–65, 182, 184–85, 198–99, 202–4, 217–18

Vajpayee, A. B., 25, 147–51; 1978 visit to USSR, 161–63; 1979 visit to PRC, 165–66
Vietnam, 18, 36, 50, 53–54, 87, 112, 164–68, 188, 193, 206–7

World War II, 1–2

Yahya Khan, 24, 33–34, 59–61, 69; 1970 visit to USSR, 52–53; 1970 visit to U.S., 56–57; 1970 visit to PRC, 56–57

Zhdanov, A. A., 2
Zia ul-Haq, 158–59, 217
Ziaur Rahman, 140

ABOUT THE AUTHOR

Robert C. Horn is Professor of Political Science and a member of the Asian Studies Faculty at California State University, Northridge. He teaches courses on Soviet foreign policy as well as international politics and international organization. He also serves as the advisor to the university's Model United Nations program.

Dr. Horn was educated at Wittenberg University and at the Fletcher School of Law and Diplomacy, receiving his Ph.D in 1969. His dissertation on Soviet policy in Indonesia in the Sukarno and immediate post-Sukarno periods was completed after a year's research in Indonesia and extensive travel through Southeast Asia and Eastern Europe.

Dr. Horn has published numerous articles, chapters, and reviews on Soviet foreign policy. These studies of Soviet policy in Southeast and South Asia, Sino-Soviet relations, and Soviet-American relations have appeared in scholarly journals such as *Asian Survey, Orbis, Pacific Affairs, Survey*, and in edited works. A recent contribution was his chapter on "The Soviet Union and Asian Security" in Chawla and Sar Desai's *Changing Patterns of Security and Stability in Asia* (Praeger, 1980).